PRAISE FOR *HIRING VETERANS*

"There is a 'War on Talent' in American businesses, and companies both big and small are looking directly to the military community to help fill their ranks with that talent. Matt's second book on veteran hiring is laser focused on the employers and is a must read for any organization looking to build a 'Veteran Ready' hiring program. Every chapter is a home run complete with expertise, best practices, tips, and more and is a blueprint for success. In today's business environment, if you want to outperform your competitors, then hiring veterans and military spouses is a smart decision and *Hiring Veterans* is required reading."

—**Adam L. Rocke**, Colonel (Ret), US Army, senior director at the US Chamber of Commerce Foundation, Hiring our Heroes

"In *Hiring Veterans*, Matt Louis provides compelling reasons for companies to hire veterans in their own self-interest, rather than as a sacrifice. He then lays out a step-by-step process for companies to not only hire veterans but also support and retain veterans, to the benefit of both veteran employees and the organization. This book is an excellent resource for any company that wants to improve its own functioning by tapping into one of the greatest sources of talent our country has to offer, our nation's veterans."

—**Keith D. Renshaw, PhD,** professor and department chair in psychology and director of the Military, Veterans, and Families Initiative, George Mason University

"America's military veterans bring a host of skills, experiences, and expertise to the talent marketplace. But many employers have difficulty recognizing the unique characteristics of our veterans, and, more importantly, many simply do not know how to assess the value veterans can bring to a business. Matt Louis simplifies this dilemma in this easy-to-read yet exceedingly insightful book that erases the mystery of hiring those who have served all of us in the armed forces."

—**Lieutenant General Guy C. Swan III,** US Army (Ret), vice president of the Association of the United States Army (AUSA), former Commanding General of United States Army North (Fifth Army), and West Point Class of 1976

"Matching the skills and abilities of the modern military veteran to the needs of corporate America is a worthy challenge. In this book, Matt Louis shares a timely blueprint for the company looking to recruit and retain top military talent. He covers it all—from the why to the how, and outlines a path to success for the savvy company seeking to work with some of our nation's finest."

—**Dr. Kate Hendricks Thomas,** academic
researcher, storyteller, and US Marine veteran

"Matt Louis has done it again! His first book, *Mission Transition,* provided an in-depth field manual for transitioning service members to follow. This time he delivers a complete guide to help bridge the civil-military divide. This book is the most comprehensive how-to guide for organizations that intend to recruit and hire veteran talent. Matt's insights are based upon his personal experience and extensive inputs from recognized experts across the veteran employment landscape. This resource should be standard issue for human resources and non-veteran hiring managers."

—**Brian Niswander,** Air Force veteran
and founder of *Military-Transition.org*

"In a business climate where winning the war for talent is at the top of every CEO's priority list, Matt Louis's *Hiring Veterans* is an indispensable resource for every leader and human-resource professional committed to fielding a winning team. With classic military precision, Matt provides the reader with a step-by-step program for attracting, training, and retaining America's veterans to maximize their impact on any business. It's a great opportunity for companies and leaders to do well by doing good."

—**Doug McCormick,** managing partner
for HCI Equity Partners

"*Hiring Veterans* is essential reading for anyone interested in improving their organization. Matt Louis has clearly articulated important steps, perspectives, and cultural dimensions that help guide readers without prior service on how to build a more inclusive environment that sets veterans and organizations up for success."

—**Chris Kondo,** global social investment strategist for 3M

"*Hiring Veterans* is the must-read for any business owner, manager, recruiter, or human resources professional seeking amazing talent. Regardless of whether you are in need of one or hundreds, this amazing and well-organized blueprint to hiring success is a gift from a true expert and veteran. It truly is the one-stop shop for hiring, onboarding, supporting, and leveraging the talents of our nation's armed forces and their loved ones. Do yourself and your organization a favor by reading and sharing this gem. This pool of incredibly agile, diverse, and reliable talent is ready for a new mission; it's now our duty to pay it forward."

—**Chris Galy,** senior vice president and
chief people officer, Couchbase

"*Hiring Veterans* is a must-read for anyone involved in the hiring process at every company. It shows how to move from hiring veterans for diversity's sake to recognizing the invaluable skill sets of veterans, to maximizing these skills to increase profitability and efficiency, and to creating an inclusive culture of high performance. My organization has realized tremendous growth because of Matt Louis's guidance. *Hiring Veterans* can help yours realize the same."

—**Harrison Bernstein,** founder and executive
director of Soldiers to Sidelines

"Matt Louis has delivered again. This book presents a well-articulated and accessible guide for business leaders to understand how to leverage the diversity and capabilities of our military veteran population in the civilian workforce."

—**Dr. Kristin N. Saboe,** author of *Military
Veteran Employment*, industrial-organizational
psychologist, and Army veteran

"*Hiring Veterans* is a well-thought-out guide to assisting non veterans in the hiring process of such talent. As a retired executive spanning both industry and consulting, I witnessed firsthand the disconnect with civilians recognizing and appreciating the skills veterans possess. This book helps bridge the gap and helps companies recognize talent and experience that [are] readily transferable to our market economy."

—**Kurt Babe,** managing director (ret) for Deloitte Consulting

"Given his background as a soldier and a business leader, Matt's book provides all the reasons why companies should have a veteran hiring strategy—and the steps for how to go about it. Creating and sustaining a culture, while simultaneously finding people that fit the culture, challenges leaders every day as we try to take care of our employees, our customers, and grow our business. Veterans are a group of people who not only understand the value of culture, but also seek out organizations who are committed to creating positive cultures. No matter how many years a veteran spent in the military or the rank they achieved, they all learned that the way to successfully accomplish *the mission* is through working together as a team."

—**Scott J. Zigmond,** USMA '88, vice president of
sales and marketing at Performance Services, Inc.

"*Hiring Veterans* provides the 'secret decoder ring' for tapping into a powerful reservoir of talent to help any company thrive and win. From the why to the how to the where, Matt Louis provides the recipe for success in harnessing vets to help any company in the war for talent. I only hope my competitors don't read and implement the proven tactics in this book!"

—**Tom Pettit,** chief operating officer of
S&P 500 company Generac Power Systems

"Matt brilliantly provides a complementary guide for US employers to leverage veterans as a competitive advantage. *Hiring Veterans* is a valuable tool for enterprises of all types and sizes. He includes numerous options to employers, including proposals to leverage the veteran workforce to accomplish diversity and inclusion goals. Our nation has spent significant resources recruiting and developing veterans—we should not let that go to waste; instead, we should find opportunities to leverage those investments to create value for our organizations. Matt's practical guide for employers is a must-read and a must-use!"

—**Jon Brickey,** senior vice president and
cybersecurity evangelist at Mastercard

"I've been asked, 'What can we do to recruit more military veterans to our company?' My answer will now be, 'Get this book!' *Hiring Veterans* is definitely the most comprehensive resource available to corporate America to establish programs that successfully recruit and retain veterans. Its practical approach and step-by-step guide will jump-start organizations on this honorable and needed task."

—**Alan Hill,** volunteer coach for the
Eagle Group of MN Veterans

"As a West Point grad, veteran, executive recruiter of fifteen years and a career coach for three years who has helped thousands of transitioning veterans, I can vouch for two things: the talent of our graduates and the potential they hold for prospective employers, and the difficulties they face in successfully making the transition from the military. While these veterans certainly own a good share of the effort in making that transition a success, they tend to succeed better at organizations that attempt to meet them halfway in those efforts and carry through on that promise after they are employed. I strongly recommend Matt's first book, *Mission Transition*, as the guide for the former; and I would encourage all employers to take advantage of this guide for the latter."

—**Scott Leishman,** West Point Class of 1977 and career coach

"Matt Louis has written a great book for helping companies unlock veterans' potential. In today's environment where getting an immediate impact from new hires and then retaining them is critical, the framework Matt lays out is invaluable for business leaders. He provides ideas, tools, and examples to follow, from recruiting to onboarding and training. As someone who has implemented hiring programs, I find it clear that the companies that take advantage of *Hiring Veterans* will get their new-hire veterans rapidly engaged and contributing, and the veterans who land in these companies will be empowered and have a high degree of satisfaction."

—**Peter G. Fontana,** USMA '91, high-tech industry
director of engineering and operations

"Our men and women in uniform that serve in the Armed Forces have been exposed to such dynamic change in technology, social dynamics in our society, and an incredible understanding of leadership to accomplish the mission over the past few decades. This has resulted in a rich and diverse talent pool that furthers national security by appropriate workplace placement in their second or third careers in life. Our veteran group of employees at BGI are 72 percent of our corporate workforce and their role of serving continues with tremendous impact. As CEO, I am constantly encouraging our hiring teams to put these highly skilled Americans into the right fit for corporate productivity, delivery excellence, and their own personal and professional growth. I am aware of the incredible upside of bringing veterans into the workplace. In *Hiring Veterans*, Matt Louis has created sound methods that are relevant to putting the pieces together. His expertise makes this a vital tool for executive and hiring leadership in every organization. His relevancy and understanding of the fit between the mature competencies veterans bring to the table and industry needs across the global enterprise is paramount to achieving the objective of keeping strength and talent in our workforce. Every corporate leader across this country should run to this source of information."

—**Phil Dismukes,** CEO and founder of BGI LLC

"Successful corporations understand the value of inclusion and diversity. Veterans are a key component of a diverse corporate landscape; however, their experience is a language that is often misunderstood. *Hiring Veterans* is a translator to facilitate adding veterans to any organization. Recruiting, growing, and retaining veterans will deliver tremendous returns for any business willing to make the investment. Matt Louis has teed up the *Why* and the *How* to hit veteran talent home runs."

—**Scott Williams,** USMA '91, US Army
LTC (Ret) and aerospace executive

"Matt Louis has been serving our country since he entered the US Military Academy in 1987. I met him then, as I was two years ahead of him at West Point, and have watched him through his service in uniform and thereafter as a committed patriot who deeply cares for service members and their families. Matt's writing, speaking, and working on behalf of those who have served our nation are exemplary, and the calling he feels to help them is sincere. This book is essential for veterans seeking employment in the corporate sector but even more important for corporate leaders in need of skilled talent to compete in the global economy and 21st century. I strongly endorse reading *Hiring Veterans*. Our country has an enormous reserve of talent from those who served in uniform and wish to continue delivering impact to organizations across all industries."

—**Rob Holmes,** cofounder of ForgeNow

"Our future all-volunteer force depends on the ability of our national economic contributors to understand, acknowledge, and articulate military experience as a critical component in achieving their strategic business goals and objectives. Younger generations need tangible evidence of career pathways stemming from military service, and who better to validate the value of service than employers committed to veteran talent. Matt Louis's *Hiring Veterans* is the perfect guide to help employers create the framework to attract, hire, retain, and develop a sustainable pipeline of future organizational leaders matriculating from today's military."

—**Marnie Holder,** veteran services program officer,
National Veterans Memorial and Museum

HIRING VETERANS

HIRING VETERANS

HOW TO LEVERAGE
MILITARY TALENT
FOR ORGANIZATIONAL GROWTH

MATTHEW J. LOUIS
Lieutenant Colonel (USA Retired)

with Dr. Anthony R. Garcia, Sr.

CAREER
PRESS

This edition first published in 2023 by Career Press, an imprint of
Red Wheel/Weiser, LLC
With offices at:
65 Parker Street, Suite 7
Newburyport, MA 01950
www.careerpress.com
www.redwheelweiser.com

ISBN: 978-1-63265-209-6
Library of Congress Cataloging-in-Publication Data

Names: Louis, Matthew J., author.
Title: Hiring veterans : how to leverage military talent for organizational
growth / Matthew J. Louis ; with Dr. Anthony R. Garcia, Sr..
Description: Newburyport, MA : Career Press, 2023. | Includes
bibliographical references and index. | Summary: "A practical guide for
prospective employers who want to hire veterans. It addresses this
primary question: How can employers better prepare for and employ
transitioning service members to improve the productivity and
competitiveness of their organizations?"-- Provided by publisher.
Identifiers: LCCN 2023012778 | ISBN 9781632652096 (trade paperback) | ISBN
9781632652102 (ebook)
Subjects: LCSH: Veterans--Employment--United States. | Career
changes--United States. | Employee selection--United States. | BISAC:
BUSINESS & ECONOMICS / Human Resources & Personnel Management | BUSINESS
& ECONOMICS / Economics / General
Classification: LCC UB357 .L588 2023 | DDC 362.860973--dc23/eng/20230508
LC record available at https://lccn.loc.gov/2023012778

Cover design by Sky Peck Design
Interior by Steve Amarillo / Urban Design LLC
Typeset in Adobe Minion Pro, Bebas Neue, and Proxima Nova

Printed in the United States of America
IBI

10 9 8 7 6 5 4 3 2 1

To those organizations that took a chance on a new kid fresh off his Army experience—and those that have supported him since. To the Kelley School of Business at Indiana University, which provided me the mental space to deprogram from the military and the education to function in the real world. To Procter & Gamble, my first post-military employer and a longtime supporter of veteran efforts, you taught me the basics of business and corporate culture. To General Electric, my second employer and a longtime supporter of veterans, who provided a basis for understanding business processes. And to Deloitte, my last employer, whose incredibly supportive culture enabled me and fellow veterans like me to thrive on all that we brought to the organization.

CONTENTS

FOREWORD

A year ago, I sought out Matt's expertise in asking him to join the External Advisory Council for Military and Veterans Affairs at JPMorgan Chase & Co. For those same reasons, I'd urge you to take heed of his newest offering if, like me, you value improving the productivity and competitiveness of your organization. As I write this, several recent events illustrate its importance. Today is 22 September 2021. I'm writing from a hotel room in midtown New York City reflecting on the fact that we just marked the twentieth year since the attacks of 9/11. Ironically, we reached this anniversary only days after the United States removed its last military forces from Afghanistan. These events serve as reminders of the sacrifices service members and their families have made over the last two decades to help keep our nation safe and protect our liberties and way of life.

Alone, these two milestones would be sufficient to signal the importance of *Hiring Veterans*. However, they occur during the outbreak and continued persistence of the most devastating global pandemic of the modern age, which has increased awareness of the sacrifices the few (in this case, first responders and healthcare workers) make on behalf of the many. There has also been a reawakening to the challenges faced by many minorities and those living in underserved communities that has created a demand for change and captured the attention of many companies, challenging their sense of what it means to be good corporate citizens.

Today, the diversity, equity, and inclusion (DEI) landscape is receiving increased attention as organizations search for best practices in implementing and sustaining employee-focused programs that provide a competitive edge to attract and build a diverse and qualified workforce. While a diverse workforce has always been conveniently viewed as a force multiplier by most modern companies, it has become a differentiator that potential employees will use to determine if it's a place they would like to work. What is needed is a guide for organizations that provides a clear road map for implementing an employee-focused DEI strategy. *Hiring Veterans* is one such resource—focused on building an environment that attracts veterans, transitioning service members, and military spouses.

Ten years ago, eleven companies saw an opportunity to make a difference by addressing the high unemployment rate experienced by veterans and formed a coalition (then known as the 100,000 Jobs Mission) to address this need. Today, that coalition (renamed the Veteran Jobs Mission) is more than 250 companies strong, representing nearly every industry—many of which are highlighted in this book. While this coalition has committed to developing and sharing best practices among themselves and others looking to establish veteran-focused programs, there still exists a void for a singular resource that consolidates this knowledge into a complete package accessible to organizations of all sizes. *Hiring Veterans* serves this purpose and much more.

The book discusses the opportunities that organizations can leverage to support the military community. This is no mere academic treatise. Like Matt's first book, *Mission Transition,* this is a genuine operations manual that uses case studies to highlight insights from organizations that successfully employ these techniques to support veterans, service members, and their families. The "Veteran Assimilation Process" provides a practical road map to follow with examples every step of the way, from deciding to launch a veteran support program, to acquiring the necessary tools to execute the entire "employment life cycle," to tracking realistic metrics to measure its success.

Hiring Veterans reminds us that it's not enough to hire veterans and military spouses but that we must offer them a way to flourish in our organizations. The "Veteran Support Program" template can be used by large and small companies, whether you are a one-person operation or have several resources to support your efforts. The appendices alone are packed full of rich information that provides the practitioner with a gold mine of relevant tools and lessons that have been proven to produce results.

And so, if your company already has an established veterans program, use this book to evaluate your current efforts and level of maturity, and then challenge your organization to take it to the next level. If you are starting out, or simply evaluating the prospect of launching a veteran support program, use this book as a guide to ensure you, your colleagues, and prospective veteran and military spouse hires benefit from a program that will be considered best in class!

Mark Elliott
Head of Military and Veterans Affairs, JPMorgan Chase & Co.
September 22, 2021

WHY WRITE THIS BOOK?

We live in the greatest country on the planet earth. There are many reasons why that is so. One significant reason is due to the competitiveness and vibrancy of our economy. One of the drivers over time of that economy—certainly over the last seventy years—has been a talent pool of experienced, trained, dedicated professionals who rose through the ranks to lead many of our business and governmental organizations: veterans of our military services.

But the presence of this talent pool and its influence in these same organizations have shrunk significantly in recent decades. Veteran presence among corporate leadership is, in fact, at an all-time low, as are the percentages of Americans both currently serving on active duty and who have served at any time in the past. Moreover, these percentages are forecasted to continue their downward trend for the foreseeable future. These trends, combined with the inadequate transition support that veterans receive upon leaving the service, have resulted in a civil-military divide whereby this valuable talent pool and the organizations they could productively serve are separated by a common language—much like the British and Americans. This inability to communicate, coupled with a decreasing veteran population, has led to a dearth of veteran presence in most civilian organizations, with prospective employers seemingly incapable of adequately understanding the value or applicability of veteran talent.

Yet we collectively hold within our hands one of the keys to enabling the competitiveness of our economy and rewarding our shareholders in the process. Veterans—and the character, work ethic, and productivity they instantaneously bring—are abundant and available (see page xviii). Moreover, as an essential component of a diverse workforce, they bring a depth of capability and inclusive mindset that would benefit any organization. **We need to find a way to help them cross that civil-military divide and assimilate to a new way of being.**

The US Department of Defense

The US Department of Defense is the nation's largest employer, encompassing more than 3.5 million individuals—more than the employees of Amazon, McDonald's, FedEx, Target, and General Electric *combined*.[1] As of 2019, this figure consisted of:

- 2,613,369 uniformed personnel
  - ◇ 1,326,200 active-duty members
    - 479,785 Army members
    - 332,528 Navy members
    - 327,878 Air Force members
    - 186,009 Marine members
  - ◇ 40,830 Coast Guard members
  - ◇ 1,038,198 Ready Reserve members
  - ◇ 199,756 Retired Reserve members
  - ◇ 8385 Standby Reserve members
- 896,160 civilian personnel[2]

Every year, more than 200,000 uniformed personnel transition off active duty. And the Department of Labor tells us that more than eight million veterans are active participants in the civilian labor pool today.[3]

Doing so requires a stretch from both sides of the divide. While veterans must certainly make increased and concerted efforts to market themselves effectively, there are steps organizations can take to meet them halfway. Focused hiring programs, affinity groups, acclimation support, and mentoring efforts are part of a comprehensive approach employers should leverage to hire and retain veterans and their spouses. But insufficient numbers are taking advantage of this opportunity today.

We live in a very divided world at present. But this is one divide whose closure is within our grasp, and the resulting benefits may exceed most others. Over my career, I have witnessed how organizations have successfully done so. And I feel it is high time to leverage their success. This work is a field manual—a practical guide—to enable yours to do the same and one that highlights the best practices of leading organizations in today's economy.

This effort is not about charity. It is not about patriotism. It is about optimizing your rightfully selfish aims as a profit-seeking enterprise in a free-market economy. Hiring and retaining veterans and military spouses effectively is a competitive economic weapon. All organizations—small, medium, or large, for-profit, nonprofit, commercial, or governmental—benefit from successfully wielding it. Done well, the effort to fully utilize this valuable talent pool holds the potential to significantly increase the productivity of your organization and, by extension, the entire economy. And that is something we can **all** get behind!

OPPORTUNITY BY ANOTHER NAME

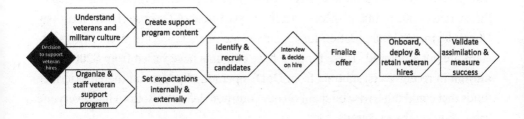

"A man who is good enough to shed his blood for his country is good enough to be given a square deal afterwards. More than that no man is entitled, and less than that no man shall have."

—**Theodore Roosevelt,** speech to veterans, Springfield, IL, July 4, 1903[1]

Teddy could not have foreseen the current civil-military gap in the country when he made this statement more than one hundred years ago, but I'm not sure it would have changed his sentiment. He is obviously talking about veterans (male and female), and I would contend that by "a square deal," he is referring to full employment. He also states that all veterans should at least have that opportunity, but nothing more. It is a grand notion.

But how does President Roosevelt's sentiment stand up against today's world? Do today's employers accept his premise? Why should they? What is it about today's veterans that should justify full employment? And even with that justification, how should employers bring this talent onboard their organizations?

This book addresses these important questions. Let's start with *why*. For starters, it's good business. Consider that the nation's military community comprises approximately thirty-seven million individuals who wield $1.2 trillion in annual buying power.[2] Establishing a good reputation among this group would bear significant benefits. Even more importantly, veteran employment is critical to both the national economy and the country overall. Although veterans make up only about 8 percent of the nation's adult population and just more than 6 percent of the civilian labor pool, they have an outsized influence over the future of the country's all-volunteer force that defends our freedom, protects our liberty, and enables capitalism to thrive. If military service is not seen as providing a gateway to successful civilian careers, future participants in the nation's all-volunteer military may be dissuaded from serving. It is thus a matter of national security: "The success of veterans after service, and the positive perception of veterans as assets to their employers and communities, is vital to the success of our military."[3] Moreover, the Department of Defense (DoD) must pay Unemployment Compensation for Ex-Servicemembers (UCX) to states whose veterans are not employed. These funds, whose amounts have varied from **$200–900+ million** in recent years, subtract from DoD's operating budget and thereby sacrifice funds that could otherwise be spent on our common defense.[4] Bottom line: everyone wins when you hire veterans.

The World Economic Forum regularly cites the most problematic factors for doing business in the United States, and there are very few that an organizational leader can directly influence.[5] Other than innovation, infrastructure, and financing, the factor that leaders can most easily influence is the makeup of their workforces. Most organizations routinely cite skilled, sufficiently educated labor with a superior work ethic as one of their most needed resources—and one they routinely find in inadequate supply.

And yet, there is a readily available talent pool in sufficient quantities meeting this description hiding in plain sight. Veterans of the US armed forces have the skills, training, character, and work ethic that most organizations overwhelmingly desire. Veterans are perhaps one of the most valuable components of diversity and inclusion efforts. They emanate from an already diverse talent pool (31 percent of active-duty service members come from racial and ethnic minority groups), bring a bevy of transferable skills, and are readily available. With more than 200,000 of them matriculating from the military annually, they represent an ongoing just-in-time talent play. And their impact is palpable. Cumulative Gallup workplace studies uncovered a 22 percent increase in productivity at organizations that create inclusive environments that include veterans.[6]

COMPANIES IN THE COCKPIT

"In sum, veterans are an optimal strategic resource for challenging times."

Brynt Parmeter, Senior Director, Non-Traditional Talent
| Head of Walmart Military & Veterans Affairs

Furthermore, as illustrated in the academic research summarized in "The Business Case for Hiring a Veteran: Beyond the Clichés," veterans draw from their unique and specialized military experience to apply relevant and market-connected knowledge, skills, and competencies within an organization.[7] (See the list below.)

The Value of a Veteran in a Competitive Business Environment[8]

Veterans are entrepreneurial. Military veterans are twice more likely than non veterans to pursue business ownership after leaving service. The five-year success rate of ventures owned by veterans is significantly higher than the national average.

Veterans assume high levels of trust. The military service experience engenders a strong propensity toward an inherent trust and faith in co-workers and a strong tendency toward trust in organizational leadership.

Veterans are adept at skills transfer across contexts/tasks. Service members and veterans develop cognitive heuristics that readily facilitate knowledge/skills transfer through their military training in disparate tasks and situations.

Veterans have (and leverage) advanced technical training. Military experience, on average, exposes individuals to highly advanced technology and technology training. This accelerated exposure to high technology contributes to an enhanced ability to link technology-based solutions to organizational challenges.

Veterans are comfortable/adept in discontinuous environments. Cognitive and decision-making research has demonstrated that the military experience is positively correlated to the ability to accurately evaluate a dynamic decision environment and subsequently act in the face of uncertainty.

Veterans exhibit high levels of resilience. Military veterans exhibit high levels of resilient behavior because of their military experience. Veterans develop an enhanced ability to bounce back from failed professional or personal experiences more quickly and more thoroughly than non veterans.

Veterans exhibit advanced team-building skills. Veterans are more adept at 1) organizing and defining team goals and mission, 2) defining team member roles and responsibilities, and 3) developing an action plan. Further, research also suggests that those with prior military service have high efficacy for team-related activities. Veterans exhibit an inherent and enduring belief that they can efficiently and effectively integrate and contribute to a new or existing team.

Veterans exhibit strong organizational commitment. Research has demonstrated that military veterans bring this strong sense of organizational commitment and loyalty to the civilian workplace.

Veterans have (and exhibit) cross-cultural experiences. Individuals with military backgrounds 1) have more international experience, 2) speak more languages/more fluently, and 3) have a higher level of cultural sensitivity as compared to age-group peers that have not served in the military.

Veterans have experience/skill in diverse work settings. Those with military experience are (on average) highly accepting of individual differences in a work setting and exhibit a high level of cultural sensitivity regarding such differences in the context of workplace interpersonal relationships.

Moreover, a recent survey by the Center for a New American Security found that more than 90 percent of HR managers said veterans are promoted faster than their non veteran peers, and 68 percent said that veterans performed better or much better than their non veteran peers. More than 75 percent also said that veterans are easier or significantly easier to manage than their non veteran peers. In short, "Veterans bring a level of dedication and professionalism that promotes the bottom line while lower turnover increases institutional knowledge and cuts costs."[9]

COMPANIES IN THE COCKPIT

"Another similarity is the military's dedication to its mission. Tesla has a mission—it is changing the world and saving the environment. This mission focus has resonated with veterans, many of whom have turned down opportunities with more money to be part of this mission. They see themselves as having a bigger purpose and being a part of something larger than themselves."

Dustin Whidden, former Tesla Veterans Program Manager

Why is this? On average, veterans are more educated than their civilian peers, with 97 percent having a high school education or higher.[10] Further, veterans are 160 percent more likely than non veterans to have a graduate degree or other advanced degree.[11] Most have had hands-on experience, technical training, licenses, and certifications that prepare them for the corresponding civilian certification.[12] Also, most senior non-commissioned officers (NCOs) and officers enter the workforce with an active security clearance, which may be helpful in roles that require it, ease the burden of accessing military installations for recruiting purposes, and provide additional confidence in their authenticity. At a minimum, possession of a security clearance indicates the passage of a rigorous background investigation.

Security Clearances

Organizations obtain security clearances for employees who may be sending, receiving, or developing information that the government has deemed important to national security. The process for doing so may be lengthy and cost several thousand dollars. The largest group of individuals with security clearances is in the military. There are three levels of clearance:

LEVEL	CAPABILITY	REINVESTIGATION
Confidential	Enables access to material that, if improperly disclosed, could be reasonably expected to cause some measurable damage to national security.	Every 15 years
Secret	Enables access to material whose unauthorized disclosure could be expected to cause serious damage to national security.	Every 10 years
Top Secret	Enables access to information or material that could be expected to cause exceptionally grave damage to national security if released without authorization.	Every 5 years

Obtaining a security clearance entails passing a thorough background investigation that may involve a polygraph (lie detector test). Investigating agencies evaluate an individual's "loyalty and allegiance to the United States, including any information relevant to strength of character, honesty, discretion, sound judgment, reliability, ability to protect classified or sensitive information, and trustworthiness" to determine eligibility for a security clearance.[13]

COMPANIES IN THE COCKPIT

"USAA values the core work ethic that veterans bring with them from the military. USAA is a company whose culture is aligned with a purpose-driven mission. Given the military's similar orientation, veterans adjust to that aspect relatively easily. Another thing that veterans bring is their learning agility. They tend to be more adept at creating order from chaos."

Marcus "Ohley" Ohlenforst, Military Talent Strategist, USAA Talent Acquisition

Moreover, veterans demonstrate many "soft skills" such as professionalism, teamwork, interpersonal and emotional intelligence, critical thinking, and the ability to solve problems, many of which they developed during military service.[14] In sum, veterans have the skills that US employers say are needed for success in the workplace. (See Figure 1.)

Most Important Skills Cited by Employers for Workplace Success	Skills Strengthened or Enhanced by Military Service
• Professionalism / work ethic • Teamwork / collaboration • Oral and written communication • Critical thinking / problem-solving • Ethics / social responsibility	• Professionalism • Work ethic / discipline • Leadership & management skills • Mental toughness • Adaptation to different challenges

Figure 1. Demand and Supply of Workplace Skills[15,16]

As this would indicate, and indeed as our collective post–World War II experience shows, veterans can become the backbone of our organizations and communities.

COMPANIES IN THE COCKPIT

"Veterans serve in some of our most business-critical roles within JPMC, such as providing network infrastructure services, cybersecurity and technology controls, and financial risk data and controls. Each of these functions allows the firm to maintain daily banking operations and deliver a level of business resiliency that are key to operating in an increasingly hostile global cyber networking environment."

Rhett Jeppson, JPMorgan Chase Military and Veterans Affairs Team

But as the veteran population relative to the nation's population has decreased, so has its presence and leadership in civilian institutions. Veteran presence among corporate leaders is at an all-time low. *The Wall Street Journal* reports that the percentage of large publicly held corporations whose CEOs had a military background is 2.6 percent![17] Even if you expand that group to include all S&P 500 board members, the percentage with a military background is still less than 5 percent.[18]

And those percentages are forecasted to continue their downward trend. As a result, research confirms that hiring managers maintain negative biases when confronting veterans due to this growing civil-military gap.[19] Those biases tend to result in the *under*employment of veterans. Underemployment occurs when a person engages in work that doesn't fully use their skills and abilities. A recent survey by LinkedIn found that 76 percent of the top industries hire veterans at a lower rate than their civilian peers and that veterans are more than 30 percent more likely to be underemployed than their civilian peers.[20] While the simple answer would be to address such biases and hire more veterans, several complicating factors have prevented this from becoming a reality.

DEFINITION OF A VETERAN

The Department of Veterans Affairs defines a veteran as "a person who served in the active military, naval, or air service, and who was discharged or released therefrom under conditions other than dishonorable."[21]

Most veterans do not easily transition from the military to the civilian world. While many government support systems attempt to support that transition, they are collectively insufficient. And while many well-intentioned nongovernment support systems try to close this gap, the critical "last mile" of support—focused hiring efforts, onboarding support, affinity groups, mentoring programs, and their like—tends to rest at the feet of their prospective employers.

However, most organizations struggle with this "last mile" of support. The Corporate Executive Board (CEB) Corporate Leadership Council found that organizations tend to struggle with three aspects of veteran hiring:

- ♦ Attracting high-quality candidates,

- ♦ Translating military experience to civilian careers, and

- ♦ Transitioning veterans into the workforce.[22]

Most civilian organizations are not organized to successfully hire veterans. A Korn Ferry study documented that 80 percent of organizations do not have veteran-specific recruiting programs. The study also noted that 71 percent of organizations do not provide hiring managers or recruiters training on veteran hiring, and 52 percent do not provide onboarding or transition support to veteran hires.[23] Even worse, the US Chamber of Commerce recently documented that 90 percent of small businesses do not intentionally hire veterans.[24] And so, despite the enormous potential upside that this talent pool offers, few organizations are taking advantage. It is a missed opportunity.

This book is for those organizations not benefitting from the presence of veteran talent. And the size of your organization matters not. While the case studies featured in this book are primarily from large, blue-chip organizations within the Fortune 500 or the federal government—all of which have ample resources to enable this goal—your organization need not be among those groups to partake of this productive talent pool. The case studies herein featuring smaller organizations will show you the way.

COMPANIES IN THE COCKPIT

"Many companies have good intentions regarding veterans, but they lack sufficiently detailed processes to deal with the reality of transitioning veterans. Some companies say they want to hire veterans, but they haven't thought through how they will organize and staff programs to do so."

Chris Newton, Workforce Development Manager at Cajun Industries

To capitalize on this opportunity, we must address the root causes imperiling successful veteran transitions. The responsibility for addressing them is shared among the veterans themselves, their prospective employers, and the governmental entities that created them in the first place. My first book, *Mission Transition,* focused on the veteran's approach to transition. The primary audience for this work is employers interested in hiring and retaining veterans. Employers are the flip side of the same coin regarding veteran employment concerns. They share the goal of having the transitioning veteran be optimally productive in the most efficient and effective manner possible.

The primary question this work attempts to resolve is: How can employers better prepare for and utilize transitioning veteran talent to improve the productivity and competitiveness of their organizations?

This book is organized by a process that provides answers to this question. Each chapter will detail a step in the process. Highlighted icons throughout the book will indicate what part of the process is discussed in that chapter. Each chapter is followed by a summary of "Keys to Success" to emphasize specific topics. Where detail exists that is more specific to the needs of smaller employers, I call it out. This process mirrors the process advocated for veterans in my first book, which is no coincidence. Your efforts will be most successful when pursued in parallel with the veterans'. See Figure 2 for the recommended approach for employers intent on supporting veterans.

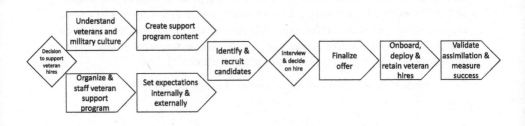

Figure 2. Veteran Assimilation Process

This book will focus on how to hire veterans and how to help employers effectively and efficiently manage veterans throughout all phases of the employment life cycle, shown in Figure 3.

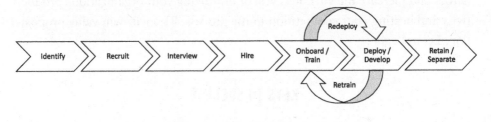

Figure 3. Employment Life Cycle

A veteran's complete transition must address multiple dimensions: employment, education, healthcare, and family support, among others. While the book will address many of these, this effort focuses on veterans' employment since full employment tends to assuage issues related to the other social determinants of health.

Also, this book was written as a *practical guide,* to be implemented a chapter at a time. I expect you will come back to the material again and again over time in your journey to hire veterans.

COMPANIES IN THE COCKPIT

"The military trains veterans to understand and accept accountability and responsibility. The military trains veterans to obey orders, live drug-free lives, lead others, organize chaos, and earn certifications applicable in industry. In short, through these experiences, veterans are eminently trainable. By comparison, most college graduates can merely prove that they know how to go to school."

Chris Newton, Workforce Development Manager at Cajun Industries

Thank you for taking the time to understand the nature and culture of our veterans and transitioning service members. Few human capital investments will be worth more over time. You represent the economic engine by which veterans can assimilate back into society as productive members and propel themselves, their families, and your organization forward in doing so. My fervent hope is that applying these ideas will improve your process of assimilating more of these heroes and increase the virtuous cycle of improving your organization's productivity and beating your competition in the process. It's a win-win value proposition. Let us begin . . .

KEYS TO SUCCESS

- ◆ Your ability to effectively engage and attract veterans as a talent pool represents an organizational productivity opportunity and potential competitive advantage.

- ◆ Recognize your limitations, with whom you are dealing, and the opportunity this talent pool could afford your organization.

- ◆ When you design hiring programs for inclusion, you design your organization for the betterment of all.

- ◆ Understand that this is not a "broken" talent pool; this is a misunderstood and underutilized talent pool.

- ◆ This group will need more support than a typical new hire—throughout their transition as they acclimate and develop with mentorship.

CHAPTER 1

UNDERSTAND THE VETERAN AND MILITARY CULTURE

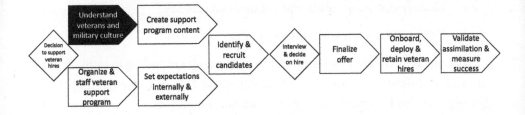

"What our servicemen and women want, more than anything else, is the assurance of satisfactory employment upon their return to civil life. The first task after the war is to provide employment for them and for our demobilized workers. . . . The goal after the war should be the maximum utilization of our human and material resources. . . . We must make provision now to help our returning service men and women bridge the gap from war to peace activity. When the war is over, our men and women in the Armed Forces will be eager to rejoin their families, get a job, or continue their education and to pick up the threads of their former lives."

President Franklin D. Roosevelt,
Message to Congress, November 23, 1943[1]

As employers, we live in an age of abundance regarding support and incentives for hiring veterans. There may have never been a time when so many programs existed. Google "veteran hiring initiative," and you'll see what I'm saying. The president of the United States (POTUS) has signed executive orders. Federal and state government agencies have put forth guidelines in support. And many of your fellow employers have announced hiring campaigns for veterans—all good. But when the rubber meets the road—when the actual hiring commences— some may find the act is not as easy as it sounds. Although recent studies reveal improvements,[2] many wide-ranging reasons explain why the retention rates of newly hired veterans have historically been low. My first book, *Mission Transition*, addresses how veterans themselves drive many of them. This book addresses how employers drive some of those reasons—and poses some ideas for improving your approach. For those new to hiring veterans, this book aims to help you optimize your approach from the outset.

In this chapter, we discuss how to:

♦ Comply with the primary requirement for success.

♦ Identify company values and cultural dimensions.

♦ Define differences with military culture.

The outcome of this chapter should be a thorough grounding in military culture and its differences from your own, accompanied by an understanding of the first requirement for veteran hiring program success.

Let's be clear from the outset: *All good intentions to support veterans transitioning into your organization will fail if your senior executives do not support it with sufficient human and monetary resources.* This is step one. Based on a study by Syracuse University's Institute for Veterans and Military Families, senior leadership engagement is the most important factor in overcoming cultural obstacles related to veteran-focused employment initiatives. Goodwill alone is insufficient to overcome these barriers and sustain enduring commitments to such programs. "Executive level commitment is essential to motivate the culture change necessary to institutionalize programs and processes positioned to sustain a focus on veterans' employment within a private-sector organization."[3] We revisit this topic in Chapter 3 when we discuss the appropriate staffing and governance of these programs. Executive-level champions are the first key to success.

COMPANIES IN THE COCKPIT

"To ensure success, you need to have:

♦ Buy-in from both senior leadership and front-line managers—both recruiters and production/operations.

♦ Senior leadership overtly demonstrate appreciation to veteran employees. It shows both the value of the employee and the program.

♦ A full-time resource dedicated to veteran hiring can help train others who will interface with veterans throughout the employment life cycle. This should not be an additional duty for the regular civilian recruiter."

Dustin Whidden, former Tesla Veterans Program Manager

With that requirement met, let's next address one of the fundamental requirements in understanding veterans and enabling their successful assimilation: understanding cultural differences and making them transparent. The advantages of hiring for a culture fit are significant. Multiple studies demonstrate that when there is a good fit between the employee and the organization, the employee:

♦ Will report greater job satisfaction. Between 50 and 90 percent of job satisfaction directly correlates to culture fit.[4]

♦ Is more likely to continue employment with the organization. Leadership IQ reports that 89 percent of employees who quit or get fired in their first 18 months do so because of a lack of culture fit.[5]

♦ Will show higher job performance levels. Studies demonstrate a strong correlation ($R^2 = .43$) between culture fit and greater mental and physical health, which leads to better job performance.[6]

The basis for this understanding lies in mapping how the values and beliefs of the military compare with that of your organization. Values form the basis for behavior, and the collective behaviors of the organization form culture. Let's review each service's core values. (See Table 1-1.)

Army[7]	◆ Loyalty ◆ Duty ◆ Respect ◆ Selfless service ◆ Honor ◆ Integrity ◆ Personal courage
Marine Corps[8] and Navy[9]	◆ Honor ◆ Courage ◆ Commitment
Air Force[10]	◆ Integrity first ◆ Service before self ◆ Excellence in all we do
Space Force[11]	◆ Character ◆ Connection ◆ Commitment ◆ Courage
Coast Guard[12]	◆ Honor ◆ Respect ◆ Devotion to duty

Table 1-1: Values of Each Service

In Table 1-2, list your organization's values and compare them to the military values list.

Military Values	Your Organization's Values
◆ Honor and integrity	◆
◆ Commitment, loyalty, and duty	◆
◆ Courage	◆
◆ Leadership by example	◆
◆ Selfless service	◆
◆ Respect	◆
◆ Excellence	◆
◆ Discipline	◆

Table 1-2: Military Values Comparison

Upon reflection, you're likely to find both similarities and differences. These similarities and differences will drive behaviors that you will likely see in veterans, which collectively form the basis for what you perceive as the military's culture.

COMPANIES IN THE COCKPIT

"USAA takes an integrated approach to our Military Talent Strategy. The approach builds upon the foundation established by our Corporate Strategy and is informed by the USAA Standard, which has embedded our shared military core values. We accomplish this by coming together through enterprise collaboration, coordination, and alignment to achieve a greater collective impact of all that we do for the military community. This concerted focus demonstrates how USAA is truly made for the military community—because we understand, care, and share their values, attitudes, and beliefs."[13]

Marcus "Ohley" Ohlenforst, Military Talent Strategist, USAA Talent Acquisition

Table 1-3 highlights typical cultural dimensions of military and civilian organizations.[14] Compare how the behaviors of military organizations differ from civilian ones. You'll see a range of behaviors, just as there is a range of organizations. These behaviors offer both similarities to—and differences with—the behaviors of the military. Which of these represent behaviors in your organization? In your experience working with veterans, what other differences have you observed? Use the empty rows at the bottom of the table to enter your thoughts. How do these behaviors compare with your organization? Populate the last column with your thoughts and observations.

Cultural Dimension	Military Organizations	Larger Civilian Organizations	Smaller Civilian Organizations	Your Organization
Purpose	Mission	Money	Money	
Leadership Basis	Team	Individual	Team	
Organizational Structure	Hierarchy	Matrix	Hierarchy	
Power Basis	Formal	Personal	Personal	
Onboarding Process	Structured, thorough	Unstructured, limited	Minimal	
Training Administration	In-person, classroom environment, provided automatically	Self-service, virtual, provided upon request	Minimal	
Compensation & Benefits	Public	Private	Private	
Assumption of Responsibility	Sooner, more	Later	Sooner, more	
Recognition & Rewards	Public	Private	Public or private	
Rank/Level in Organization	Publicly known	Privately known	Privately known	
Occupational Specialty	Deep knowledge	Deep knowledge	Deep and broad knowledge	

Table 1-3: Typical Military and Civilian Cultural Dimensions

Cultural Dimension	Military Organizations	Larger Civilian Organizations	Smaller Civilian Organizations	Your Organization
Personal Initiative	Muted	Expected	Encouraged	
Rules of Engagement, Standard Operating Procedures	Spoken, written	Unspoken, unwritten	Undocumented	
Work Intensity Duration	Shorter bursts, sprints	Longer-term, marathon	Combination	
Time in Grade/Role	Shorter	Longer	Shorter	
Talent Models	One	One or more	One or more	
Career Management	Top-down	Bottom-up	Bottom-up	
Receptiveness to Change	Accepting	Fearful	Accepting	
Thrives On	Chaos	Order	Chaos	
Frequency of Feedback	More frequent	Less frequent	More or less frequent	
Requesting Help	Not encouraged	Encouraged	Encouraged	
Lifestyle Choices	Few, if any	Many	Many	
After-work Interaction	Much	Little	Some	
Employee Category	Just-cause	At-will or just-cause (unions)	At-will	
Governing Law	UCMJ, oath of office, enlistment contract	Constitutional law, employment agreement	Constitutional law, employment agreement	

Table 1-3 (continued)

In compiling this table, you will have drafted a definition of your organization's culture. Now let's focus on the differences and ponder why they exist. Understanding the reasons for these differences will significantly impact your ability to help veterans successfully assimilate into your organization.

PURPOSE

One of the most significant differences you need to help veterans come to terms with is your organization's purpose and their unique role in furthering it. They are coming from an organization whose mission was as patriotic as it comes (defending the free world), involved contributing to a cause that was greater than themselves, and whose outcome had life-or-death consequences for those involved. Finding motivation was easy for them when their service focused on their team, unit, and country every day. The nature of their service was selfless. This mission gave their lives deep meaning and personal satisfaction during their time in service. They identified with it and internalized it. Supervisors measured them in their annual efficiency reports on their ability to display the above military values, and they took great pride in doing so. Now, things are likely different for them. Unless you are a nonprofit, your organization's purpose looks quite different from what they were used to.

COMPANIES IN THE COCKPIT

"Coming into the corporate world, veterans have no perspective. This is unfamiliar territory for them. There is a certain fear factor at play. They are used to a specific structure and processes to get things done, but that system no longer exists. They have to overcome that fear by realizing that they bring something incredibly valuable with them, leadership. What they don't know is how to translate what they've done so that civilians can understand."

Beau Higgins, Senior Manager, Amazon Military Recruiting Center of Excellence | Worldwide Operations Talent Acquisition

Assuming your organization is in the private sector, your main reason for existing is to make money—pure and simple. This is, of course, as it should be. No apologies are needed for fulfilling your intended function in a market economy. To you, this is no great insight. To veterans, it may be a revelation. To compound matters in the eyes of the veteran, motivations at a personal level may also include the accumulation of power, recognition, or some other goal they may see as being selfish. Statistics tell us that veterans may have difficulty finding purpose and motivation in supporting what—on its surface—may seem to be a selfish mission. One study found that 64 percent of veterans say they felt a greater sense of meaning and purpose in the military than they do in their current job.[15] A separate study found that active-duty service members have higher rates of well-being than all American workers, but employed veterans fare worse than the general workforce.[16] So, how do you help transitioning veterans avoid becoming a statistic and successfully fulfill their intended role in your organization?

You do so by helping them find new meaning in their work—by helping them redefine their personal mission to align with your organization's product or service. Studies tell us that veterans want to do work that allows them to promote global health, grow spiritually, protect the environment, save lives, develop deep camaraderie, improve the lot of humankind, and provide social services.[17] **You must help them look past the core reason for your business's existence (making money) and tie their personal value to what your organization does or enables.** You must help them redirect their basis for aligning with your organization and committing to its mission. For example, I work in professional services. I serve clients with significant business challenges that require an outside perspective to help resolve them. In doing so, I'm not only helping improve their lot in life, I'm helping improve the lot of all *their* customers as well. Service is still the basis of my work (albeit for different purposes and in other capacities than when I was in the military), and it is that on which I thrive. Service is still what gets me out of bed in the morning, just as it did when I was in the military. All veterans will need to come to a similar realization to find their "new normal." And if they are struggling with that, they need to feel comfortable asking for help.

COMPANIES IN THE COCKPIT

"There are some visible ways in which the culture of the military and corporations differ (e.g., dress code, hierarchy) and some ways that may not be as visible (e.g., rules of behavior, roles, and status). The transition from 'serving the country' to 'serving the customer' can challenge a veteran's sense of purpose. It can help to see your organization's positive impact by providing products and services your customers want and need. We find that it's important for our veterans to believe that our company operates with integrity and makes a positive impact in our communities."

Rhett Jeppson, JPMorgan Chase Military and Veterans Affairs Team

LEADERSHIP BASIS

One result of living the selfless-service value in the military is that the team or unit always took precedence. It was the basis for getting things done. Even if individuals had a significant accomplishment supporting their team, the military's focus on servant leadership resulted in them posing that accomplishment as part of the greater team effort. Much of the basis for a service member's annual evaluation report was their team's or unit's performance. Military members might brag to others about what their team or unit accomplished, but that likely had little to do with their individual efforts. And in doing so, the first word they used was *we* and never *I*.

Your view is likely very different. You probably view these veterans as individuals with specific strengths and skills that you desire to acquire, not those of their teams. In interviews and on résumés, you are interested in hearing about particular efforts that the candidate—not their team—took to enable success. Doing so is very difficult for veterans. For perhaps the first time, they find themselves needing to speak in the singular ("I") rather than plural ("we") voice.

To compound things in the eyes of the veteran, this focus on the individual continues beyond their hire date. In many organizations, personal evaluations and rewards tend to have more to do with individual efforts than that of their teams. Internal promotion boards and evaluation review boards tend to focus on individual contributions and individual potential, just as in the initial hiring process. We see this in society on most social media outlets, where the focus is almost entirely on the individual. Identifying what percentage of posts highlight the team's efforts versus the individual would prove my point.

However, because of their experience working in teams, veterans can significantly increase coordination and cooperation in any organization they join. But they will need support in learning how to thrive in a culture in which organizations emphasize individual efforts. They will need to adjust their expectations in working with individuals on their teams in the short term. Those individuals will have different motivations than their former military peers. Understanding those motivations and factoring that into their approach will be key to success. To enable their long-term success, they will need to make an ongoing adjustment at evaluation or promotion time. Just as they did in documenting their accomplishments in leaving the military, they will need to learn to characterize their team's achievements in the form of what they personally enabled. Here is a little tactic that can help:

1. Have them create a folder in their email software program for personal plaudits.

2. Whenever someone sends them a complimentary or thankful message for something they or their team enabled, have them store that message in this newly created folder.

3. Come evaluation or promotion time, they can collate those messages into a cohesive document that will inevitably and charitably speak to their individual contributions.

This approach is an easy way to help them get used to selling themselves.

"Once veterans get on the inside of the organization, they come to realize there is nothing magical at work. Leadership is leadership, regardless of where you are. However, they must tailor their approach to fit the culture, as some leadership styles in the military don't translate over directly into the civilian world."

Beau Higgins, Senior Manager, Amazon Military Recruiting Center of Excellence | Worldwide Operations Talent Acquisition

ORGANIZATIONAL STRUCTURE

Military units are hierarchical structures. They are purposely designed to enable the exercise of authority and direction necessary for propagating missions and tasks. It's why they call them *commands*. For example, a team leader reports to a squad leader, who reports to a platoon leader, who reports to a company commander, and so on (see Table 1-4 on pg. 17 for details on the scope of responsibility by level). Veterans implicitly understand how such organizations work—how directives are given and to whom they are accountable for their actions. In such organizations, that accountability chain tends to be singular—they are accountable to a single individual.

Your organization likely doesn't work that way. Most organizations are structured in the form of a matrix, in which the accountability chain has multiple dimensions. In such organizations, veterans would likely be receiving direction from, and thus be accountable to, multiple individuals simultaneously. Such an approach has its benefits. A matrix structure tends to be looser and allows for more flexibility and responsiveness. It tends to promote collaboration, information flow, and knowledge sharing. Employees tend to be grouped by talents or clustered by projects within it. They may work on different projects simultaneously while communicating with multiple peers and reporting to multiple decision-makers. Because employees report to multiple individuals in positions of authority, a matrix structure also allows for more career development and professional growth options. Lateral moves, which are more widely available, are viewed as advancements within the organization. You understand this implicitly; however, this is foreign territory to most veterans.

For them to succeed in this new environment, you'll need to coach veterans on how to work within it. For a matrixed organization to succeed, the multiple dimensions of the matrix must be integrated in some way. A positive way to encourage veteran engagement is to pose part of their responsibility as enabling that integration. You might coach veterans to position themselves as champions of collaboration, coordination, information flow, and knowledge sharing. However, doing this successfully will require them to leave their level (or job title) at the door. Coming from an environment in which their military rank carried much weight, they must understand that their former rank has no place in their new organization. In fact, they may find themselves working with, if not reporting to, people who are junior to them. This is something to which they will likely need to adjust. You will need to teach that the collective viewpoints of the team will help reduce ambiguity and result in a more well-rounded solution.

POWER BASIS

John R. P. French Jr. and Bertram Raven defined six different bases of power:[18]

- Reward Power—the perceived ability to give positive consequences or remove negative ones

- Coercive Power—the perceived ability to punish those who do not conform with your ideas or demands

- Legitimate Power—the perception that someone has the right to prescribe behavior due to election or appointment to a position of responsibility

- Referent Power—the association with others who possess power

- Expert Power—having distinctive knowledge, expertise, abilities, or skills

- Informational Power—based on controlling the information needed by others to reach an important goal

The military primarily leverages Legitimate, Reward, and Coercive power. Let's call this a *formal* power structure or basis. To the veteran, this makes total sense and is consistent with the military's command-and-control environment. Imagine if a combat leader had to take the time to explain the rationale for every single order. By contrast, civilian organizations tend to leverage Referent, Expert, and Informational power. Collectively, let's call this a *personal* power basis.

COMPANIES IN THE COCKPIT

"Given USAA's brand and reputation in the military community, some transitioning veterans have an expectation that USAA is their next PCS [Permanent Change of Station], but it's not. USAA has a corporate culture whereby the average service member that matriculates into USAA takes a while to learn how to lead through influence. The culture of USAA is collaborative, which may be different from the military environment these veterans are coming from."

Marcus "Ohley" Ohlenforst, Military Talent Strategist, USAA Talent Acquisition

This difference will have broad implications for how veterans must adjust their leadership style in your organization. They should understand that they will no longer be *directing* or *commanding* anyone. They will, however, be *coaching, guiding, mentoring,* and *inspiring* others. It's still leadership; it just occurs in different ways. You will need to teach veterans that effective leaders in the civilian world motivate others to achieve significant results by leveraging personal power.

COMPANIES IN THE COCKPIT

"It can be a challenge for some veterans to transform their leadership styles to adapt to the new environment in which they are working. To be effective at Amazon, they have to learn that they can't just yell or scream to motivate people. They must learn to leave their rank behind and flex practical elements of their leadership style for applicable situations."

Beau Higgins, Senior Manager, Amazon Military Recruiting Center of Excellence | Worldwide Operations Talent Acquisition

ONBOARDING PROCESS AND TRAINING ADMINISTRATION

Upon joining the military, all veterans go through a basic training experience that teaches them how to be a professional soldier, marine, sailor, or airman from the ground up. A series of courses specific to an individual's military occupation follows and teaches them their craft in a crawl-walk-run succession of learning steps. The process is structured, formal, in-person, and automatically programmed and provided.

Most civilian organizations do not enable a similar experience. Over the years, budgetary considerations and technology enablement have resulted in an onboarding experience that is more abbreviated and virtual. Moreover, most organizations are anxious to immediately leverage a veteran's strengths honed during their years in the military—not have them tied up in an onboarding experience or training classes. As a result, a veteran's expectations for a formal indoctrination process are usually not met. Organizations tend to quickly assign them to a role in what, to them, feels like a sink-or-swim environment with little training or support.

The takeaway is to set clear expectations up front with incoming veterans regarding the onboarding process and whatever initial training they are to receive. If a formal program is in the offing, let them know when and where it will take place. If supporting material is available online, direct them to its location and encourage them to take advantage of it as soon as it's feasible. Further, encourage them to take advantage of as many self-development opportunities as possible while augmenting this "academic" material with the real-world lessons learned from their new peers and teammates. Veterans should view this as an excellent opportunity to broaden their new internal network. We cover much more on this topic later in the book.

COMPENSATION AND BENEFITS

Veterans are used to crystal-clear transparency on this topic—for both themselves and everyone else. Military pay tables and tables for most benefits are public knowledge and easily available online. If you knew a military member's rank, time in service, and geographic location, you could easily calculate nearly to the penny how much that person netted in every paycheck. As a result, there was never much debate around this topic. Everyone knew what everyone else was making, and what you made was what you made—end of story.

That is not how you treat this topic. While guidelines and pay bands likely exist, nearly all compensation and benefits result from a negotiated settlement with employees and are subject to being revisited. Moreover, most of the information regarding pay bands and specifics around individual pay packages below executive levels is typically closely held and normally not publicly available.

You will need to set clear expectations with veterans early on regarding how to treat this topic. What information you share regarding their compensation and benefits is meant for their eyes only—just as it is for their new peers in the organization. Compensation is not a topic they should be openly discussing, and if they have any questions or concerns regarding it, they should address them with either their immediate supervisor or HR.

ASSUMPTION OF RESPONSIBILITY

The military tends to confer significant responsibility on its members at relatively young ages. As one of my old platoon sergeants told me, "War is a young person's game." It's a fact of life in the military. In its paper "Lost in Translation: The Civil-Military Divide and Veteran Employment," the Center for a New American Security states, "Civilian employers generally lag government agencies, let alone the military, in conferring rank and responsibility. Few employers will immediately put a transitioning veteran, or any employee, in a position comparable in responsibility and management to their last job in the military."[19] Exceptions occur when the transitioning veteran has done an exceptional job translating their specific skills to benefit the prospective employer, which often doesn't happen. So, you must understand that veterans are used to taking on significant responsibilities from the outset and will tend to get bored or turned off if that's not the case. As stated previously, they learn and adapt to new environments very quickly. Thus, it becomes more important to staff your veteran hiring teams with individuals effectively trained in recognizing how best to place veteran talent in your organization.

RECOGNITION AND REWARDS; RANK/LEVEL IN ORGANIZATION

In the military, veterans wore uniforms—every single day. On that uniform were displayed their rank insignia, individual and unit medals or badges won, the patch of the unit to which they belonged, and other particulars that would relate their role, organization, and accomplishments in a very public manner. As a military member, they would be able to garner a thorough understanding of a fellow service member's history and capabilities without uttering a single word. (See Figure 1-1 and Figure 1-2 for military ranks, and Figure 1-3 on page 18 for understanding the relationship among them.) Moreover, they usually would take great pride in wearing that uniform, part of which sprang from the very public manner in which many of those badges, awards, and rank were conferred. Typically, military units hold large public ceremonies for award presentations, promotions, or changes in command.

Rank	Army	Marines	Navy	Air Force	Space Force	Coast Guard
E-1	Private	Private	Seaman Recruit (SR)	Airman Basic	Specialist 1 (Spc1)	Seaman Recruit (SR)
E-2	Private (PV2)	Private First Class (PFC)	Seaman Apprentice (SA)	Airman	Specialist 2 (Spc2)	Seaman Apprentice (SA)
E-3	Private First Class (PFC)	Lance Corporal (LCpl)	Seaman (SN)	Airman First Class (A1C)	Specialist 3 (Spc3)	Seaman (SN)
E-4	Corporal (CPL) -------------------- Specialist (SPC)	Corporal (Cpl)	Petty Officer Third Class (PO3)	Senior Airman (SrA)	Specialist 4 (Spc4)	Petty Officer Third Class (PO3)
E-5	Sergeant (SGT)	Sergeant (Sgt)	Petty Officer Second Class (PO2)	Staff Sergeant (SSgt)	Sergeant (Sgt)	Petty Officer Second Class (PO2)
E-6	Staff Sergeant (SSG)	Staff Sergeant (SSgt)	Petty Officer First Class (PO1)	Technical Sergeant (TSgt)	Technical Sergeant (TSgt)	Petty Officer First Class (PO1)
E-7	Sergeant First Class (SFC)	Gunnery Sergeant (GySgt)	Chief Petty Officer (CPO)	Master Sergeant (MSgt) -------------------- First Sergeant	Master Sergeant (MSgt)	Chief Petty Officer (CPO)
E-8	Master Sergeant (MSG) -------------------- First Sergeant (1SG)	Master Sergeant (MSgt) -------------------- First Sergeant	Senior Chief Petty Officer (SCPO)	Senior Master Sergeant (SMSgt) -------------------- First Sergeant	Senior Master Sergeant (SMSgt)	Senior Chief Petty Officer (SCPO)
E-9	Sergeant Major (SGM) -------------------- Command Sergeant Major (CSM)	Master Gunnery Sergeant (MGySgt) -------------------- Sergeant Major (SgtMaj)	Master Chief Petty Officer (MCPO) -------------------- Fleet/Command Master Chief Petty Officer	Chief Master Sergeant (CMSgt) -------------------- First Sergeant -------------------- Command Chief Master Sergeant	Chief Master Sergeant (CMSgt)	Master Chief Petty Officer (MCPO) -------------------- Fleet/Command Master Chief Petty Officer
Senior Enlisted Advisors	Sergeant Major of the Army (SMA)	Sergeant Major of the Marine Corps (SgtMajMC)	Master Chief Petty Officer of the Navy (MCPON)	Chief Master Sergeant of the Air Force (CMSAF)	Chief Master Sergeant of the Space Force (CMSSF)	Master Chief Petty Officer of the Coast Guard (MCPOCG)

Figure 1-1. Enlisted Military Ranks[20]

Understanding Military Ranks

Military ranks consist of enlisted ("E") and officer ("O") ranks (Warrant Officers—a specialized officer rank for individuals with highly skilled expertise in their assigned area—are referred to by "W"). A numeral that indicates the level of rank within the enlisted or officer corps (the higher the number, the higher the rank) follows this letter designation. Officers supervise enlisted personnel, and enlisted personnel make up more than three-quarters of the military population. Enlisted ranks above E-4 are called Non-Commissioned Officers (NCOs). Officer ranks lower than O-4 are known as Junior Military Officers (JMOs). Officer ranks above O-6 are called Flag ranks, as Generals (Army, Marines, and Air Force) and Admirals (Navy and Coast Guard) are always accompanied by a flag displaying their rank at ceremonial functions. Almost all officers and most senior NCOs (E-7–E-9) have at least an undergraduate degree. Nearly all enlisted personnel have a high school diploma or GED equivalent. Officers receive their commissions from three sources:

◆ The nation's Service Academies (US Military Academy, US Naval Academy, US Air Force Academy, US Coast Guard Academy, and the US Merchant Marine Academy).

- The Reserve Officer Training Corps (ROTC).

- Officer Candidate School.

As Table 1-4 indicates, the military spends considerable resources educating and training its members, outfits them with translatable skill sets, and places them in significant positions of authority at relatively early points in their careers.

Rank	Army	Marines	Navy	Air Force	Space Force	Coast Guard
W-1	Warrant Officer 1 (WO1)	Warrant Officer 1 (WO)	USN Warrant Officer 1 (WO1)	N/A	N/A	N/A
W-2	Chief Warrant Officer 2 (CW2)	Chief Warrant Officer 2 (CWO2)	USN Chief Warrant Officer 2 (CWO2)	N/A	N/A	Chief Warrant Officer 2 (CWO2)
W-3	Chief Warrant Officer 3 (CW3)	Chief Warrant Officer 3 (CWO3)	USN Chief Warrant Officer 3 (CWO3)	N/A	N/A	Chief Warrant Officer 3 (CWO3)
W-4	Chief Warrant Officer 4 (CW4)	Chief Warrant Officer 4 (CWO4)	USN Chief Warrant Officer 4 (CWO4)	N/A	N/A	Chief Warrant Officer 4 (CWO4)
W-5	Chief Warrant Officer 5 (CW5)	Chief Warrant Officer 5 (CWO5)	USN Chief Warrant Officer 5 (CWO5)	N/A	N/A	N/A
O-1	Second Lieutenant (2LT)	Second Lieutenant (2ndLt)	Ensign (ENS)	Second Lieutenant (2nd Lt)	Second Lieutenant (2nd Lt)	Ensign (ENS)
O-2	First Lieutenant (1LT)	First Lieutenant (1stLt)	Lieutenant Junior Grade (LTJG)	First Lieutenant (1st Lt)	First Lieutenant (1st Lt)	Lieutenant Junior Grade (LTJG)
O-3	Captain (CPT)	Captain (Capt)	Lieutenant (LT)	Captain (Capt)	Captain (Capt)	Lieutenant (LT)
O-4	Major (MAJ)	Major (Maj)	Lieutenant Commander (LCDR)	Major (Maj)	Major (Maj)	Lieutenant Commander (LCDR)
O-5	Lieutenant Colonel (LTC)	Lieutenant Colonel (LtCol)	Commander (CDR)	Lieutenant Colonel (Lt Col)	Lieutenant Colonel (Lt Col)	Commander (CDR)
O-6	Colonel (COL)	Colonel (Col)	Captain (CAPT)	Colonel (Col)	Colonel (Col)	Captain (CAPT)
O-7	Brigadier General (BG)	Brigadier General (BGen)	Rear Admiral Lower Half (RDML)	Brigadier General (Brig Gen)	Brigadier General (Brig Gen)	Rear Admiral Lower Half (RDML)
O-8	Major General (MG)	Major General (MajGen)	Rear Admiral Upper Half (RADM)	Major General (Maj Gen)	Major General (Maj Gen)	Rear Admiral Upper Half (RADM)
O-9	Lieutenant General (LTG)	Lieutenant General (LtGen)	Vice Admiral (VADM)	Lieutenant General (Lt Gen)	Lieutenant General (Lt Gen)	Vice Admiral (VADM)
O-10	General (GEN)	General (Gen)	Admiral (ADM)	General (Gen)	General (Gen)	Admiral (ADM)
Wartime Only	General of the Army	N/A	Fleet Admiral	General of the Air Force	N/A	Fleet Admiral

Figure 1-2. Officer Military Ranks[21]

Imagine their confusion when they enter an entirely new world where their new "uniform," whether formal or casual dress, has no such publicly visible signs of their past accomplishments or level in the organization. Upon reviewing the outward appearance of others in the organization, they will be unable to instantaneously understand those individuals' backgrounds or their roles in the organization. And so, veterans must be taught that they will need to work much harder to understand the backgrounds of their new peers, which will require a deeper level of communication than they might be used to. (If your organization has an online organization chart or list of personnel biographies, please point your veterans to these resources.) It would help if you taught them to avoid

Rank	Education	Military Role	Military Training	Translatable Skill Sets	Military Personnel Supervised	Equivalent Civilian Role	Civilian Personnel Supervised
O-7 – O-10	Advanced Degree	• Enterprise leader • Coalition leader (Joint Services, Interagency, International)	• Advanced Senior Leader education • Joint Chiefs of Staff education	• Strategic planning • National policy implementation • Enterprise policy development • Advising elected officials	10,000+	CXO (CEO, COO, CFO, CIO, etc.)	1000+
O4 – O-6 / W4 – W5	Advanced Degree	• Large-Unit leader • Staff commander	• War college • Command & General Staff College	• Advanced leadership • Organizational controls • Policy development • Long-term planning	3000+ (O-6) 1000+ (O-5)	President, vice president	600+
O-1 – O-3 / W-1 – W-3	Undergraduate Degree	• Small-unit leader	• Officer Basic & Advanced training • Technical schools	• Tactical planning • Team building • Basic leadership • Mentoring • Operational experience • Organizational administration	150 (O-3) 40 (O-1/2)	Director, operations manager, business analyst, engineer	~250 30 16 8
E7 – E9	Undergraduate Degree	• Large-unit leader • Senior Staff leader/ member	• Advanced professional and advisor courses	• Strategic management • Advanced advisory • Organizational administration	200+ (E-9) 40–200 (E-7/8)	Supervisor	8–40
E5 – E6	Undergraduate Degree or High School / GED	• Small-unit leader	• Basic leadership & technical schools	• Basic leadership • Team building • Coaching	10–60	Team leader	3–12
E1 – E4	High School / GED	• Member of team	• Basic training & technical schools	• Teamwork • Performance under pressure • Accountability • Honesty, loyalty	0	Analyst, programmer, generalist, specialist	2 1 1 0

Table 1-4: Education and Experiences of Military Ranks[22]

assumptions about anyone based on physical appearances alone. To paraphrase Stephen Covey, they will need to seek first to understand the other person before asking to be understood. Although veterans will initially find this frustrating, it is another excellent opportunity to broaden their new internal network.

In recruiting veterans, consider the breadth and depth of responsibility that the individual had, which tends to correspond to their rank. Table 1-4 and Figure 1-3 provide some perspective on how military rank relates to the scale and scope of their roles and, as such, the roles for which transitioning service members may be viable candidates within your organization.

Beyond the physical display of awards and rank, your organization also likely has few public ceremonies to recognize individual accomplishments, such as a promotion or an achievement of some sort. In my experience, those awards tend to be slower in coming and of a different nature (monetary) than in the military— and represent yet another departure from a typical veteran's experience. It would help to encourage them to adjust expectations and consider implementing such an approach within their sphere of influence. As long as they take a consistent, fair, and equitable approach to make such recognition public, it should go a long way to motivating the people under their charge—just as it did in the military.

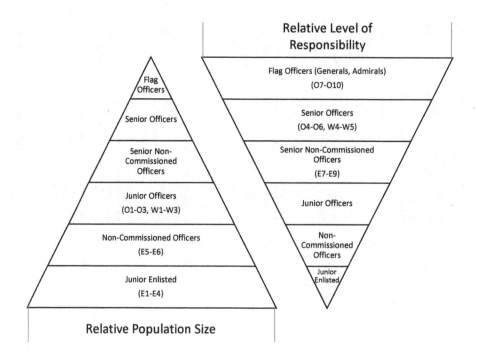

Figure 1-3. Relationships among Military Ranks

COMPANIES IN THE COCKPIT

"Schlumberger tends to hire JMOs [Junior Military Officers; officer ranks below O-4] for project management. Our ideal model is a service academy graduate with a top-tier MBA. Their career progression takes the form of a rotational program. They spend a year in the field learning the business from the ground up, then go on to another business function and then another. The purpose is to groom them for leadership roles within the company. This process gets them exposure to all aspects of the business and multiple geographies in an effort to create general managers."

Nick B. Tran, Manager, Community and Veteran Affairs at Schlumberger

OCCUPATIONAL SPECIALTY

In addition to rank, military members are assigned various military occupational specialties (MOS). The Army, Marines, and Coast Guard use this acronym, while the Air Force uses an Air Force Specialty Code (AFSC) and the Navy a Naval Enlistment Classification (NEC) to refer to the same thing. These codes refer to the functional capacity in which the veteran served in the military and are akin to corporate functions. The military trains its members to be deeply proficient in their specialty, especially among enlisted ranks, which, depending on the organization's size, may or may not translate well in the civilian workplace. Larger civilian organizations similarly value depth in corporate function specialization, whereas smaller civilian organizations, whose employees typically span multiple functions, require breadth and depth of expertise. Most military skill specialties translate directly to the civilian world (see Figure 1-4). It is interesting to note that only about 15 percent of military members serve in a combat specialty role, countering the prevailing stereotype. Flipping that statistic, even though *all* transitioning veterans have the soft skills that you desire, about 85 percent of veterans work in roles whose skill sets are immediately accretive to your organization.

Occupational Specialties	Army	Air Force	Space Force	Coast Guard	Marines	Navy	Personnel per Occupational Specialty	
Administrative	5,073	13,253	—	—	11,933	20,393	50,652	3.9%
Combat Specialty	133,791	4,603	45	—	43,664	15,458	197,561	15.1%
Construction	14,353	4,991	—	—	6,119	3,849	29,312	2.2%
Electronics	28,934	28,552	4	—	14,333	50,455	122,278	9.3%
Engineering	67,538	69,368	2,777	—	33,180	57,968	230,831	17.6%
Managerial	13,601	6,942	757	—	2,684	6,732	30,716	2.3%
Healthcare	36,788	24,214	1	—	—	31,622	92,625	7.1%
Human Resources	18,278	10,091	9	—	3,140	8,744	40,274	3.1%
Machine Operator	4,153	6,695	—	—	2,399	9,402	22,649	1.7%
Media and PR	5,686	7,122	—	—	1,932	4,063	18,803	1.4%
Protective Service	23,655	35,804	—	—	5,257	14,918	79,634	6.1%
Support Service	10,323	6,381	—	—	2,097	9,901	28,702	2.2%
Transportation / Logistics	59,441	52,130	21	—	30,513	48,524	187,629	14.3%
Vehicle / Machine Mechanic	44,481	47,360	2	—	18,042	49,821	159,706	12.2%
Unspecified Code	3,077	5,382	2,741	—	966	8,540	20,706	1.6%
Total	469,172	322,888	6,357	40,208	176,259	340,390	1,312,078	100.0%

Figure 1-4. Military Occupational Specialties[23]

TIME IN GRADE AND TALENT MODELS

Similar to the transparency associated with compensation, the time frame that military members spent within a particular rank was relatively well defined and publicized. While it became more variable at senior ranks, veterans typically had a general sense of when they should expect their next promotion. Early in their careers, they could anticipate rising through the ranks relatively quickly and progressing in the scope and scale of their leadership responsibilities. Toward the end of their careers, military members who served more than twenty years became cognizant of mandatory retirement dates associated with specific ranks.

Veterans are likely to join your organization as experienced hires at some level beyond an entry-level role. And chances are, the time they spend in those roles will be somewhat variable—likely more so than occurs in the military. Also, unlike the military and by law, there is no mandatory retirement (although there are permissible exceptions).[24] And so, veterans should expect to spend more extended time frames within their assigned roles. To reduce this ambiguity, ensure that training on career paths for various talent models is part of your onboarding experience, if not part of the recruiting and interviewing processes. Doing so will set expectations for the veteran and allow proactive career management.

Speaking of talent models, you should understand that the primary talent model used in the military was "up or out." If service members didn't realize a promotion within standard time frames established by the military, there were removal dates by rank within which they needed to depart the service. Military members clearly understood these expectations, which were not subject to debate. Your organization may offer a similar "up or out" talent model, but the terms of the "out" may be more variable and subject to negotiation. Moreover, you may provide alternatives to this "up or out" model. Some organizations maintain talent models that allow for specialization or long-term focus on a particular aspect of the business. These models tend to enable a steadier employment scenario and realize fewer monetary benefits than their "up or out" peers. In some organizations, employees can move from one talent model to another over their career, which provides for greater flexibility in their long-term career growth.

Whatever the specifics of the talent models in your business, an optimal approach is to communicate them to the transitioning veteran at the soonest opportunity, preferably during the recruiting cycle before they onboard. Doing so will help set expectations, enable the veteran to start work with eyes wide open, and reduce frustration with—and turnover due to—this cultural dimension.

CAREER MANAGEMENT

Akin to talent models is the topic of career management. The performance management system links to the career management system in the military, and institutionalized governance oversees both. Service members understand well the series of training courses and possible assignments needed to realize their next promotion. Moreover, these expectations are regularly reinforced by their chain of command at every review cycle, when supervisors assess individuals as being worthy of the next level. As such, responsibility for career management in the military includes a "top-down" component usually not present in most civilian organizations, which tend to leave responsibility for such direction to the individual—especially at more senior levels.

And so, as above, organizations should make clear to transitioning veterans the expectation that this responsibility will tend to fall on their shoulders. To be successful, veterans will need to take more personal initiative than they have previously in their careers.

PERSONAL INITIATIVE

In the military, service members follow orders. Those orders are usually the result of a very formal military decision-making process (MDMP).[25] That structured process produced orders that removed ambiguity for those charged with executing them, although their input wasn't solicited. However, once service members started executing those orders, critical thinking and personal initiative were required for success, as situational realities are always different from their imagined plans.

As a result, you will encounter two types of veterans: those who had input into the organizational decision-making process and those who did not. Those who had input tend to take personal initiative and help drive decisions through a formal process and make adjustments on the fly once the operations driven by those decisions encounter reality. They have a bias for taking action. Those who did not have input do not tend to take personal initiative but are very adept at making course corrections to successfully adapt to changing circumstances in making plans a reality.

Your organization likely takes a less-structured approach to formal decision-making and likely solicits input from many areas in the organization to inform those decisions. And so, you will need to help transitioning veterans adjust to this new reality. Those who provide input into the formal military decision-making process should expect something that works but is less structured than their prior approach. And those who did not have input in the past may well be asked for their input, so they should prepare to offer it. Both should still expect to exercise personal initiative in making decisions based on incomplete or inconclusive information. Dealing with this ambiguity and applying judgment and problem-solving skills should be a stated expectation (more on this to come).

STANDARD OPERATING PROCEDURES

The military has a manual or a procedure for seemingly everything—from maintaining individual weapons to conducting large-scale unit movements. If there was an opportunity to screw something up, leaders tended to implement a documented process to preempt failure. These documents, which leaders published in the form of manuals or directives, were broadly distributed and widely available. Moreover, leaders expected that service members had them readily available as a reference in performing the operation called for in the manual. When lives were on the line, precision was required.

· ·

COMPANIES IN THE COCKPIT

"I find that almost every industry has a unique 'language,' and learning that language in a new role with any organization adds yet another layer to adapting to a new job and a new culture. Organizational language also holds the key to some of the 'unspoken rules,' which can lead to not realizing when and why a rule may have been broken. That first broken rule conversation can be quite jarring for a newly transitioned service member having come from a place where rules were clearly defined."

Brynt Parmeter, Senior Director, Non-Traditional Talent
| Head of Walmart Military & Veterans Affairs

Access to the same level of detailed instruction tends to vary in the civilian world. Larger organizations, or those governed by the Department of Labor, the Equal Employment Opportunity Commission (EEOC), or the Occupational Safety and Health Administration (OSHA), largely maintain required documentation. Also, most organizations that require employees to maintain industry-recognized certifications will maintain needed documentation. However, while you likely have a significant set of policies that govern behavior, they are probably not published in hard copy format and physically present where they may be applied—the standard most veterans experienced. Moreover, most civilian organizations don't have lives at stake in what they do, so the thoroughness in your policies and procedures may lack what veterans experienced in the military. Thus, veterans might encounter less-than-perfect guidance at times. They may experience some ambiguity in performing tasks and need to develop a comfort level in dealing with them to succeed. In fact, for junior enlisted veterans, I would go so far as to say that ambiguity is the enemy of early transition success. Anything you could do to meet them halfway here would be helpful.

To that end, you might provide some checklists for expectations in their first days. You would also benefit from training veterans to understand that managing ambiguity is a competency that involves being adaptive and flexible as conditions change, which includes:

- Shifting gears or changing course quickly and efficiently when priorities change.

- Making decisions with incomplete information.

- Moving among multiple tasks without having to finish each one.

- Maintaining a positive attitude when faced with uncertainty.

- Viewing the situation inquisitively and seeing it as an opportunity to grow.

A related aspect is the use of lessons learned from past performances of a task to inform future efforts, which is an area where you can leverage the experience of veterans to improve your organization. The military has this down to a science, and several civilian academics have noted as much. Service members regularly conduct formal After Action Reviews (AARs) following an operation. These "blameless autopsies" capture lessons gleaned from the operation just completed, which are then documented in a central database for others in the organization to access and from which to benefit. Over time, this practice creates a learning organization that is continually improving. Assuming this is of interest, use your veterans to help lead the way. They will enjoy sharing a skill set and feel like they add significant value to their new workplace.

WORK INTENSITY DURATION

Military activities can be very intense, both physically and mentally. But most tend to be relatively short in duration (measured in days or weeks). Also, as noted, these activities tend to have little ambiguity associated with them—at least from the outset. And finally, military members are always considered either on duty or on call.

This experience stands somewhat in contrast to activities they will likely experience in your organization, which will almost certainly not be as physically intense as most military activities but may be more strenuous on a mental level. Further, activities in your organization likely last longer (measured in months and years) than their military experience. Given their duration and more ambiguous nature, veterans may become mentally exhausted.

And so, supervisors should coach veterans to give themselves a break and make sure they build regular exercise into their daily routine. There was a reason the military emphasized physical fitness. It kept them healthy, but it also helped relieve stress. If you offer a wellness program from which they can benefit, share it. You can find a free management library that focuses on this topic online if you don't.[26]

A related topic has to do with helping veterans appropriately manage their time. They may have to juggle more responsibilities in the civilian world than in the military. But, as you well know, not all of those responsibilities are equally important. A helpful tool to consider sharing with veterans is what's known as the Eisenhower Matrix.[27] Although the Eisenhower Library cannot confirm this direct quote, our 34th president was known to comment: "What is important is seldom urgent, and what is urgent is seldom important."[28] The application of this concept takes the form of the 2 x 2 matrix reflected in Figure 1-5. You would want to coach veterans to prioritize activities that you would categorize in the upper right quadrant.

	Urgent	Not Urgent
Important	Crises; pressing problems; deadline-driven projects; paying the mortgage **Must-Do Activity; Schedule It**	Prevention; getting exercise; relationship-building; new opportunities; planning; business development; saving $ **Value-Added Activity; Do It Now**
Not Important	Interruptions; answering the phone **Non-Value-Added Activity; Delegate It**	Trivia; binge-watching TV; most social media **Non-Value-Added Activity; Do It Later**

Figure 1-5. "Eisenhower" Matrix

RECEPTIVENESS TO CHANGE

While the military has many of its processes documented, as noted previously, they paradoxically don't always follow them. Historically, this has been the lament of many of our enemy's military leaders. Our military doesn't always follow the "script" due to a cultural dynamic that encourages autonomy and flexibility when encountering the enemy. All military operations orders (OPORDS) contain a commander's intent, which informs the organization about the desired end state. Some OPORDS also include contingency plans, but most state a basic plan, assume you can't plan for everything, and depend upon service members to adapt to and overcome the situation they eventually encounter. The cumulative result of this dynamic is a military that anticipates, if not thrives on, change.

If your organization is large, it likely displays a different dynamic. The larger an organization gets, the more set in its ways it tends to become. According to an article in *Harvard Business Review* entitled "Why Big Companies Can't Innovate," the measure of success for mature public companies is profit, and the optimal means to ensuring profit is operational efficiency.[29] This focus on operational efficiency tends to preclude the flexibility needed to respond to changes in the environment and innovate accordingly. Conversely, smaller, newer organizations are designed to bring innovation to market. Their reward system thrives on matching a solution to the market's demands. So, their behavior is much more akin to what most NCOs and officers experience in the military. (Junior enlisted veterans may require more precise guidance in their civilian work—at least at its outset. They may need more proactive coaching and mentoring than their more senior veteran colleagues.)

Veterans should understand this aspect of the nature of your organization before they join. They should realize that they won't be able to alter these deep-rooted behaviors at larger, more mature companies. Still, they can always attempt to control elements within their sphere of influence. They can still train their team members to react to situations that don't match the "script." They can still make recommendations to their supervisors to address scenarios they encounter that run contrary to what that supervisor expected. In short, they should be encouraged to do what they can to help the organization succeed despite cultural aspects that may limit its ability to do so.

LIFESTYLE CHOICES

In the military, service members were told when to wake up, what to wear, what to eat, where to live, how to walk, how to talk, what equipment to use, what their salary was, and what healthcare they had, among other things. They didn't have much input on these things until later in their careers. The upside of that lack of freedom was fewer things about which to worry.

In entering the civilian world, veterans suddenly have tremendous freedom regarding nearly all these things. For some, that may seem long overdue and most welcome; but for others, those may pose an exhausting problem set that they must actively manage every day. It can be quite a shock to their systems.

To help them deal with these newfound freedoms, provide as much information early on to set expectations regarding these topics and establish boundaries. Also, encourage veterans to engage with their new veteran peers in your organization and solicit any lessons they might offer on these topics.

FREQUENCY OF FEEDBACK

Formal feedback in the military typically occurs on at least a quarterly basis in the form of documented counseling forms. Informal feedback occurs on a much more regular basis, especially during field operations, followed by After Action Reviews (AARs). Service members quickly become accustomed to receiving course corrections from helpful observers, and in the absence of this, they will proactively seek it.

Formal feedback within your organization probably occurs less frequently, and this may come as a surprise to them. So, you'll want to establish expectations around this topic. Whatever the process is for employees to receive formal and informal feedback, spell it out. Put it in writing, and make sure that supervisors in your organization follow through. If veterans aren't receiving feedback per the plan, they should solicit it from their supervisors. Don't allow veterans to drown silently without feedback, and encourage them to do something positive with it upon its receipt.

REQUESTING HELP

For better or for worse, military culture is such that it does not encourage individuals to seek help. Conformity rules the day. From the beginning of basic training, sticking out from the group was usually not a good thing; it was usually the basis for a correction or some adjustment—and those were never pleasant. Veterans tend to maintain this attitude when they transition to the civilian world. They tend to believe that seeking help is a form of weakness. But their persistence in this belief can lead to unnecessary delays or floundering on assigned tasks.

In contrast, larger, more mature civilian organizations value operational efficiency. They want to see any questions or issues addressed and resolved—pronto. Time is money, and any inefficiencies caused by unaddressed questions or employee confusion risks incremental profits. And so, individuals are highly encouraged to seek help and ask questions when they run into challenges they can't immediately address.

Thus, encourage transitioning veterans to ask questions when they have them. Teach them that doing so is not a weakness but an opportunity to eliminate confusion and potential inefficiency, which helps the organization. Teach them to listen carefully and learn from the answers provided to their queries. This simple exercise in seeking clarity can go a long way in helping veterans feel comfortable.

AFTER-WORK INTERACTION

Veterans coming from the military experienced work as not just a job; it was a way of life. *Camaraderie didn't stop at the end of the workday.* Driven by the mutual availability of on-post/base facilities and housing, they and their families tended to live, work, and play together around the clock. When they weren't deployed, days after work included:

◆ Interunit sports competitions.

◆ Social calls at all-unit clubs.

◆ Friendly games of golf.

◆ Other community events in the housing areas.

They typically shopped together at the same on-post/base stores and watched movies together at the same on-post/base theater. They openly interfaced with neighbors in military housing on nearly any topic or concern. In more trying times, it was a short drive to the on-post/base health clinic or hospital to support each other. In short, veterans were part of a mutually supportive community for nearly every need or want. Moreover, this social interaction had the additional benefit of promoting team building, networking, and social adaptation outside of work—all of which helped them and their families cope when it came to their eventual deployments and their associated challenges.

The social fabric of their new workplace will likely resemble little of this. The amount of after-work interaction between professionals will probably be far less than veterans are used to—although this is truer in larger, more mature public companies than smaller, private entrepreneurial companies. You will need to help veterans get comfortable with this new lifestyle. You'll need to help them understand that after work and as a rule working professionals go home to their separate families in their respective communities and partake in different social activities. Although your organization may sponsor some activities outside of work, those instances likely won't rise to the level to which veterans may have grown accustomed.

It may be helpful to share the perspective that this is another consequence of veterans' greater freedom upon departing the military. Moreover, people aren't necessarily opposed to getting together and interacting outside of work. Still, veterans will need to be more proactive in making that a reality, assuming it is something that might help their team. Camaraderie is equally important in their new roles, and they should be encouraged to take advantage of your organization's culturally acceptable ways of building it.

Another consequence of this increased freedom that veterans experience is that their families become much less connected to the veteran's peers at work. Your organization is likely not used to including extended family members in work activities like they are in the military. Some veterans' families may be disappointed by this lack of connectivity to their new workplace. They may expect information on benefits, pay, schedules, and other things that might concern them. You might help address this by offering to include family members in any veteran onboarding activities. Doing so may help address information gaps, form a connection, and relieve some of the stress of losing their former military contemporaries.

EMPLOYEE CATEGORY

From a legal standpoint, and as human resource professionals know, there are two categories of employees: *just-cause* and *at-will*. As the name implies, employers may terminate just-cause employees only for a good reason, and those employees are usually entitled to some form of independent review of the employer's decision to terminate them. On the other hand, employers may terminate at-will employees for any reason or no reason at all.[30] Federal employees, including the military, are one of the largest groups of just-cause employees. The others are state and local employees and union members.

As most experienced hires will join your organization under the at-will doctrine, the veterans among them may be experiencing the terms of at-will employment for the first time. You may need to help veterans understand the implications of this new category. Unless they have joined a union, veterans can no longer be terminated for only just-cause. Employer behavior that before may have required some justification may no longer require it.

GOVERNING LAW

Military behavior is governed by the Uniformed Code of Military Justice (UCMJ), a separate—and some might say, stricter—system of laws than the standard constitutional law that governs civilian activity. Violations of UCMJ tend to have swift repercussions that might include jail, fines, letters of reprimand, or discharges from the military that were less than honorable. These things—especially less-than-honorable discharges—leave a permanent stain on a veteran's record, negatively impacting their ability to thrive in the civilian world (see "Military Discharges").

Military Discharges

There are generally two types of discharges from the military: administrative and punitive. The various military services may use unique terminology to describe each of these.

- ♦ Administrative Discharges

  - ◊ Honorable Discharge: Indicates that an individual's service during their tour of duty met or exceeded the required standards of duty performance and personal conduct. It is the highest level of discharge. Recipients are eligible for all benefits they have earned.

  - ◊ General Discharge under Honorable Circumstances: Indicates an individual's service was satisfactory but involved situations where the individual's conduct or performance of duty was not so meritorious to warrant an Honorable Discharge. Recipients have usually engaged in minor misconduct or have received nonjudicial punishment. While eligible for most benefits, some services may deem recipients to be ineligible for education benefits.

  - ◊ Other than Honorable Discharge: Indicates that an individual's service included a pattern of behavior that constitutes a significant departure from the conduct expected of service members. Such conduct may include violent behavior, use of illegal drugs, or abnormal superior-subordinate relationships. Most veterans' benefits are unavailable to recipients of this discharge type.

- ♦ Punitive Discharges. These are given only after a court-martial finds a service member guilty of certain offenses under the UCMJ. Commissioned officers cannot be given a Bad Conduct Discharge or a Dishonorable Discharge by a court-martial. When an officer is convicted at a general court-martial, the officer's sentence may include a "Dismissal," which is considered the equivalent of a Dishonorable Discharge. Both types of punitive discharges deprive recipients of substantially all benefits administered by the Departments of Defense and Veterans Affairs.

◇ Bad Conduct Discharge: Reserved for those service members separated under conditions of bad conduct after conviction of serious offenses of a civil or military nature at a special or general court-martial.

◇ Dishonorable Discharge: Reserved for those service members separated under conditions of dishonor after conviction of serious offenses of a civil or military nature at a general court-martial.[31]

As noted, you will likely be hiring veterans on an at-will basis and having them sign an employment agreement to ensure compliance with organizational policies, rules, and regulations. Veterans must understand that in violations of such agreements, the primary remedy for most civilian organizations is invoking the employment-at-will doctrine and firing the employee. Compared to jail time and less-than-honorable discharges, this may not seem impactful, but there are longer-term implications.

Whether the veteran was fired or voluntarily initiated the departure from your organization, the outcome is the same: For the veteran, it entails another job hunt and the need to justify a job change on their résumé. For you, it means incurring the cost and additional work associated with backfilling yet another headcount. Veterans may need to be informed of the reality that future employers may look askance at "job hoppers" and that the long-term implication of such transgressions is a negative impact on their career earnings and a corresponding inability to build wealth. You may want to remind veterans to abide by all laws, policies, rules, and regulations. While they may be experiencing an increased modicum of freedom now that they are outside the military, they should understand that with increased freedom comes increased responsibility. They owe it to you, themselves, and their families to live up to that responsibility—or suffer the consequences.

That may seem like a lot to digest but consider that veterans are experiencing all those differences simultaneously upon departure from the service. How you can make those differences appear transparent and help the veteran acclimate into your organization will improve your chances of success in ensuring cultural assimilation, increased productivity, and reduced turnover.

Before moving forward, it will be instructive to some members of the reading audience to dispel some myths surrounding veterans and their stability as potential employees. Today's media has propagated several stereotypes that, upon closer inspection, are simply not true. Please see Appendix H.

Now that you understand veterans' cultural aspects, let's turn our attention to understanding some other basic facts that will govern our interaction with veterans and afford us some opportunities for hiring them.

KEYS TO SUCCESS

- Ensure the most senior executives in your organization directly support your veteran hiring program.

- Define the cultural similarities and differences between the military and your organization. Document the same and provide it as part of your onboarding curriculum.

- Validate that every person who encounters veterans during the employment life cycle understands and appreciates the cultural differences between the military and your organization.

- Use your understanding and appreciation of these cultural differences to engage veterans proactively throughout the employment life cycle.

CHAPTER 2

UNDERSTAND GOVERNING REGULATIONS

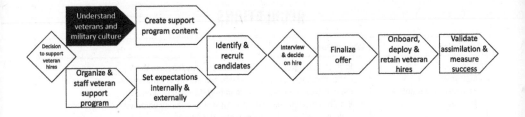

"Honor to the soldier and sailor everywhere, who bravely bears his country's cause. Honor also to the citizen who cares for his brother in the field and serves, as he best can, the same cause."

—Abraham Lincoln[1]

Employers must understand that hiring veterans comes with certain obligations—even more, if you qualify as a government contractor. Over the years, governing bodies have emplaced certain protections covering the hiring and employment of veterans in the form of laws and regulations. Maintaining compliance with these directives is not optional and might be viewed as table stakes. Ideally, employers integrate them to enable their veteran support program. Additionally, in recent years governmental entities at federal, state, and local levels have put forth tax credit incentives intended to spur the hiring of veterans. Awareness of both these obligations and opportunities should inform your veteran support program.

In this chapter, we discuss how to:

♦ Identify regulations impacting veteran employment at state and federal levels.

♦ Identify incentives for veteran employment at state and federal levels.

♦ Understand their implications for a veteran support program.

Understanding the legality of anything can be a daunting task, especially employment law. Not only are new laws and regulations constantly being added, but current ones are always in flux. Table 2-1 summarizes the major regulations impacting veteran employment as of this writing. Please seek legal counsel on their proper implementation. By the end of this chapter, you should have a reasonable grasp of the major federal and state laws and regulations currently governing veteran hiring and employment.

REGULATIONS

Regulation	What It Does
Uniformed Services Employment and Reemployment Rights Act (USERRA)[2]	♦ Protects job rights of service members, applicants to the uniformed services, and those who voluntarily or involuntarily leave employment positions to undertake military service. ♦ Prohibits discrimination in employment or adverse employment actions against service members and veterans.
Vietnam Era Veterans' Readjustment Assistance Act of 1974 (VEVRAA)[3]	♦ Prohibits employment discrimination by federal government contractors against certain veterans. ♦ Requires affirmative action for specific veterans by federal government contractors with at least fifty employees and a contract worth $150K or more.
Americans with Disabilities Act (ADA) of 1990[4]	♦ Protects against discrimination based on the presence of disabilities. ♦ Mandates that employers make appropriate and reasonable accommodations for employees with disabilities.
Family and Medical Leave Act (FMLA)[5]	♦ Entitles eligible employees of covered employers to take unpaid, job-protected leave for specified family and medical reasons with continuation of group health insurance coverage under the same terms and conditions as if the employee had not taken leave. ♦ Permits military family members to take up to twelve weeks of FMLA leave during any twelve-month period to address issues that arise during a military member's deployment to a foreign country. ♦ Allows family members of a covered service member to take up to twenty-six weeks of FMLA leave during a single twelve-month period to care for the service member who is undergoing medical treatment, recuperation, or therapy for a serious illness incurred on active duty.

Table 2-1: Regulations Impacting Veteran Employment[9,10]

Regulation	What It Does
Veterans' Preference[6]	♦ Gives eligible veterans preference in appointment over other federal job applicants. ♦ Applies to new appointments in both the competitive and excepted service; however, does not guarantee a job and does not apply to promotions, transfers, reassignments, or reinstatements.
Higher Education Act of 1965, as Amended[7]	♦ Requires institutions of higher education to promptly readmit with the same academic status a service member previously admitted to the institution but who did not attend, or did not continue to attend, because of service in the uniformed services.
Rehabilitation Act of 1973, ss Amended[8]	♦ Prohibits discrimination on the basis of disability in programs conducted by federal agencies, in programs receiving federal financial assistance, in federal employment, and in the employment practices of federal contractors. ♦ Employment discrimination standards are the same as those used in Title I of the Americans with Disabilities Act.

Table 2-1 *(continued)*

The Veterans' Employment and Training Service (VETS) of the Department of Labor manages a compliance assistance website to support your efforts.[11] If you qualify as a federal contractor (thresholds vary over time; the current threshold is a contract or subcontract with the federal government valued at $150,000 or more), the Office of Federal Contract Compliance Programs can help you remain in compliance with these requirements.[12] There are also reporting requirements to remain in compliance as a federal contractor.[13] Please take advantage of these resources, as noncompliance comes with such possible adverse side effects as monetary fines, decreased productivity, poor employee engagement, and a damaged organizational reputation.[14]

Additional Regulations (Special Hiring Authorities) Pertinent to Federal Agencies[15]

None of these authorities *entitle* a veteran (or their spouse) to an appointment, but agencies may use them to enhance a veteran's or military spouse's chance of being considered.

♦ The **Veterans' Recruitment Appointment (VRA)** program allows agencies to appoint eligible veterans without competition.

♦ The **Veterans Employment Opportunity Act (VEOA)** can be used when filling permanent, competitive service positions; it allows veterans to apply for jobs that are open only to "status" candidates, which means "current competitive service employees."

- The **Schedule A Appointment Authority**, though not specifically for veterans, allows agencies to appoint eligible applicants who have a severe physical, psychological, or intellectual disability.[16]

- **30% or More Disabled Veteran**. Allows an agency to noncompetitively appoint any veteran with a 30% or more service-connected disability.[17]

- **Disabled Veterans Enrolled in a VA Training Program**. Under terms of an agreement between agencies and the VA, a veteran who completes the VA vocational rehabilitation program may be appointed by the agency noncompetitively under a status quo appointment that may be converted to career or career-conditional. See 38 US Code chapter 31; 5 CFR 3.1 and 315.604 for details.

- **Executive Order 13518: Veterans Employment Initiative**. Created an Interagency Council on Veterans Employment to coordinate a government-wide effort to enhance veteran employment opportunities and serve as a national forum for promoting veterans' employment opportunities across twenty-four federal government agencies.[18]

- **Military Spouse Hiring Authorities**[19]

   ◇ **Executive Order 13832: Enhancing Noncompetitive Civil Service Appointments of Military Spouses**. Enables agencies to provide federal job opportunities for military spouses by using the government-wide noncompetitive hiring authority.[20]

   ◇ **Appointment of military spouses (5 US Code § 3330d)**. Likewise enables a hiring manager to noncompetitively appoint a military spouse who meets certain criteria to any position in the competitive service for which they are qualified. There is no grade-level limitation.[21]

While most state laws reinforce the mandates of USERRA and other federal laws, they also tend to stipulate additional requirements for employers, especially as it relates to service in the National Guard or Reserve or preference in employment. These may apply to all business locations within these geographies, regardless of the location of your headquarters. You will find a summary table and additional detail regarding compliance requirements on all states and territories in the Resources section of my website (*www.matthewjlouis.com*). As of this writing, however, all states and territories have adopted USERRA-like protections. In addition, most have adopted laws enabling veteran preference for public employment (exceptions include Alabama, Arkansas, Illinois, New York, Ohio, South Carolina, Guam, and the Virgin Islands), and many have adopted laws enabling the same for private employment. Among those that have yet to do so, several have bills pending or legislative discussions underway.

INCENTIVES

Your investment in veteran talent may have financial and reputational rewards.

FINANCIAL INCENTIVES

Financial incentives for hiring veterans include:

- Tax credits:
    - The Work Opportunity Tax Credit (WOTC).
    - Differential Wage Payment Credit for activated military reservists.
    - For disabled veterans, the Disabled Access Credit and the Architectural Barrier Removal Tax Deduction.
    - Individual state tax credit programs.
- Veterans benefits:
    - VA Veteran Readiness and Employment (VR&E) program.
    - Special Employer Incentives (SEI) program.
    - The Department of Labor's CareerOneStop Business Center.

Tax Credits

Federal, state, and local tax authorities provide the following financial incentives for hiring veterans in the form of tax credits:

The **Work Opportunity Tax Credit (WOTC)** is a federal tax credit available to employers who hire veterans and individuals from other eligible target groups.[22] Employers claim more than *$1 billion* in tax credits under the WOTC program each year. The success and growth of this income tax credit for business are beneficial for all who participate while increasing America's economic growth and productivity. The WOTC reduces an employer's cost of doing business and requires little paperwork. It can reduce an employer's federal income tax liability by as much as *$9,600 per veteran* hired. Moreover, employers can claim as many individuals as they hire that qualify for the tax credit. Also, certain tax-exempt organizations can take advantage of WOTC by receiving a credit against the employer's share of Social Security taxes. Veterans who have a service-connected disability, are unemployed, or receive SNAP (food stamp) benefits are eligible. Applying for the WOTC is simple; the Resources section of my website (*www.matthewjlouis.com*) contains detailed instructions.

The **Differential Wage Payment Credit for Activated Military Reservists** offers employers a credit of *up to $4,000* for each Reserve or National Guard employee you pay when they are away from work serving on active duty. The IRS maintains a website that provides details and the form (Form 8932) needed to apply.

The **Disabled Access Credit** provides a tax credit to small businesses (up to $1M and less than 30 full-time employees) that incur expenditures providing access to persons with disabilities. Organizations may take the credit each year they incur such expenditures. Refer to IRS Form 8826.

The **Architectural Barrier Removal Tax Deduction** enables businesses of any size to claim a deduction of *up to $15,000 a year* for qualified expenses to remove architectural and transportation barriers to the mobility of persons with disabilities. Businesses may use the Disabled Tax Credit and the architectural tax deduction together in the same tax year if the expenses meet the requirements of both sections.[23]

State-level tax credits. Your state may also provide additional tax incentives for hiring veterans. The following states are providing incentives as of this writing: Alabama, Alaska, Maryland, Utah, Washington, West Virginia, and Wisconsin. For an updated list, please see the Resources section of my website (*www.matthewjlouis.com*). Please note that these state-level programs are constantly in flux. You should check with your accountant to understand if a program becomes available in your state or local jurisdiction when you file your annual taxes. Most states and territories maintain a state-level Veterans Affairs office that may provide assistance and financial resources for organizations hiring veterans, so please reach out to those offices for guidance.[24]

Veterans Benefits

In hiring veterans, you are onboarding individuals who likely have access to valuable education, job training, and medical benefits that may accrue to your organization.

The US Veterans Affairs's **Veteran Readiness and Employment (VR&E) program** assists employers nationwide with information on incentives for hiring eligible veterans and works to match veterans with available employers.[25] The VR&E also:

- ◆ Offers vocational and employment services to veterans with service-connected disabilities to help them obtain suitable employment.

- ◆ Subsidizes veterans' salaries so that employers pay an apprentice-level wage while training veterans via on-the-job training programs.

- Offers specialized tools, equipment, and workplace modifications—at no cost to employers—to eligible veterans with disabilities.

- Provides counselors to work with disabled veterans to provide supportive services.

- Provides a Veteran Employment Toolkit with a voluminous list of third-party resources to support your veteran-hiring efforts.[26]

Through the VA's **Special Employer Incentive (SEI)** program, employers may also receive an incentive to hire veterans facing extraordinary obstacles to employment, which includes reimbursement of as much as 50 percent of the veteran's salary for up to six months.[27]

The US Department of Labor's **CareerOneStop Business Center** exists to help employers looking to recruit, hire, train, and retain employees. While not its sole function, much of its focus is on helping employers hire veterans. To that end, the department deploys local veteran employment representatives to its 2,500 American Job Centers nationwide. These representatives help connect you to state and local resources and funding for workforce training.[28] They also offer a helpful toolkit.[29]

REPUTATIONAL INCENTIVES

Several recognition programs exist at the federal, state, and local levels to recognize your efforts in supporting veterans. The point of applying for them is to portray your organization in a positive light in the minds of veteran talent seeking careers post-service. Moreover, the hiring of veterans further enhances your organization's reputation by boosting your diversity and inclusion efforts (more on that in Chapter 6). While summarized here, you will find more detail on these programs in Chapter 9.

Presently, the following opportunities exist at the national level:

- The Department of Labor offers the **HIRE Vets Medallion Program.**

- Employer Support of the Guard and Reserve (ESGR) offers several progressive awards, including:

  ◇ Patriot Award and Spouse Patriot Award,

  ◇ Seven Seals Award,

  ◇ Above and Beyond Award,

  ◇ Pro Patria Award,

- ◇ Extraordinary Employer Support Award, and

- ◇ Secretary of Defense Employer Support Freedom Award.

- ◆ *Chief Executive* magazine, in concert with the Thayer Leader Development Group at West Point, sponsors the annual **Patriots in Business Award.**

- ◆ VETS Indexes sponsors an annual **Employer Awards** program.

- ◆ Disabled American Veterans (DAV) sponsors an annual **National Commander Employer Awards Program.**

- ◆ The American Legion sponsors **National Veterans Education & Employment Awards** every year.

- ◆ Viqtory conducts annual surveys to determine whether applicant companies and schools meet criteria to be considered **Military Friendly** in one of several categories.

Additional programs tend to exist at the state and local levels. See relevant details in the Resources section of my website (*www.matthewjlouis.com*).

IMPLICATIONS

This combination of requirements and opportunities presents a framework for your organization to structure its veteran hiring program. See Table 2-2 for a handy means by which your organization may specify the pertinent regulations and incentives. Populating this template will clarify your obligations and opportunities. You'll find a downloadable version in the Resources section of my website (*www.matthewjlouis.com*).

It should go without saying, but I'll state it nonetheless: employers taking advantage of tax credit incentives should do so with veterans' best interests in mind. There have been reports of employers maintaining hired veterans only long enough to qualify for the tax incentive. I would hope that no employer reading this book would engage in such perverse behavior. The sons and daughters of America who fought for the freedom that enables businesses to thrive economically deserve much better. Moreover, it makes little sense to kill the "golden goose" of a competitive economic weapon. Enough said.

With the regulatory boundaries of our veteran support program now established, let's turn to the task of organizing and staffing the program. That is the subject of our next chapter.

Applicable Regulations and Incentives	Federal		State & Local	
Regulations	*Name*	*Implication*	*Name*	*Implication*
	e.g., VEVRAA	If qualifying as a contractor or subcontractor, submit an annual VETS-4212 report	e.g., Maryland Code	Maintain compliance with Title 13 (Militia) § 13-704 to 13-706, Title 3 (Employment Standards and Conditions) § 3-714—Hiring and promotion preferences—Veterans and veterans' spouses
Incentives	*Name*	*Implication*	*Name*	*Implication*
	e.g., WOTC	1. Complete IRS Form 8850 by the day the job offer is made 2. Complete ETA Form 9061 3. Submit the completed and signed IRS and ETA forms to your State Workforce Agency	e.g., Hire Our Veterans Tax Credit	Apply by submitting Application Forms A & B, Qualified Veteran Employee's Self-Certification Form(s), copies of W-2s or pay stubs, and copies of DD214 to the Maryland Department of Commerce

Table 2-2: Applicable Regulations and Incentives Template

KEYS TO SUCCESS

◆ Understand in detail the regulatory obligations pertaining to your organization at federal, state, and local levels.

◆ Take advantage of all applicable programs and incentives for hiring veterans at federal, state, and local levels.

◆ Do so with the best of intentions in fully utilizing the veteran talent pool as the competitive economic weapon they represent.

CHAPTER 3

ORGANIZE AND STAFF A VETERAN SUPPORT PROGRAM

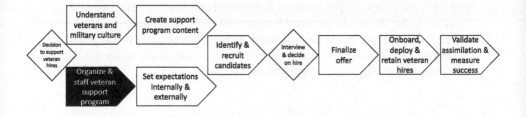

"Wounds are not always visible as veterans return; so, help when help is not asked for, and aid when those who need appear to suffer quietly."

—Byron Pulsifer[1]

Now that you understand the obligations and opportunities associated with veteran support programs, we can work on organizing and staffing one. In doing so, it's important to understand that successful groups are intrinsically linked to, if not an organic component of, your business's everyday inner workings and processes. If viewed as distinct or separate, products of the program will also be considered distinct or separate. This is not the goal. The infrastructure and governance espoused herein must be a natural outgrowth of your existing organizational approaches. While I highlight examples from other organizations, the makeup of your veteran support program must be unique to your organization. It may not look like any of those noted, and that's okay. In this chapter we cover how to:

- Define the scope of the veteran support program.

- Establish veteran program leadership, governance, and reporting processes.

- Define the roles and responsibilities of a veteran talent translator.

- Define the conditions for success and establish supporting organization policies.

By the end of this chapter, you should be prepared to begin staffing the support program and have the basis for communicating its intent, as I will describe in Chapter 5.

A Note to Federal Agencies

While Executive Order 13518: Veterans Employment Initiative has necessitated the creation of your Veteran Employment Program Office (VEPO)[2] to promote veterans' recruitment, employment, training and development, and retention, it has largely left the organization, staffing, content, and its creation up to you. Please utilize the content below and its references to establish yours.

DEFINING THE SCOPE OF THE VETERAN SUPPORT PROGRAM

Ideally, your veteran support program is just one component of the broader organization's overall diversity and inclusion efforts. The decision as to the ultimate scope of your veteran support program has a lot to do with the extent to which your organization would like to be military- or veteran-friendly (more on that in Chapter 5). It also has to do with two key dimensions: Training and Cultural Awareness (which is mainly internal to your organization) and Education and Preferences (which may be internal or external to your organization). See Figure 3-1. Ideally, a veteran support program would include both internal and external preferences and in-depth training and cultural awareness programs for *all* employees. At a minimum, your program should somehow address each of these dimensions. Consider the following:

- **Personnel:** Employment preferences for veterans, their spouses, and family members—including clarity on whether these include enlisted members, officers, Guard or Reserve members, or Department of Defense (or Homeland Security) civilians.

♦ **Value Chain:** Preferences for veteran-owned organizations that supply your organization services or raw materials, or sales policies that favor veterans, such as veteran discounts. These could also involve working with community members to improve their awareness of veteran issues or veteran service organizations to improve their efficiency in providing services to veterans.

♦ **Internal Policies/Functions:** Supportive infrastructure that could include an affinity group for veterans, mentor program for new veteran hires, a corporate philanthropy focused on veteran causes, employee assistance tailored to veteran needs, and veteran support throughout the entire employment life cycle.

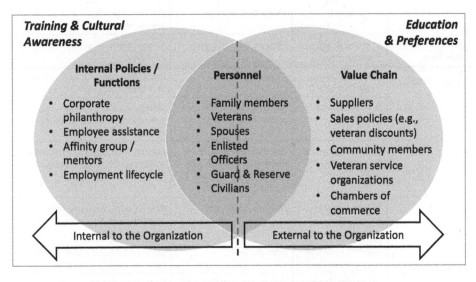

Figure 3-1. Sample Scope of a Veteran Support Program

Understanding the potential spectrum that your veteran support program could encompass, you can define the scope of your organization's program. See Table 3-1 for an *example*. You'll find a downloadable template in the Resources section of my website (*www.matthewjlouis.com*) to complete your own.

Scope Dimension	Components	Policies / Benefits	Policy / Benefit Definition
Personnel	Hiring Targets: Officers, Enlisted, Spouses, Wounded Warriors	◆ Hiring preferences. Additional points in federal hiring. ◆ Targeting specific subsets of the population	◆ All other evaluative components being equal, the veteran gets hired. ◆ Targets with at least four years of experience; enlisted ranks E-6 and below, officer ranks O-3 and below
	Veteran Employees	Promotion preferences	All other evaluative components being equal, the veteran gets promoted.
	Civilian Employees	Mandatory training programs for managers of veterans	All managers of veterans must complete a course on how to best manage them.
	Guard & Reserve Employees	Differential pay when activated or deployed; USERRA compliance	No member's employment status will be negatively impacted by activation or deployment status.
Internal Policies / Functions (Internal to the Organization)	Affinity Group	Business resource group enabling a "tribal" community	Every new veteran hire included.
	Mentor Program	Veteran-based mentor program	Every new veteran hire is assigned a veteran mentor.
	Non veterans	Onboarding training	Every employee is provided training on veteran hires as part of onboarding.
	Employee Assistance Programs	Employer support group	Veteran needs are segmented and prioritized.
	Corporate Philanthropy Programs	Philanthropic funding	Designated percentage of funds goes to veteran-related causes.
	Veteran Onboarding Program	Mandated for all veteran-related hires	All veteran-related new hires must complete the program within 90 days of hire.
	Veteran Employment Information Fair	Organizational subject matter experts made available to answer veteran-related questions	Open to all employees, but mandatory attendance for all veteran-related hires.
Value Chain (External to the Organization)	Veteran Suppliers	Business preferences	All other evaluative components being equal, the veteran business receives the contract.
	Veteran Customers	Sales discount	Standard 5 percent discount on all items not already discounted.
	Community Members	Exposure to veteran needs and capabilities	Participation in military holiday celebrations (e.g., Veterans Day, Memorial Day, Fourth of July).
	Veteran Service Organizations (VSOs)	Education on how to serve veterans more efficiently or effectively	Any philanthropic donations to VSOs include access to organizational lessons learned in dealing with veterans.
	Chambers of Commerce	Coordination on veteran-related education and hiring efforts in local communities	Participation at the state and local levels in helping to educate other organizations about veteran support programs.

Table 3-1: Veteran Support Program Scope Template

The ultimate scope of your program could be as narrow or broad as you would like, depending on the guidance of your organization's leaders and your program leader's ability to manage all its dimensions effectively. As we will discuss, it is crucial to measure the performance of all components using quantifiable metrics for which the program leader is accountable. It is also vital that the performance along all in-scope dimensions ultimately demonstrates positive outcomes, "moving the needle" of the entire organization. It would be unwise to adopt a specific component as part of your program if there is little expectation that its outcome would positively affect the organization.

COMPANIES IN THE COCKPIT

"Across Amazon, we have veterans at multiple levels engaged in supporting veteran initiatives. Amazon's Global Military Affairs team has invested heavily in hiring, retaining, and engaging the military community. Our best initiatives triangulate where Amazon can uniquely deliver value, where the military need is the greatest, and where there is a clear Amazon business interest."

Beau Higgins, Senior Manager, Amazon Military Recruiting Center
of Excellence | Worldwide Operations Talent Acquisition

Note the varying scopes of veteran support programs in some leading companies in Table 3-2. There is no singular "right" answer; whatever you decide to implement must make sense for your organization alone.

| Organization | Veteran Support Program Scope | | |
	Personnel	Internal Policies / Functions	Value Chain
ADP[3]	◆ All veterans ◆ Spouses	◆ All corporate functions ◆ Military Strong & Allies Business Resource Group ◆ Mentoring program ◆ Military leave and pay policies to support reserve component associates and their families	◆ Participation in military holiday celebrations (Veterans Day, Memorial Day) ◆ ADP Foundation philanthropic support of selected veteran organizations ◆ Supplier diversity

Table 3-2: Sample Veteran Support Program Scopes

Organization	Veteran Support Program Scope		
	Personnel	Internal Policies / Functions	Value Chain
JPMorgan Chase[4]	◆ All veterans (global) ◆ Spouses	◆ All corporate functions ◆ Business resource group ◆ Mentoring program ◆ Military leave and pay Policies to support National Guard / Reserve associates and their families ◆ Manager training of non veterans ◆ Support of Service Academy Interns, Secretary of Defense Fellows, SkillBridge Interns	◆ Participation in military holiday celebrations (Veterans Day, Memorial Day) ◆ Philanthropic support of select veteran organizations ◆ Mortgage-free homes for vets ◆ Supplier diversity ◆ Small business incubation—Bunker Labs ◆ Small business access to capital—Veterans LLC ◆ Leadership of the Veteran Jobs Mission coalition
Procter & Gamble[5]	◆ Junior Military Officers (JMOs) Non-Commissioned Officers (NCOs)	◆ All corporate functions ◆ Filling site technicians ◆ Affinity group ◆ Mentor program ◆ Cultural training of non-vets	◆ Preferences for disadvantaged supplier groups
Prudential[6]	◆ All veterans ◆ Spouses	◆ All corporate functions ◆ Business resource group ◆ Military leave policy to support National Guard / Reserve associates ◆ Third-party training program	◆ Philanthropic support of VSOs ◆ Military wellness initiative ◆ Share thought leadership with veteran organizations (e.g., IVMF) and peer companies ◆ Community events during military holidays ◆ Supplier diversity
Schlumberger[7]	◆ JMOs ◆ NCOs	◆ JMOs targeted for general management ◆ NCOs targeted for non-exempt roles	◆ Community events during military holidays
Tesla[8]	◆ All veterans ◆ Spouses	◆ Leadership positions ◆ Supervisors ◆ Skilled trades ◆ Production associates ◆ Sales & service	◆ Community events during military holidays ◆ Blood drives ◆ Donations to veteran causes ◆ Wreath laying at vet cemetery
Walmart[9]	◆ All veterans ◆ Guard & Reserve ◆ Military spouses	◆ All corporate policies and functions ◆ Military Family Promise, turning jobs into careers for spouses through enlightened transfer policy ◆ Enhanced Military Leave of Absence Policy, encouraging associates to serve in the Reserve and Guard ◆ Third-party training program	◆ Walmart Find-a-Future program ◆ Walmart SERVES (veteran and military family Associate Resource Group) ◆ Coalition for Veteran-Owned Business ◆ Philanthropy via Walmart.org ◆ Share thought leadership with strategic partners

Table 3-2 (continued)

Organization	Veteran Support Program Scope		
	Personnel	Internal Policies / Functions	Value Chain
US State Department[10]	◆ All veterans ◆ Family members	◆ All civil service and foreign service vacancies ◆ Veteran Employment Training for all HR personnel and hiring managers ◆ Veteran Employment Information Fairs for veteran employees ◆ Annual hiring team training on engaging with veterans	◆ Veterans Innovation Partnership (VIP) Fellowship program ◆ Diplomats in Residence at US universities ◆ Career fairs at TAP centers and other commercial venues; includes classes on résumé preparation and job-hunting skills
Xavier University[11]	◆ All veterans—any discharge status ◆ Active duty ◆ Guard & Reserve ◆ Spouses ◆ Dependents	◆ Early separations for undergraduate education ◆ Mid-career separations for graduate education	◆ Campus-wide recognition of Memorial Day, Veterans Day ◆ Hosting military-friendly speakers ◆ Public recognition of student veteran accomplishments

Table 3-2 (continued)

Please note, however, that most of these organizations maintain a veteran-themed affinity group. As I relate in Chapter 4, this should be a priority effort in program execution as these group members will be significant contributors to your program's success.

COMPANIES IN THE COCKPIT

"With the Military Family Promise, Walmart guarantees a job at a nearby store or club for all military personnel and military spouses employed by the company who move to a different part of the country because they or their spouse have been transferred by the US military."

Brynt Parmeter, Senior Director, Non-Traditional Talent
| Head of Walmart Military & Veterans Affairs

Wounded Warrior Hiring Programs

Some portion of your program's personnel scope may include wounded warriors and be designed to recruit and hire severely wounded veterans. After all, diversity and inclusion efforts are essential to business growth in today's economy, and adding veterans with disabilities can help add to your organization's bottom line. In doing so, you might consider some parameters in organizing the effort:

◆ Specific standards for those that would qualify for the program. Criteria for federal agencies, for example, include those who:

◇ Suffer from injuries or illness incurred in the line of duty after September 10, 2001, *and*

◇ Receive or expect to receive a Department of Defense or Veterans Affairs disability rating of 30 percent or greater in categories such as Loss of Limb, Loss of Vision / Blindness, Spinal Cord / Paralysis, Permanent Disfigurement, Loss of Hearing / Deafness, Severe Burns, Traumatic Brain Injury (TBI), Post Traumatic Stress Disorder (PTSD) and any other condition requiring extensive hospitalization or multiple surgeries, *or*

◇ Receive a Department of Defense or Veterans Affairs combined rating equal to or greater than 50 percent for any other combat or combat-related condition.

◆ Any regulations that support your effort. As an example, federal agencies have hiring authorities that support and enable their programs:

◇ Schedule A (persons with disabilities) (5 CFR 213.3102(u)).

◇ Veterans Recruitment Appointment (VRA) (5 US Code 3301, 3302).

◇ 30 Percent or More Disabled Veterans (38 US Code 4214 and Public Law 107-288).

◆ Specific support provided or benefits of membership in the program.

See Appendix D for more information on considerations for hiring disabled veterans.

ESTABLISHING VETERAN PROGRAM LEADERSHIP, GOVERNANCE, AND REPORTING PROCESSES

When identifying a leader for your veteran support program, you should keep a few things in mind:

◆ While the leader need not be a veteran, it sure does help. The immediate respect and relational value of being one of "their own" go a long way. More practically, given that veterans typically maintain a security clearance, it eases the burden of overcoming security measures on military installations when trying to access candidates. Access to these installations is even easier for military retirees.

◆ That said, the leader should *not* be a veteran who has recently transitioned from the military. The leader should have at least five years' experience in a civilian organization (ideally, yours) and be sufficiently able to relate to organizational leadership and staff.

◆ Among others you may assign, consider assigning the leader responsibility for:

◇ Hiring and training support program staff.

◇ Developing and maintaining curricula and processes for:

- Training recruiters, interviewers, hiring managers, and others associated with the employment life cycle

- Training the balance of civilians in the organization

- Training veteran mentors

◇ Liaising with internal and external veteran communities

◇ Supporting onboarding sessions for veterans

◇ Monitoring successful acclimation of veterans

See Appendix B for a sample formal job description for a veteran support program leader and Appendix F for a persona matrix that lists summary responsibilities of program personnel.

COMPANIES IN THE COCKPIT

"In my role, I act as a translator of military skills and serve as an in-house advocate for veterans. My goal is to serve as a type of 'Rosetta Stone' for veterans looking for opportunities within Amazon that best match their unique skill sets to Amazon's wide-ranging needs."

Beau Higgins, Senior Manager, Amazon Military Recruiting Center of Excellence | Worldwide Operations Talent Acquisition

The program leader should be accountable and regularly report to senior organizational leadership. Table 3-3 contains some examples.

Organization	To Whom Its Veteran Support Group Reports
Procter & Gamble	Chief Diversity & Engagement Officer[12]
JPMorgan Chase	Chief Diversity, Equity, and Inclusion Officer[13]
Tesla	Chief People Officer[14]
Walmart	Senior Vice President, Global Talent[15]
USAA	Vice President, Talent Acquisition[16]
Prudential	Senior Vice President, Inclusive Solutions[17]
Schlumberger	General Counsel[18]
Cajun Industries	Chief Executive Officer[19]
Xavier University	Vice President for Enrollment Management and Student Success[20]

Table 3-3: Examples of Organizational Reporting Structures

To whom some of these leading programs report varies, and that is perfectly fine. Your program may report to any of those. What they all have in common, however, is what's important:

- ◆ All have sponsorship from senior leadership in the organization.

- ◆ All have leaders accountable to that senior leadership.

- ◆ Though not evident from Table 3-3, all have linked their veteran support programs directly to their organization's values—their *why*, their reason for existing.

To whom will your veteran support program leader report? Why? Note it here:

A Consideration for Especially Large or Global Organizations

Organizations with exceptional scale risk having insufficient oversight within their veteran support program. One veteran leader or executive advocate may not be enough to reach all intended audiences in the enterprise. Addressing this concern, Brynt Parmeter, Senior Director, Non-Traditional Talent/Head of Walmart Military & Veterans Affairs, noted: "Taking a view of veterans and military spouses as components of a larger, nontraditional hiring population enables large organizations like Walmart to scale such programs without exceptional overhead in each division to oversee a veteran-specific effort. Nontraditional hiring efforts simply become an extension of the existing human resources infrastructure in all parts of our business."[21]

Beyond mere oversight is what gets communicated to those leaders. Appropriate governance involves regular updates on program progress. Key performance indicators, or metrics, enable quantifiable measurements of your program's progress and its value to the organization. In doing so, they hold the program's leadership accountable for its results. Ideally, these metrics include micro (output-based) measures such as recruiting, participation, and retention rates and macro (outcome-based) measures such as organizational productivity, increased revenue, cost savings, or margin improvement. These outcome measures should support, if not be identical to, the organization's strategic goals. Figure 3-2 shows the ideal relationship among these measures. Consider including both types of measures and using them to update organizational leadership regularly.

Figure 3-2. Relationship between Program and Organizational Measures

COMPANIES IN THE COCKPIT

"The core of USAA's business strategy is exceptional service to its members. We believe that our employee experience should be equal to our membership experience. In addition, we are committed to setting an aspirational goal that focuses our talent acquisition efforts on seeking out veterans and military spouses. Twenty percent of USAA employees are veterans or military spouses; however future employees do not need to have served in the military to work at USAA."

Marcus "Ohley" Ohlenforst, Military Talent Strategist, USAA Talent Acquisition

The frequency of reporting and the metrics reported also vary among leading programs. Here are some examples:

- Procter & Gamble's Veterans Affinity Group leader meets with the CEO and the company's Diversity Council twice a year. The Affinity Group leader regularly reports on metrics, including recruiting, active participation, and progress on activities underway.

- Walmart tracks and reports hiring figures publicly and to Walmart leadership quarterly.

- USAA's VetsLeaD program regularly reports the retention of veteran hires to the program's executive sponsor and to USAA leadership upon request.

- Prudential reports the geographic and demographic breakdown of new hires, what roles they have assumed, how they are performing, and status on all other programmatic activity at both enterprise and organizational levels quarterly.

- Performance Contractors reports the numbers and status of new veteran hires and rehires to their Human Resource and Training directors quarterly. The report includes details on how many are in craft training, how many have certified with the National Center for Construction Education and Research (NCCER), and how many have received promotions.

- Xavier University's Student Veteran Center reports twice a year on the following metrics: total veteran-related enrollment (veterans, active duty, Guard/Reserve, spouses, dependents), year-over-year retention/attrition, cumulative GPA, student engagement (appointments with the Center's staff), and career outcomes (percentage of students employed, in graduate school, or volunteering full-time within six months).

The particulars of each program are uniquely tailored to each organization, as they should be for yours. What's essential is the commonality of all successful programs:

- Regular reporting takes place.

- Quantifiable metrics monitor the value realized against an established goal.

- The program leader is accountable for both.

Table 3-4 provides a *sample* of how to define your program's metrics and reporting process. You will find a downloadable template of the same in the Resources section of my website (*www.matthewjlouis.com*).

Metric Type	Metric	Operational Definition (how it is measured)	Reporting Frequency	To Whom It Gets Reported
Output-based	First-year retention	Percentage of new veteran hires employed by the organization beyond the first anniversary of their hire date	Quarterly	Chief Executive Officer
Outcome-based	Productivity	Outputs (# of products produced within X time) / Inputs (labor hours worked over X time)	Quarterly	Typically tracked by the Chief Financial Officer

Table 3-4: Veteran Support Program Metric Template

Percentage of Workforce Goals

Many organizations have specific goals regarding what percentage of their workforce they desire to be composed of veterans. The government actually *requires* contractors governed by the Vietnam Era Veterans' Readjustment Assistance Act (VEVRAA) to develop a written affirmative action program and establish a hiring benchmark for protected veterans every year or adopt the national benchmark provided by the Office of Federal Contract Compliance Programs (OFCCP).[22] The reasons for the goal and its size vary significantly by each organization and have much to do with their industry, types of work, the role veterans play, and the degree to which they desire to appeal to external audiences, including government and the general public. Here are some examples:

- Schlumberger's veteran population is just shy of 8 percent, and its goal is 10 percent.[23]

- In the US, JPMorgan Chase wants its veteran hiring efforts to match OFCCP targets for the US market.[24]

- Tesla wants veteran hires to reach 7 percent of its total workforce.[25]

- USAA has established an aspirational goal for military hiring north of its current 20 percent and includes both veterans and military spouses.[26]

- Xavier University's goal is to have military-affiliated students comprise 10% of its full-time undergraduate population.[27]

If you choose to track this, note that this percentage is often challenging to capture, given that veterans have to self-identify. Consider adding an opt-in box as part of your application form with promises to assign a mentor and include in your veteran support group. Use verbiage such as "Have you ever served in the military?" Finally, consider that veteran hiring program initiatives must continually persist in their efforts to maintain or grow these percentages, given inevitable personnel turnover.

COMPANIES IN THE COCKPIT

"Procter & Gamble has been recruiting veterans since the Civil War. In fact, 50% of P&G CEOs have military experience. Veterans represent 1–2% of the company population and are present within every company function."

John Myers, Procter & Gamble Veterans Affinity Group Lead

Please note that the organization's finance function produces most outcome-based metrics because they tend to measure the entire organization's performance. So, your program's responsibility would be to monitor these to detect how your veteran hires helped "move the needle" for the overall organization. There is nothing wrong with monitoring the outcomes of specific portions of the organization (say, a particular function, location, or organizational department) to detect the impact of veteran hires in that area. Just be aware that you may need permission from executive leaders to do so.

The means for reporting these metrics and their trends typically come in the form of an executive dashboard of some sort, with cascading detail for the more detailed, output-based program measures for each hiring life cycle component. See Figure 3-3 for an Executive Dashboard template. See Appendix C for a sample cascading dashboard. See the Resources section of my website (*www.matthewjlouis.com*) for downloadable versions of both. You would, of course, tailor this to your organization's needs. ADP, for example, likes to track the details of veteran hiring by location. On the other hand, the State Department prefers to review progress by the major portions of its workforce (Civil Service, Foreign Service) and by Veteran Status and Veteran Preference Code.

Overall Summary: ⃝

Lifecycle Component	KPI	KPI Trend	Status v Goal	Summary Highlights		Organization Strategic KPI	Strategic KPI Trend
Identify				• A • B • C			
Recruit				• A • B • C			
Interview	OUTPUT MEASURES			• A • B • C	OUTCOME MEASURES		
Hire				• A • B • C			
Onboard / Train				• A • B • C			
Deploy / Develop				• A • B • C			
Retain / Separate				• A • B • C			

Legend: ⃝ On Track ⬤ Behind Plan ⬤ Off Track *As of: [DATE]*

Figure 3-3. Veteran Support Program Executive Dashboard Template

DEFINING THE ROLE AND RESPONSIBILITIES OF A VETERAN TALENT TRANSLATOR

At its outset, an organization's veteran support program ideally includes a resource dedicated to acting as an intermediary between its civilians and its military members. Some may term this "talent development." Such a role will help overcome the civil-military divide. As with the program leader, this individual is optimally both a veteran and a tenured member of your organization. During program startup, members of your organization's military-themed affinity or business resource group (BRG)—perhaps with support from human resources—might assume the responsibilities of this talent translator. Again, this BRG should take priority during your program's initiation.

Responsibilities for this role might include:

◆ Working with learning professionals to develop and manage the curricula associated with veteran-related programs.

◆ Training veteran recruits on résumé preparation and terminology translation.

◆ Translating veteran résumés for civilian consumption.

- Working with recruiting and hiring managers to translate job descriptions.

- Participating in veteran interviews, if not leading them.

- Reviewing all program training materials for mutual understanding.

- Facilitating program events, such as onboarding sessions.

- Facilitating the training of employees who interact with veteran recruits and new hires, including recruiters, interviewers, onboarding personnel, and first-line managers.

- Training additional facilitators as the program scales and coordinating their participation in veteran-related programs.

- Monitoring the execution of veteran-related programs and incorporating continuous improvement feedback from each.

- Acting as a resource for career counselors and all civilian managers of veterans.

- Maintaining a database of potential veteran hires.

- Maintaining a library of veteran-related educational materials.

- Vetting software programs or apps that may improve the efficacy of any of the above.

As it scales, your program may require additional staff beyond the above-noted leader and talent translator, especially if your organization spans multiple businesses or divisions. To cite a few examples, administrative support, marketing, and communications could quickly grow to become a more dedicated program need. Also, you may find that what starts as part-time support eventually becomes full-time. Such evolutions are welcome challenges and signs of positive growth!

See Figure 3-4 for a sample program organization chart. Your structure should scale with the maturity of your program; this figure illustrates the staffing of a more mature program. Please see Appendix F for a list of responsibilities for these roles.

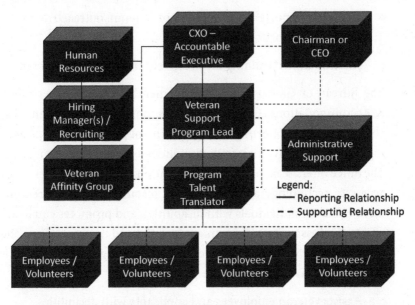

Figure 3-4. Sample Veteran Support Program Organization Chart

As an example of how a leading federal agency organizes, the State Department maintains three offices that oversee veteran recruitment, hiring, and training:[28]

- The Bureau of Global Talent Management's Office of Talent Acquisition (GTM/TAC) attracts interested and competitive veterans and disabled veterans to the State Department. A dedicated veteran outreach specialist coordinates veteran recruitment, including their "Diplomats in Residence" based at universities across the United States. Other responsibilities of this specialist include:

  ◇ Leads information sessions for veterans of all branches of the military.

  ◇ Attends career fairs on military bases and other commercial venues.

  ◇ Conducts classes on résumé preparation and job-hunting skills.

  ◇ Utilizes the State Department's Talent Database to connect qualified veterans with open vacancies.

  ◇ Manages online and social media advertising, including audience engagement.

◇ Regularly reports on the status of veteran outreach for each recruitment portfolio.

◇ Attends annual training on effectively engaging with veterans.

♦ The Bureau of Global Talent Management's Office of Accessibility & Accommodations (GTM/OAA) is responsible for developing disability policies, supporting State Department programs, and providing services to individuals with disabilities as required by regulation. The office offers reasonable accommodation solutions, ensures equal access to technology and information resources, oversees recruitment efforts of individuals with disabilities, and promotes equal and effective access to State Department facilities and transportation. The GTM/OAA employs a Selective Placement Program Coordinator (SPPC) that has the following responsibilities:

◇ Assists veteran employees and applicants with disabilities.

◇ Assists service members in their Wounded Warrior and Operation Warfighter programs.

◇ Maintains a Talent Database of Schedule A-eligible applicants that they regularly circulate to office hiring managers.

◇ Coordinates with State Department HR specialists to fill their vacancies with qualified candidates from the Talent Database before posting vacancy announcements on USAJOBS.

◇ Coordinates a SharePoint site to track referrals and placements of wounded warriors.

◇ Educates hiring managers and bureau executives on the use of hiring tactics for individuals with disabilities, such as:

♦ Schedule A hiring authority (as noted in Chapter 2).

♦ Workforce Recruitment Program, a Department of Labor and Department of Defense program for college students (including veterans returning to school) with disabilities that helps them find summer or permanent jobs.[29]

♦ The Bureau of Global Talent Management's Office of Civil Service Talent Management (GTM/CSTM) contains a Veteran Employment Program Manager who:

◇ Monitors, reviews, and evaluates all veteran hiring activity.

◇ Supports Veteran Employment Information Fairs.

◇ Comanages the Veterans Innovation Partnership (VIP) Fellowship program.

DEFINING THE CONDITIONS FOR SUCCESS AND ESTABLISHING SUPPORTING ORGANIZATION POLICIES

Another program leader's responsibility is to ensure necessary financial support and the presence of supportive organizational processes and policies. The executive sponsor would be a likely source of financial support, although the organization's philanthropic foundation could be another, if one exists. Supporting processes needed throughout the employment life cycle will vary with the nature of the program but may include some of the following:

- Identifying:
  ◇ An existing military-themed affinity group.

  ◇ Knowledge of the best sources of military talent.

  ◇ Means of accessing military installations.

  ◇ Materials necessary for participating in relevant job fairs.

- Recruiting:
  ◇ A small team of recruiters dedicated to veteran recruiting.

  ◇ Training materials for all recruiters on best practices for recruiting veterans.

  ◇ A human resource leader who understands the advantage of a veteran recruiting team: they can supply talent year-round and on-demand, whereas academic recruiting teams are usually beholden to the regular matriculation schedule of those institutions.

  ◇ An application that veterans can understand.

  ◇ A strategy for using social media to recruit veteran talent.

- Interviewing:
  - A trained cadre of professionals capable of understanding veterans.
  - Scripted competency-based questions aimed at uncovering transferable skill sets.
- Hiring:
  - Offer packages that contain sufficient education on compensation and benefits.
  - A policy to send messages to the managers and senior managers of new veteran hires upon their arrival.
- Onboarding:
  - Policies that encourage former military personnel to self-identify as veterans.
  - A program that assigns every new veteran hire a mentor.
  - An affinity group for veteran peers in the organization.
  - A "fast-start" program providing the "inside scoop" on how to succeed in the organization (e.g., understanding organizational culture and understanding how to complete annual work reviews).

COMPANIES IN THE COCKPIT

"We can attribute much of our recent success to our 'Find-a-Future' program, which helps individuals:

1. Identify their current state of skills and competencies via a personal audit
2. Identify personal goals that comprise their future state
3. Identify activities and pathways that enable achievement of that future state."

Brynt Parmeter, Senior Director, Non-Traditional Talent
| Head of Walmart Military & Veterans Affairs

- Training:
  - Access to classrooms with audiovisual capabilities sufficient for teaching classes—or their virtual equivalent.

◇ Curricula 1) for transitioning veterans on the nature of their roles and the culture of the organization and 2) for civilians on the nature of veterans and means for engaging with them.

◇ Processes for retraining veterans to support redeployment elsewhere in the organization.

◆ Deploying:

◇ Policies that assign veterans to roles that contribute to the organization's strategic goals and objectives.

◇ Policies that ensure goal-setting to encourage organizational commitment.

◇ Processes that ensure supervisors establish clear assignment expectations and then follow up to ensure compliance.

◆ Developing:

◇ Policies to provide veterans early, frequent, informal performance feedback.

◇ Transparent policies regarding training requirements, appraisal or review cycles, reward systems, and career path expectations.

◇ Policies that enable redeployment of talent pending performance feedback to allow an optimal "fit."

◆ Retaining:

◇ Processes supportive of ongoing service in the National Guard or Reserve.

◇ Processes supportive of military spouses and portable careers.

◇ Processes for addressing segments of the business that underperform in retaining veterans.

◆ Separating:

◇ Processes for successfully outplacing those veterans not able to be retained.

◇ Exit-interview process to understand reasons for turnover to address root causes.

◇ Policies that enable reemployment of separated individuals.

In total, this list may serve as "table stakes" for the infrastructure of a successful veteran support program. Succeeding chapters further expand upon these items by highlighting best practices from several prominent organizations with leading veteran support programs.

USAA's Top-10 Best Practices for Successful Veteran Hiring Programs

1. It is essential to have an executive champion for military hiring efforts, with stated goals that support the organization's mission, values, and culture.

2. Ensure hiring programs meet business needs and are supported by developmental efforts to retain the talent.

3. Prioritize reviewing military talent as part of the candidate pool.

4. Include veterans on review panels when a veteran is in the candidate slate.

5. Ensure your career website is veteran-friendly. Highlight veteran programs and testimonials in addition to displaying veteran employer accolades.

6. Establish a focused effort on military-friendly messaging in job postings.

7. Post your jobs on military-friendly job boards.

8. Conduct routine military acumen training for Talent Acquisition employees.

9. Segment military candidates in a talent community to provide targeted outreach.

10. Offer resources and ongoing updates for hiring leaders to ensure meaningful, succinct, and informative resources with dedicated content for military recruitment.[30]

Most organizations would already have supporting policies in each area, but they may not be specific to veterans. The responsibility of the veteran support program leader is to review all such policies and suggest modifications that would support the execution of the previously mentioned "table stakes" processes. See Table 3-5 for a template and some *examples*. See the Resource section of my website (*www.matthewjlouis.com*) for a downloadable version.

Phase	Process	Supporting Policy
Identifying	Means of accessing military bases	Recruiters accessing military bases must have a security clearance.
	Materials necessary for participating in relevant job fairs	All materials provided to prospects at job fairs must be brand compliant and reviewed by the veteran talent translator.
Recruiting	An application that veterans can understand	Veterans must be allowed to self-identify during the application process.
	A small team of dedicated veteran recruiters	All recruiters must be cross-trained on veteran hiring.
Interviewing	A trained cadre of professionals capable of understanding veterans	A veteran should accompany any untrained interviewer in an interview with a veteran.
	Scripted competency-based questions to uncover a veteran's transferable skills	Veterans should be provided sample interview questions ahead of the interview.
Hiring	Offer packages containing sufficient education on the components of the organization's compensation and benefits	Veterans may take 50 percent longer than non veterans to respond to offer letters to enable time to answer their questions.
	Send messages to the managers and senior managers of new veteran hires upon arrival	A welcome letter from a new hire veteran's manager should accompany any offer letter.
Onboarding	A program that assigns a mentor to every new veteran hire	Every new hire veteran will be provided a mentor within 30 days of their start date.
	An affinity group for veteran peers in the organization	All new veteran hires will enroll in the organization's veterans business resource group.
Training	Access to classrooms with audiovisual capabilities sufficient for teaching classes	To the extent possible, integrate veterans with their civilian peers in attending all functional training. Reimburse reasonable expenses for procuring space for teaching courses outside of the organization if all available space in the organization is reserved.
	Curricula for transitioning veterans and their civilian managers	All veterans will attend a veteran-specific onboarding curriculum within 120 days of their start date. All veterans' non veteran managers and senior managers must pass the online curriculum regarding the management of veterans within 30 days of the veteran's start date.
Deploying	Establish goals to encourage organizational commitment	All veteran hires will work with assigned managers to document annual performance goals within two weeks of their start date.
	Ensure supervisors establish clear assignment expectations and then follow up to ensure compliance	Supervisors will perform initial counseling within 48 hours of assignment. Performance counseling will take place every four weeks.

Table 3-5: Template for Generating List of Supporting Policies

Phase	Process	Supporting Policy
Developing	Provide veterans early, frequent, informal performance feedback	Veterans will receive formal performance feedback quarterly and informal feedback monthly for the duration of their first year.
	Transparency regarding training requirements, appraisal or review cycles, reward systems, and career path expectations	Training requirements, appraisal cycles, reward systems, and career path options and requirements are mandatory topics discussed in veteran onboarding courses.
Retaining	Address segments of the business that underperform in retaining veterans	Veteran performance and retention will be segmented by location and reported quarterly.
	Support ongoing service in the National Guard or Reserve	The veteran support program leader will maintain the ESGR Statement of Support.
Separating	Successfully outplace veterans not retained	HR will attempt to outplace every separating veteran.
	Conduct exit interviews to understand reasons for veteran turnover and address the root causes	Veteran affinity group members will conduct exit interviews with all separating veterans and document causes for their separation.

Table 3-5 (continued)

Sample Walmart Supporting Policies

◆ Since those who serve, and have served, and their families make Walmart a better company and make communities and the nation stronger, building and fostering top-of-mind awareness as the Employer of Choice is the cornerstone.

◆ Building and fostering a whole person, whole family, whole community framework via four pillars: employment, education, entrepreneurship, and health and wellness.

◆ Engaging, supporting, and empowering veteran and military family associates and their allies through Walmart SERVES, the veteran and military family Associate Resource (affinity) Group.[31]

The resulting list of policies, once enacted, will better position your veteran support group—and your organization—for success.

With your veteran support program now organized and staffed, we can turn our attention to creating the content necessary to enable its success.

KEYS TO SUCCESS

♦ Successful programs tend to be components of the broader organization's overall diversity and inclusion efforts.

♦ Make the scope of your veteran support program a conscious choice. Directly link the program to the organization's values and its purpose for being.

♦ Veteran support program leaders are optimally veterans or retirees who have significant experience in the civilian world post-military, ideally within your organization.

♦ Make veteran support program leaders accountable to an individual at the executive level of the organization who has sponsorship from the chief executive.

♦ Ensure program leaders regularly track and report on metrics intended to measure the value and trends of veterans in the organization.

♦ Ensure needed enabling area infrastructure is in place. Sufficient financial resources and a robust set of supporting processes will support success.

♦ A competent veteran talent translator can be a significant source of added value to any veteran support program.

CHAPTER 4

CREATE SUPPORT PROGRAM CONTENT

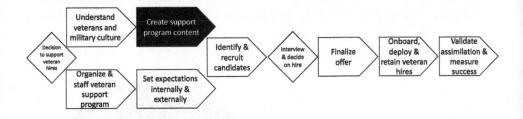

"Surround yourself with the best people you can find, delegate authority, and don't interfere."

—Ronald Reagan[1]

President Reagan may not have been referring to the administration of veteran programs, but Ol' Dutch's words certainly apply. And the program you are constructing will help emplace some of the best people you can find. Having defined the outline of our program in the previous chapter, you must now create its guts—the explicit content you will use to execute the program with all audiences, internal and external. The good news is that you won't need to start from scratch. In recent years, many sources have become available that will give you a jumpstart on your effort, as many governmental and nongovernmental organizations are anxious to help you help veterans. However, much work exists to tailor the plethora of available materials to your organization's needs. In this chapter, we discuss how to:

◆ Enable a veteran affinity group.

◆ Enable a veteran mentoring program.

◆ Create an onboarding curriculum.

◆ Create a training program for both veterans and civilian employees.

◆ Orchestrate delivery of support program content.

After this chapter, you should have the content to enable a veteran support program and a synchronization plan for delivering it to incoming new veteran hires.

In approaching the content of this chapter, please understand and subsequently support the sequential networking process and resulting assimilation of the veteran hire. As I established in my award-winning book *Mission Transition,* the sequential process of engaging first with veteran peers and then gradually expanding to other elements of the employee base supports the assimilation process significantly. (See Figure 4-1.) This approach again underscores the importance of prioritizing affinity group initiation.

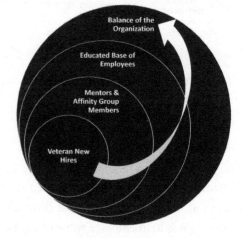

Figure 4-1. Veteran Networking Assimilation Process

ENABLING A VETERAN AFFINITY GROUP

Affinity groups, alternately known as business resource groups (BRGs), are employee-run groups that voluntarily form an informal network within an organization. I distinguish them from employee resource groups (ERGs), which take on the air of a social club in some circles. BRGs have teeth; they serve a bottom-line purpose. They execute a mission whose outcome directly impacts the organization's goals—financial or otherwise.

Enabling a veteran affinity or business resource group must be a priority for two important reasons. First, the members of this business resource group serve as primary resources and offer significant bandwidth to generate or tailor the content needed for your support program—and act as a source of referrals for more members of the same talent pool. Second, they are a necessary means of practically and successfully enabling the reintegration of veterans into civilian society. Why? These groups enable three factors that, as Sebastian Junger notes in *Tribe: On Homecoming and Belonging*, affect a veteran's transition back into civilian life—and are not well enabled by modern US society. First, these groups act as a cohesive and egalitarian tribal society, which helps mitigate the effects of any trauma. Modern societies like the US are the exact opposite: hierarchical and alienating. Second, the groups don't see the veteran as a victim. They're not excused from fully functioning in society. Finally, and most importantly, "Veterans need to feel that they're just as necessary and productive back in society as they were on the battlefield."[2] These groups act as societies that provide the social resilience that modern US society lacks.

Veteran affinity groups typically have two primary purposes: enabling a community of like-minded individuals and recruiting the best of that same community from outside the organization. Members should not be limited to only veterans, however. Spouses, family members, and other non veteran supporters can often relate directly to the paths veterans have traversed and be very influential in supporting the group's purpose.

A Family Member's Perspective

"As the son of a career Marine, I witnessed the highest demonstration of commitment that went beyond family. I saw first-hand the loneliness of separation but understood that my father's job was bigger than our family . . . and I was proud. As a result, in the course of my career, I faced on numerous occasions colleagues that couldn't understand the responsibilities veterans had when in the service. I spent a lot of time explaining what service members did—their responsibilities, commitments, stresses, and hardships—all of which made them incredible additions to our organization."

Kurt Babe, Retired Managing Director, Deloitte Consulting

In establishing these groups, leaders will want to address several design and implementation elements:

♦ Determine whether participation is an additional duty or part of a veteran's assigned role (e.g., chargeable time).

♦ Define the group's governance structure and frequency of meetings.

♦ Define members' assigned roles and responsibilities and how performance against those will be tracked and reported.

♦ Identify how they will market the program internally and externally.

♦ Define by whom, to whom, and on what frequency program success will be measured and reported.

♦ Determine the level of leadership support, budget, and resources required.

♦ Identify similar groups in other organizations that could partner on shared goals.

Table 4-1 illustrates sample activities for such groups. Only budget and imagination should limit these goals.

Sample Community-Building Goals	Sample Recruiting Goals
♦ Support local veteran service organizations (VSOs), especially veteran collaboratives. ♦ Participate in any nearby Soldier for Life—Transition Assistance Program (SFL-TAP) instances. ♦ Ensure organizational philanthropic events include veterans causes. ♦ Celebrate Memorial Day and Veterans Day by participating in some sort of veteran-related event (e.g., run a 5K). ♦ Support the Marine Corps' annual Toys for Tots campaign. ♦ Support any internal veteran support programs (e.g., RED Friday events[3]). ♦ Facilitate internal veteran networking—conduct quarterly social gatherings. ♦ Support any nearby veteran-related events (e.g., Honor Flights, Warrior Games, Wheelchair Olympics). ♦ Network with veteran affinity groups from other local organizations and mutually support local veteran initiatives. ♦ Support local chambers of commerce or rotary clubs in furthering their veteran-related programming.	♦ Actively support company veteran recruiting and retention efforts—ensure BRG participation in all veteran recruiting events. ♦ Participate on new veteran hire interview panels. ♦ Offer to act as mentors to new veteran hires or coordinate a program for doing so. ♦ Partner with local colleges that have a Student Veterans of America (SVA) chapter. ♦ Refer qualified, high-potential veterans from your network. ♦ Support or sponsor veteran internship opportunities available via DoD's SkillBridge program.[4] ♦ Formally sponsor transitioning veterans via American Corporate Partners.[5] ♦ Support or sponsor veteran fellowship opportunities available via the US Chamber of Commerce's Hiring Our Heroes program.[6] ♦ Support the organization's social media strategy for veterans. ♦ Participate in the formation of veteran-related organization policies (e.g., military leave, workplace accommodations, diversity supplier programs).

Table 4-1: Sample Veteran Affinity Group Goals

Once established, the veteran affinity group leader should track performance against these goals to ensure effective use of time and treasure. Most organizational leaders will want to quantify and understand their return on these investments. To do so, consider leveraging the metric frameworks noted in Chapter 3. The veteran program leader might also consider taking periodic surveys of group members to ensure the group meets their needs effectively and to solicit feedback and continuous-improvement ideas.

Finally, and to ensure effective coordination, the veteran support program leader works closely with the veteran affinity group leader. In representing the affinity group's views and inputs, the veteran affinity group leader will be a significant source of primary research on all veteran-related topics supporting the broader veteran support program.

Companies in the Cockpit

"After fulfilling our 2016 pledge to hire 25,000 veterans and military spouses over five years, Amazon made a new pledge in July of 2021 to hire 100K US veterans and military spouses over the next three years."

Beau Higgins, Senior Manager, Amazon Military Recruiting Center of Excellence | Worldwide Operations Talent Acquisition

ENABLING A VETERAN MENTORING PROGRAM

Mentoring programs enable a more experienced person (the mentor) to work with a less experienced person (the mentee) to share skills and insights that will help the mentee grow in their career and life. When combined with affinity groups and formal onboarding, mentoring programs are a sound method for improving the retention of targeted groups.

The best mentoring programs implement two types of mentoring, which would coincide. The first type is the traditional approach, where a more-tenured employee is paired with a newly hired one. The other type is called peer mentoring, in which a peer sponsor—someone of similar age and experience—offers guidance and support within the first year of employment. JPMorgan Chase provides a playbook that documents its Pathfinder Mentoring Program for newly hired veterans.[7]

Such leading in-house mentoring programs consist of several components you should tailor for your organization (see *samples* in Table 4-2). Leverage your veteran support program lead and affinity group lead for creating this content. I've provided a downloadable template in the Resources section of my website (*www.matthewjlouis.com*) that your leads may utilize. As these organizations have done, you might consider documenting your approach in a handbook that includes topics such as: program structure and eligibility, definitions of roles, expectations of commitment, best practices, available resources, conversation topics, and relationship assessment.[8]

Component	Traditional Mentoring	Peer Mentoring
Participation Criteria	◆ *Mentor: Employees (ideally veterans) with more than five years of tenure with the organization or part of an executive leadership development program* ◆ *Mentee: Newly hired veterans*	◆ *Mentor: Veterans with 1–3 years of tenure with the organization* ◆ *Mentee: Newly hired veterans*
Pairing Methodology / Considerations	◆ *Career compatibility* ◆ *Experience level* ◆ *Location* ◆ *Personal interests*	◆ *Same location* ◆ *Same role level* ◆ *Same organizational function* ◆ *Similar service background (e.g., branch, officer/enlisted, Guard or Reserve, gender)* ◆ *Similar veteran type—experienced (those familiar with—and not familiar with—your industry) or recently transitioned (from the military and graduating student veterans)*
Commitment	◆ *Open-ended time frame* ◆ *Meetings once per month* ◆ *In person or virtual*	◆ *1-year relationship* ◆ *Meetings twice per month* ◆ *In person*
Ground Rules	◆ *Pairing and mentoring initiation takes place within 60 days of hire* ◆ *Mentoring handbook provided to mentors ahead of relationship* ◆ *Establish concrete goals and develop an action plan* ◆ *Share responsibility for the relationship* ◆ *Respect each other's time*	◆ *Pairing and mentoring initiation takes place within 30 days of hire* ◆ *Mentoring handbook provided to mentors ahead of relationship* ◆ *Establish concrete goals and develop an action plan* ◆ *Share responsibility for the relationship* ◆ *Respect each other's time*
Conversation Topics	◆ *First-year career objectives* ◆ *Finding meaning at work* ◆ *Career development; progression within the organization* ◆ *Networking* ◆ *Compensation and benefits* ◆ *Recognition programs* ◆ *Veteran affinity group efforts*	◆ *Military vs. organizational values* ◆ *Military vs. organizational culture* ◆ *Military vs. organizational leadership* ◆ *Influencing others* ◆ *Military vs. organizational structure* ◆ *Managing ambiguity* ◆ *Military vs. organizational communication styles* ◆ *Organizational behavior, conduct, and collaboration expectations*

Table 4-2: Mentoring Program Structure

While most organizations would desire to maintain mentoring programs in-house, there are opportunities for outside programs to provide mentors. For example, American Corporate Partners offers a more traditional mentoring program for service members transitioning into civilian roles, student veterans, or veterans seeking advancement in their civilian careers.[9] Also, Veterati offers an algorithmic matching technology to connect your new veteran hires with more tenured veterans in industry.[10]

ESTABLISHING A VETERAN AFFINITY GROUP OR MENTORING PROGRAM

If your organization is new to creating such programs, a relatively straightforward approach has proven to be successful:

1. Conduct a business needs assessment. Determine the quantifiable business goals these programs can help your organization achieve.

2. Benchmark best practices. Identify and incorporate the lessons of organizations that have succeeded in hiring and retaining veterans using such programs (see page 76).

3. Set goals and objectives. Just as you did in Chapter 3 for the overall veteran support program, identify outcome measures for which these program leaders are accountable.

4. Design the program. Create the structure and content needed to enable a tailored version of Table 4-1 and Table 4-2 for your organization.

5. Publicize the program. Use the stakeholder analysis and communication plan approaches noted in Chapter 5 to inform and enroll priority stakeholders in the efforts.

6. Execute the program. Ensure identified leaders have needed resources and program participants receive the training required for success.

7. Evaluate and continuously improve the program. Track and report the outcome performance measures identified above and implement helpful feedback from surveys the programs might periodically conduct.

Leading organizations offer several learnings in designing and executing these essential programs. Incorporating these may prevent you from relearning these hard-earned lessons:

- Align the program with the organization's culture.

- Ensure the program has a clear charter linked to quantifiable business goals.

- Ensure the program has adequate resources and leadership support.

- Improve the program continuously based on regular feedback.

- Align these efforts with related programs.

CREATING AN ONBOARDING CURRICULUM

An onboarding program for veterans ideally takes place in the very early days of their tenure at your organization. Coming from the military, they are used to early, direct leadership engagement to explain organizational direction, expectations, and norms. Your organization's onboarding program could take one of two forms:

- A dedicated, veteran-only class delivered centrally and periodically. New courses would include new veteran hires since the last class. Organizations taking this approach emphasize the importance of initiating tribal behavior.

- A dedicated but shorter veteran-only briefing coupled with onboarding sessions with the balance of employees. Organizations taking this approach place a premium on getting veterans acclimated with the rest of the non veteran new hire population soonest.

Regardless of the form, the content for the veterans would be similar, if not identical. In creating this content, there are two things to keep in mind:

- As this content will be among the first things these new employees experience, it should represent the best of the organization. Military organizations attempt to put their best foot forward from the outset, understanding that first impressions have a significant impact. Consider doing the same.

- The onboarding curriculum should be specific to a veteran audience, enabling internal tribal behavior to begin. So, leveraging your veteran talent translator to help compose it would be wise.

When composing the onboarding curriculum, consider that it should reflect the topics in the earlier mentoring discussions:

- How organizational values compare to the military
- How organizational culture compares to the military
- How organizational leadership styles compare to the military
- How organizational structure compares to the military
- How organizational communication styles compare to the military
- How to network and the benefits of networking within the organization
- How to influence others within the organization
- How to manage ambiguity in your daily work
- Understanding organizational behavior, conduct, and collaboration expectations
- Defining first-year career objectives
- Finding meaning at work
- Understanding the typical career progression within the organization (i.e., promotion timing expectations)
- Understanding what career development support/processes exist within the organization (e.g., training, mentoring)
- Understanding compensation and benefits and how they are different from the military
- Understanding recognition programs and how they are different from the military
- Understanding the support offered by the organization's veteran affinity group
- Understanding other internal or external support structures, groups, or elements and how to utilize them

- Understanding advice, guidance, and lessons learned from veteran program leaders and executive sponsors (see the Resources section of my website [*www.matthewjlouis.com*] for some examples)

- Understanding how to perform—and the resources that enable—administrative tasks (e.g., timekeeping, payroll, scheduling, accessing employee assistance programs)

Two case studies illustrate the different approaches: Deloitte and ADP.

Deloitte's Career Opportunity Redefinition & Exploration (CORE) curriculum includes a CORE Success program for recently hired veterans, part of a series of milestones within a veteran's first year of employment that facilitates assimilation and supports retention. It is intended to be administered within a new veteran hire's first ninety days, consists of an in-house, all-day workshop, and limits its audience to only those new veteran hires. Facilitators include tenured in-house veteran affinity group members, sometimes coupled with outsourced professional facilitators. Additional veteran affinity group members act as table coaches for groups of three to four new hires. The program includes the following content and ends with an unstructured networking reception:

- Adapting: understanding the similarities and differences between military and civilian work culture

  - Adopting a new culture

  - Managing ambiguity

- Interacting: developing skills for successfully engaging with others in a civilian work setting

  - Communicating differently

  - Influencing others

  - Leading differently

- Engaging: finding fulfillment and connectedness in a civilian job

  - Strategic networking

  - Finding meaning at work[12]

On the other hand, ADP takes an approach that integrates veterans into training programs of the mainstream employee population from the beginning of their tenure. Their onboarding training is conducted in-house within their first weeks and months. For those elements unique to veterans, ADP provides veterans a mentor and opportunities to participate in mentoring circles for selected topics most needed by recently transitioned veterans.[13]

Deloitte and ADP conduct their programs in-house, but that is not the only option for supporting incoming veteran talent. Prudential produced a unique veteran hiring program, VET Talent, in collaboration with Workforce Opportunity Services (WOS).[14] The role of WOS is to create relevant job descriptions, identify viable candidates, and develop appropriate curricula with local universities that administer the program. The VET Talent program had three phases:

- An *academic* phase, where the candidates learned their new role while they earned a stipend.

- An *apprenticeship* phase, during which candidates were employees of WOS and acted as consultants to Prudential. (For more on apprenticeship programs, see Appendix E.)

- A *hiring* phase, at both Prudential and other major companies.

Prudential grew the program's scope and administered it at all their major domestic sites. It expanded to include officers, enlisted, and military spouses, and applied to many roles where they hire more than six people within a six-month window. The program resulted in several hundred veteran hires and an ever-increasing talent pipeline. To help other organizations do the same, Prudential shared its VET Talent learnings with many other large and small companies.[15]

CREATING A TRAINING PROGRAM FOR VETERANS AND CIVILIAN EMPLOYEES

Once you successfully onboard your veterans, the next assimilation challenge is ensuring they have the technical skills to be effective in their new roles. Doing so involves implementing a training program, which you might administer in one of several ways: as a series of classes, over a shorter period, in-house, or not. Regardless of the administration approach, the integration of veterans into the balance of the employee population is most important. Whether the onboarding approach was partially or wholly unique to incoming veterans, try not to separate them from the rest of the incoming training population for functional training. These training experiences have the dual purpose of cultural assimilation and technical orientation/development for veterans.

COMPANIES IN THE COCKPIT

"Those veterans most successful at Walmart are those who are able to adapt quickly to changing environments, just as they did in the military. The sooner a transitioning service member can get out of their traditional military mindset and its various cultural dimensions, the better. Thus, we have found that 'mainstreaming' veterans into established training programs is more successful than separate training programs."

Brynt Parmeter, Senior Director, Non-Traditional Talent
| Head of Walmart Military & Veterans Affairs

A corporate training curriculum is not only for veterans, however. Most organizations that have adopted a dedicated veterans program stated that training the managers of incoming veterans was a best practice. Understanding that most managers in today's corporate setting do not have experience with military members, these individuals must receive some training of their own to enable their new veteran hires to succeed. For fashioning these materials, consider such sources as your organization's veteran affinity group, the Institute for Veterans and Military Families (IVMF), PsychArmor, the Department of Defense–funded Veteran Supportive Supervisor Training, or the Community Resources in the Department of Labor Education and Training Administration's WorkforceGPS.[16] Federal agencies may reference the Office of Personnel Management's annual Veterans Employment Training.[17] Topics in this training session might include:

- ◆ Understanding veterans and the military:
    - ◇ Organizational values and military values.
    - ◇ Organizational culture and military culture.
    - ◇ Organizational leadership styles and military leadership styles.
    - ◇ Organizational structure and military organizational structure.
    - ◇ Organizational compensation and benefits and military compensation and benefits.

- ◊ Organizational recognition programs and military recognition programs.

- ◊ Purpose and meaning of work.

- ◆ Welcoming and onboarding military new hires, including the military new hire's spouse and family:

  - ◊ Orientation to the new hire's team.

  - ◊ Connection with a veteran affinity group or mentor.

- ◆ Setting expectations for military new hires:

  - ◊ Understanding metrics.

  - ◊ Setting goals.

  - ◊ Career progression.

  - ◊ Reward systems.

  - ◊ How the organization supports veterans.

  - ◊ Reserve or National Guard service.

- ◆ Communicating with military new hires:

  - ◊ Organizational terminology.

  - ◊ Military terminology.

  - ◊ Networking within the organization.

  - ◊ Influencing within the organization.

- ◆ Training military new hires:

  - ◊ Participation in preprogrammed training.

  - ◊ Exposure to additional self-paced training.

- ◆ Coaching/providing feedback to military new hires:

  - ◊ How to conduct feedback sessions.

  - ◊ Recommended frequency of feedback sessions.

For federal hiring managers, additional topics might include:

◆ Benefits of hiring veterans.

◆ Veterans' preference.

◆ Special appointing authorities.

◆ How to cultivate a ready recruitment source of veterans.

◆ Where to find resources for the veteran employment process.

◆ Recruitment strategies that will increase veteran hiring.

Ideally, this training includes a handbook or reference guide that managers of veterans can take with them for future use. There will be many details inherent in these training materials that you will want these managers to apply, and attendees won't be able to recall them all.

A couple of stories from Procter & Gamble's veteran affinity program illustrate the value of such training. In the first story, a former pilot new hire was assigned to a manager that didn't understand veterans. This manager did not attend the training sessions offered by the veteran affinity group, and the former pilot quit out of frustration. By contrast, a second story has one of the veteran affinity group mentors having lunch with one of their mentees. The mentee spent much of the lunch comparing his military experience to his experience at the company. He lamented that he was always much busier in the military and much happier as a result. Following that lunch, the mentor called the mentee's manager, sent him some training materials, and provided guidance on addressing the issue. Long story short, the mentee began to enjoy his work and eventually got promoted in that role.[18]

ORCHESTRATING DELIVERY OF SUPPORT PROGRAM CONTENT

Consider two dynamics of veterans to deliver this content effectively:

◆ They arrive with varying degrees of both military and civilian experience.

◆ They will need support over an extended period to effectively assimilate.

A veteran is not a veteran is not a veteran. Tailor the content of your program to the level of experience of individual veterans. Put yourself in their shoes.

Individuals only value training that they see as accretive to their incoming experience level. You wouldn't treat a non-retired NCO with no industry experience coming into your organization like a retired officer with a graduate degree. It's best to tailor onboarding and training content and initial assignment protocols to individual population types. (Chapter 8 contains guidance on tailoring veteran assignments.) Table 4-3 illustrates a sample approach.

Instruction Type	Instruction	Possible Incoming Veteran Populations				
		Hire without Industry Experience	Hire with Industry Experience	Hire from Undergraduate School	Hire from Graduate School	Retiree hire
Briefing	Welcome Briefing	✓	✓	✓	✓	✓
Program	Onboarding Training	✓	✓	✓	✓	✓
Meeting	Informal Check-ins	✓	✓	✓	✓	✓
Briefing	Veteran Affinity Group Briefing	✓	✓	✓	✓	✓
Program	Mentor Pairing	✓	Optional	Optional	Optional	Optional
Briefing	Executive Champion Meeting	✓	✓	✓	✓	✓
Program	Veteran Assimilation Training	✓	Optional	✓	✓	✓
Meeting	Formal feedback	✓	✓	✓	✓	✓

Table 4-3: Sample Program Content Delivery by Population Type

Beyond tailoring by veteran experience type, consider the timing of its delivery. Spacing the content delivery over the new hire's first year to enable a constant drumbeat of "tribal" activity with veteran peers has proven to be an effective retention strategy. Moreover, the sequencing of these programmatic activities matters. For example, you want the incoming veteran population to be greeted immediately—ideally by veteran peers, shortly followed by a welcome from a senior executive sponsoring the program. This approach would resonate with veterans, who are used to such practices when reporting to military units. Similarly, you would want to pair the incoming veteran with a mentor before any assimilation training. The mentor can help the incoming veteran apply the content provided in that training. See Figure 4-2 below for a sample approach.

Figure 4-2 table:

Veteran Population Type	Hire without Industry Experience	Hire with Industry Experience	Hire from Under-Graduate School	Hire from Graduate School	Retiree Hire
Week 1			• Welcome briefing • Informal supervisor check-in		
Month 1		• Onboarding training • Personal goal identification		• Informal supervisor check-in	
Month 2	• Executive champion meeting • Paired w/ mentor	• Executive champion meeting • Paired w/ mentor (optional)		• Informal supervisor check-in	
Month 3		• Veteran affinity group briefing • Mentor touch-point (optional)		• Informal supervisor check-in	
Month 4			• Affinity group activity • Formal supervisor feedback		
Month 5	• Mentor touch-point • Veterans assimilation training	• Affinity group activity • Veterans assimilation training (optional)		• Affinity group activity • Veterans assimilation training	
Month 6	• Mentor touch-point • Informal supervisor check-in			• Mentor touch-point (optional) • Informal supervisor check-in • Affinity group activity	
Month 7	• Mentor touch-point • Affinity group activity			• Mentor touch-point (optional) • Affinity group activity	
Month 8			• Affinity group activity • Formal supervisor feedback		
Month 9	• Mentor touch-point • Informal supervisor check-in			• Informal supervisor check-in • Affinity group activity	
Month 10	• Mentor touch-point • Affinity group activity			• Mentor touch-point (optional) • Affinity group activity	
Month 11	• Mentor touch-point • Affinity group activity			• Mentor touch-point (optional) • Affinity group activity	
Month 12			• Affinity group activity • Formal supervisor feedback		

Figure 4-2. Sample Timing of Program Content Delivery by Population Type

With the content of your program now composed, it is time to lay the groundwork with internal and external audiences before formally initiating the hiring life cycle with prospective veteran talent. That is the topic of the next chapter.

KEYS TO SUCCESS

◆ If it doesn't already exist, first enable a veteran affinity group. Leverage that affinity group in creating your support program content.

◆ Create and administer onboarding materials unique to incoming new veteran hire types, but integrate veterans with the balance of the employee population when conducting technical training specific to their new roles.

◆ Teaming with third parties on the composition and execution of program content has proven to be successful in some organizations. In deciding whether to do so, consider how you want to maintain control over program content and its evolution.

◆ Train managers of incoming veteran talent on the nature of veterans and the military. Provide the resources and guides to enable their successful support of transitioning veterans in their new roles.

CHAPTER 5

SET EXPECTATIONS— INTERNALLY AND EXTERNALLY

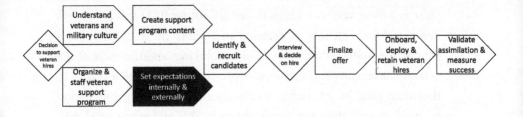

"Old men declare war. But it is the youth that must fight and die. And it is youth who must inherit the tribulation, the sorrow, and the triumphs that are the aftermath of war."

—Herbert C. Hoover[1]

President Hoover's truism applies equally today. And so, keep in mind that the program you are building will help the youth of today triumph over their battle-field experiences. With your veteran support program now defined and staffed, you have one piece of work to accomplish before you begin operating. It involves laying some groundwork with internal and external stakeholders. Its purpose is to explain why your organization is undertaking such efforts and shape expectations for what is to come. From a public relations standpoint, this is a time for your organization to shine. In this chapter, we discuss how to:

- Identify and influence internal and external stakeholders.
- Define program participant requirements.
- Update recruiting and marketing materials.

After this chapter, you will be able to successfully engage stakeholders and veteran candidates.

The overriding intent at this stage is to transform all your hiring processes to be military-friendly and portray them as such to all internal and external stakeholders. That statement raises a couple of questions:

- What hiring processes? In short, the details we will cover in Chapter 6 through Chapter 9. They will expand upon the products of your efforts in applying the material in Chapter 1 through Chapter 4.

- What does it mean to be military-friendly? What may immediately come to mind are any number of award or recognition programs. But we're not there yet; we address those in Chapter 9. At this point, let's define military-friendly as fostering an organizational culture that is supportive, appreciative, respectful, embracing, and inclusive of the veterans it recruits and employs. More tactically, and as it relates to the hiring process, let's define it as being able to be easily understood by, used by, and attractive to talent (applicants and employees) with military backgrounds (including both veterans and their spouses).

IDENTIFYING AND INFLUENCING INTERNAL AND EXTERNAL STAKEHOLDERS

Let's begin with internal stakeholders. Our internal stakeholders consist of three distinct groups other than your experienced veteran employees:

- Those acquiring veteran talent
- Those managing and working with incoming veteran talent
- Those interfacing with external stakeholders regarding the veteran support program

Sometimes individuals within these groups will overlap, as shown in Figure 5-1. Each has a stake in successfully assimilating veterans and must learn their role in enabling that outcome:

♦ The veteran hiring team must learn to thoroughly understand the many nuances and challenges veterans face in leaving military service and how to utilize tactics that will enable a veteran's successful recruiting, hiring, onboarding, and training. Among others, this group includes your veteran affinity group members.

♦ The managers and peers of incoming veteran talent must learn the military culture and which management tactics result in optimal outcomes. This group includes the balance of the employee population.

♦ Individuals interfacing with external stakeholders must learn how to accurately represent the veteran support program's overall intent, implementation process, and successful outcomes. Among others, this group includes your executive sponsors.

Figure 5-1. Veteran Support Program Internal Stakeholders

Each internal stakeholder group oversees several internal business processes in the employment life cycle. As part of their education, these stakeholders should make these internal processes as appealing to the targeted veteran as possible— that is, make them military-friendly. To demonstrate how a military-friendly culture can germinate through these processes, please see the sample characteristics in Table 5-1.

Internal Stakeholder Group	Business Processes	Sample "Military-Friendly" Characteristics
Veteran Hiring Team	Identify	◆ Have a physical presence at all sources of veteran talent, even if intermittent. ◆ Make the process inclusive of spouses and wounded warriors.
	Recruit	◆ Use experienced veterans to recruit veterans; ensure team members can translate military jargon and acronyms. ◆ Provide as much information as possible; make the entire process transparent. ◆ Tout the organization's value proposition for veteran talent.
	Interview	◆ Utilize competency-based interview questions; give interviewing veterans some idea of what types of questions to expect. ◆ Ensure that only team members understanding military jargon and acronyms conduct interviews.
	Hire	◆ Provide competitive offers that demonstrate an apples-to-apples comparison of total compensation and benefits vis-à-vis the military. ◆ Offer packages that set expectations for what to expect upon acceptance, upon joining the organization, and over the first two years.
	Onboard	◆ Provide a welcome from a senior executive that connects the organization's purpose to their role. ◆ Ensure early assignment of a mentor and membership in the organization's veteran support group.
	Train	◆ Provide targeted veteran assimilation training that focuses on values and cultural differences vis-à-vis the military.
	Retain	◆ Provide clear policies regarding service in the Guard and Reserve. ◆ Ensure membership and active participation in Employee Support of Guard and Reserve (ESGR). ◆ Participate in industry veteran hiring award/recognition programs.
	Separate	◆ Outplace veteran talent with industry peer organizations. ◆ Conduct exit interviews with all separating veterans; capture and address feedback from all interviews.

Table 5-1: Military-Friendly Business Processes by Internal Stakeholder Group

Internal Stakeholder Group	Business Processes	Sample "Military-Friendly" Characteristics
Managers and Civilian Peers of Veterans	Interview	◆ Utilize competency-based interview questions. ◆ Understand military jargon / acronyms or conduct interviews with someone that does. ◆ Be educated on military culture and its differences from organizational culture.
	Onboard	◆ Verify organizational welcome from a senior executive and early assignment of a veteran mentor. Encourage veterans to join the veteran affinity group. ◆ Establish clear expectations from the outset on the requirements of their role. Provide a career roadmap for the first two years with promotion requirements. ◆ Ensure completion of onboarding training, attempt to answer any remaining questions, and reinforce the linkage of the organization's purpose to their role.
	Train	◆ Ensure completion of veteran onboarding and reinforce key takeaways.
	Deploy	◆ Assign veterans to roles that contribute to the organization's strategic goals and objectives. Establish annual goals and clear assignment expectations.
	Develop	◆ Provide veterans early, frequent, informal performance feedback. ◆ Publish information on training requirements, appraisal cycles, reward systems, and career path expectations.
	Retain	◆ Celebrate military-themed holidays (i.e., Fourth of July, Veterans Day, Memorial Day) and support community involvement programs targeted at veteran causes. ◆ Provide early, substantive, and regular feedback to new hires; support members of the Guard and Reserve.
Veteran Support Program Emissaries	Identify	◆ Facilitate executive-level relationships at sources of veteran talent.
	Recruit	◆ Publicize the organization's value proposition for veteran talent.
	Onboard	◆ Welcome new hires and connect the organization's purpose to their role.
	Retain	◆ Celebrate military-themed holidays (i.e., Fourth of July, Veterans Day, Memorial Day) and support community involvement programs targeted at veteran causes. ◆ Publicize awards from veteran hiring recognition programs; act on feedback from veteran support group leaders.

Table 5-1 *(continued)*

Internal Stakeholder Group	Business Processes	Sample "Military-Friendly" Characteristics
Experienced Veteran Employees	Identify	◆ Refer veteran talent to the veteran hiring team and act as a networking hub in supporting transitioning veterans.
	Recruit	◆ Participate in or support the veteran hiring team.
	Interview	◆ Coach prospective veteran talent on how to answer the types of questions they should expect and participate in the interviews of veteran talent.
	Hire	◆ Offer to answer questions of prospective veteran hires, relate stories from your transition, and help set expectations for the first month to two years. ◆ Reinforce organizational principles, values, and expectations.
	Onboard	◆ Act as an instructor for onboarding training. Mentor incoming veteran talent. ◆ Enroll new veteran hires in the veteran support group; reinforce expectations of their first role and career path requirements.
	Retain	◆ Participate in the veteran support group; check in periodically with new hires. ◆ Coach members of the Guard and Reserve on activation/deployment and redeployment processes. ◆ Lead organizational efforts to celebrate veteran-themed holidays (i.e., Fourth of July, Veterans Day, Memorial Day). Facilitate community programs supporting veteran causes.

Table 5-1 *(continued)*

COMPANIES IN THE COCKPIT

"We have a small team of recruiters, mostly made up of service academy graduates. This group trains interviewers on how to conduct interviews with veterans. Within the company, our veteran recruiting team is a top contributor of talent among the academic recruiting teams in the US because they can supply talent year-round and on-demand. In contrast, academic recruiting teams are usually beholden to the regular matriculation schedule of the institutions on which they are focused."

John Myers, Procter & Gamble Veterans Affinity Group Lead

Motivating these internal stakeholders to participate in your veteran support group is usually not that difficult. Typically, these groups are already positively disposed to veterans and relish the opportunity to support them. That said, Table 5-2 offers some tactics to consider in ensuring their buy-in.

Internal Stakeholder Group	Sample Motivational Tactics
Veteran Hiring Team	◆ Rewards for achieving program goals (e.g., number of veterans hired, veteran retention levels)
	◆ Highlights in internal news stories
Experienced Veteran Employees	◆ Positive feedback/support from veteran support program emissaries and organization executives
Managers and Civilian Peers of Veterans	◆ Rewards for veteran retention levels.
	◆ Highlights in internal news stories.
	◆ Positive feedback/support from veteran support program emissaries and organization executives
Veteran Support Program Emissaries	◆ Recognition for "veteran-friendly" organization awards
	◆ Rewards for increased organizational productivity

Table 5-2: Sample Internal Stakeholder Group Motivational Tactics

As an example of striving for a military-friendly culture, Procter & Gamble's veteran affinity group maintains a regular rhythm of activities that builds camaraderie inside and outside of their organization and educates the balance of the company:

◆ They conduct a monthly lunch-and-learn with all group members via Webex so all can attend. Sample topics include influence, business impact, recruiting, and diversity and inclusion. The person briefing is usually a very senior executive (vice president level within P&G), enabling great exposure.

◆ They conduct joint happy hours with veterans groups from other local companies to enable networking opportunities.

◆ They work with each functional group in the company (e.g., HR, finance, product supply, sales, marketing) and offer veteran-specific mentoring, networking, and recruiting services to the leaders and veterans in those groups.

◆ They facilitate a military speaker series for the entire company.[2]

Now let's turn to external stakeholders. While you will find greater variety in their numbers, it is equally important to manage the perceptions of these groups proactively. Their perceptions will weigh heavily on your organization's perceived brand in the marketplace. Your organization's perceived brand will weigh heavily on how veteran talent joins your organization. Figure 5-2 portrays a typical list of external stakeholders.

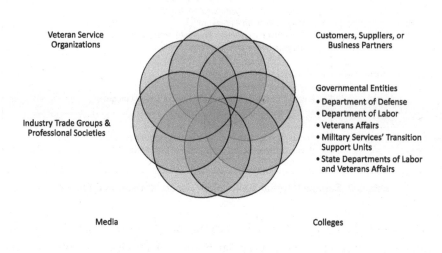

State and Local Chambers

Veteran Service
Organizations

Customers, Suppliers, or
Business Partners

Governmental Entities
• Department of Defense
• Department of Labor
• Veterans Affairs
• Military Services' Transition
  Support Units
• State Departments of Labor
  and Veterans Affairs

Industry Trade Groups &
Professional Societies

Media

Colleges

Figure 5-2. Typical Veteran Support Program External Stakeholders

Your organization will want to engage with these external stakeholder groups to set expectations proactively. You will want to influence these groups to positively perceive your organization's brand via your veteran support program. Table 5-3 illustrates some examples of how your organization might demonstrate possession of a military-friendly culture.

External Stakeholder Group	Ways to Demonstrate "Military-Friendly" Culture
Veteran Candidates and Their Families	◆ Demonstrate the presence and effectiveness of veteran affinity groups, onboarding resources, and past success in hiring veterans and military spouses. ◆ Demonstrate that selection rates, promotion rates, and retention rates of military employees (including Guard & Reserve employees, spouses, and wounded warriors) are higher than non-military employees. ◆ Demonstrate that military employee turnover is less than that of non-military employees.[3] ◆ Demonstrate that Guard and Reserve policies exceed federal requirements, the organization is a member of Employer Support of the Guard and Reserve (ESGR), and it maintains "rear detachment support" for activated or deployed personnel. ◆ Appear on "Best for Vets" employer lists of various periodicals. Receive "veteran-friendly" type organization awards.[4] Get certified as a "Veteran Ready Organization" (nonprofits only).[5] ◆ Conduct annual surveys gauging the effectiveness of the organization's veteran support program and publicize the results.

Table 5-3: Sample Tactics for Influencing External Stakeholders

External Stakeholder Group	Ways to Demonstrate "Military-Friendly" Culture
Governmental Entities	◆ Maintain relationships with local offices of the VA and Departments of Labor (American Job Centers, VETS program) and Defense (Transition Support Units of any nearby military installations), as well as state-level departments of labor and veterans affairs, to include County Veteran Service Officers (where they exist). ◆ Have no outstanding claims or violations under investigation by the US Departments of Labor or Defense, or the Consumer Financial Protection Bureau. ◆ If applicable, don't be debarred from participation in federal contracting.
Veteran Service Organizations (VSOs)	◆ Maintain active relationships with regional veteran collaboratives (see Chapter 6). ◆ Actively support national VSOs (e.g., The American Legion, Veterans of Foreign Wars, United Service Organizations (USO), Wounded Warrior Project).[6]
Colleges	◆ Actively support veteran support groups and chapters of Student Veterans of America on target college campuses. Support military-related on-campus activities. ◆ Actively recruit veterans from target campuses; include veteran alumni.
State and Local Chambers	◆ Provide programmatic materials on how to establish veteran hiring programs that they, in turn, could pass on to other local employers. ◆ Support the creation of a "Community Veteran Business Resource Group" for small or mid-size employers with limited budgets.
Media	◆ Maintain a public relations office that welcomes the presence of outside media outlets and routinely showcases the success of your veteran support program. ◆ Maintain a newsletter regularly provided to external stakeholders.
Industry Trade Groups and Professional Societies	◆ Secure recognition as a "military-friendly" brand.[7] ◆ Maintain a dialogue with trade groups or professional societies specific to your industry regarding the progress and success of your veteran support program. ◆ Include veterans in maintaining relationships with trade groups or professional societies specific to your industry.
Customers, Suppliers, or Business Partners	◆ Include veteran-owned and service-disabled, veteran-owned businesses as part of your supplier diversity program. Maintain an outreach program to attract the same. ◆ Maintain procurement infrastructure or mentoring programs to improve relationships with veteran-owned and service-disabled, veteran-owned businesses.

Table 5-3 *(continued)*

COMPANIES IN THE COCKPIT

"Our VETS (Veteran Employees That Served) Business Resource Group provides an opportunity for both veterans and non veterans to support local efforts to benefit the broader military community. These include sponsoring the annual Carry the Load Memorial Day campaign, participating in the firm's Military Home Award program, facilitating firmwide activities on Veterans Day and Memorial Day, and other local efforts like cemetery cleanups and charity runs or walks."

Rhett Jeppson, JPMorgan Chase Military and Veterans Affairs Team

By way of example, Tesla's Veteran Employment Resource Group is very involved in community support efforts. They support the Marine Corps' Toys for Tots campaign, regularly participate in blood drives, and facilitate Veterans Day and Memorial Day activities. On Veterans Day, they produce displays for each service and assemble a missing-man table. On Memorial Day, they take Tesla cars to a local veterans cemetery and lay wreaths on headstones. The group also participates in the Tesla family day and 5K run. In doing so, they donate all proceeds to the Wounded Warrior Foundation and other veteran-related causes. At the same event, they have Guard members bring out their military vehicles to display for families.[8]

DEFINING PROGRAM PARTICIPANT REQUIREMENTS

With stakeholders identified, one of the pieces of information you want to communicate to them is the organization's entry requirements. The criteria by which the hiring team judges applicants to be worthy will set the tone and the basis for the successful execution of tasks beginning in the next chapter. The application of these criteria must produce the agreed personnel scope of the program. Do applicants include only veterans? What about spouses, disabled veterans, or other family members? Whatever those answers, the point is to determine criteria that will determine which applicants get in, which don't, and why.

This effort should be thoughtful, proactive, and purposeful, and its outcome should reflect the values and culture of both the organization and the affinity group that reinforces it. As we discuss in the next chapter, these expectations should be transparent to applicants. Once they understand what—and how high—the bar is, they will more easily demonstrate their ability to leap over it. Table 5-4 provides some *sample content* to spur your thinking. Edit this list as desired.

Sample Selection Criteria	Context
Cultural match; organizational values match	Culture is the most challenging aspect for veterans to research and is critical to a good fit within your organization. You want a good match; help veterans understand what one looks like.
Education and training	Although most veterans will have degrees from formally accredited institutions of higher learning, much of their training comes from on-the-job experiences unique to their specialty. They are highly trained, but you may need to ask them to elaborate on their experiences to determine a fit.

Table 5-4: Sample Veteran Hiring Criteria

Sample Selection Criteria	Context
Certifications	Much of the training service members receive would qualify them for civilian-equivalent certifications in their fields, but often the military does not issue them. You may need to enumerate the certifications' requirements to understand if the veteran would qualify.
Work experience	
Technical skills	
Supervisory skills	Be as specific as you can in stipulating these requirements. Otherwise, veterans may struggle with where to start. They have enough difficulty here as it is. Translation of military experience is one of the most challenging things with which veterans struggle. They have these skills in spades but often fall short in relating them in a language that civilians can understand and appreciate—all the more reason to include an experienced veteran hire on your interviewing team.
Leadership skills	
Interpersonal skills	
Problem-solving skills	
Teamwork skills	
Time management skills	
Customer service orientation	
Personal motivation	Veterans leave the service for all kinds of reasons, and many do so without thinking through their next career. You want transitioning military personnel who aspire to join your organization because it is the best "fit," not people just looking for a new income source.
Compensation and benefits expectations	Most transitioning veterans don't fully appreciate the totality of their military compensation or the package you may offer them. Moreover, they tend to have little understanding of the tax implications for various portions of their benefits package. You will need to help them produce an apples-to-apples comparison for your offer to make sense.

Table 5-4: Sample Veteran Hiring Criteria *(continued)*

COMPANIES IN THE COCKPIT

"At Prudential, we spend some time assessing a candidate's cultural fit for alignment within our organization and the specific workgroup. This assessment is conducted throughout the entire talent acquisition process by evaluating every candidate through a whole-person lens. Of course, we examine hard skills such as degree attainment, certification, various credentials, and actual work experience. However, for many roles, we can train for those skills.

"For most positions, soft skills are just as important as hard skills, and this is where military talent often has the advantage. We explore the intangible ethos of collaboration, teamwork, empathy, and judgment. In addition, we celebrate candidates from nontraditional backgrounds as we drive to leverage their strengths and talents into a fully diverse and inclusive organization—recognizing that different perspectives drive better problem solving and decision making. Lastly, we highly encourage veterans and military spouses to self-identify throughout their career journey to ensure support and explore opportunities to leverage their military experience into a meaningful corporate career."

James Beamesderfer, former Vice President, Veterans Initiatives, Prudential

UPDATING RECRUITING AND MARKETING MATERIALS

Now that you know our list of stakeholders and ways to potentially influence them, you need to put in place the tactical plan by which you will influence them and create the materials with which to engage them. Some stakeholders may be unaware of your organization, its purpose, and how to engage with you, especially as it relates to veterans. Giving thought to how you would conduct purposeful outreach may pay dividends. To do so, you must answer a few questions:

◆ Which stakeholders should take priority (especially if I have a limited budget)?

◆ What are their specific information needs?

◆ How much do I need to influence them to achieve a desired state of support?

◆ By what method(s) should I engage these stakeholders for optimal effectiveness?

The answers to these questions lie in conducting a formal stakeholder analysis that includes both internal and external stakeholders. Doing so will enable you to more finely tailor your communications approach and the materials you may use to engage your intended audience. See Table 5-5 below for a Stakeholder Analysis template and *sample content*. I provide a downloadable template in the Resources section of my website (*www.matthewjlouis.com*) for your use.

Stakeholder Group	Priority	Information Needs	Level of Awareness*		Engagement Strategy
			Current	Desired	
Military Members	High	Understand opportunities and support programs at our organization.	Unaware	Supporter	Email/phone/website
Spouses	Medium		Unaware	Supporter	Email/phone/website
Transition Support Units	High		Aware	Advocate	In-person visits/website
Local Chambers of Commerce	Medium	Understand veteran employment opportunities.	Unaware	Advocate	Email/phone/in-person/website

Table 5-5: Stakeholder Analysis Template

Stakeholder Group	Priority	Information Needs	Level of Awareness*		Engagement Strategy
			Current	Desired	
ESGR	Low		Unaware	Advocate	Email/phone/website
State / Local Government	Medium		Unaware	Advocate	Email/phone/website
Veteran Collaboratives	Low	Understand existence of support program and how they might support it.	Unaware	Supporter	Email/phone/website
Local Colleges	High		Unaware	Advocate	Email/phone/website
County Veteran Service Officers	High		Unaware	Supporter	Email/phone/website
Industry Trade Groups	Medium		Unaware	Supporter	Email/phone/website
Suppliers	Low	Understand the benefits of our support program.	Unaware	Aware	Email/phone/website
Customers	Medium		Unaware	Aware	Email/phone/website
Employee Civilian Peers	Medium		Unaware	Aware	Email/website
Fellow Veteran Employees	High	Understand detailed expectations of the support program and where to find—and how to utilize—supporting materials.	Aware	Supporter	In-person meetings/email/intranet site
Employee Managers	High		Supporter	Advocate	In-person meetings/email/intranet site
Employee Trainers	High		Aware	Supporter	In-person meetings/email/intranet site
Employee Recruiters	High		Supporter	Advocate	In-person meetings/email/intranet site

*Level of Awareness spectrum: Unaware, Aware, Supporter, Advocate

Table 5-5 *(continued)*

Understanding your priority stakeholder groups' information needs and considering how you will engage them, you can now create (or update) the materials to engage our intended audiences. In general, transitioning service members are seeking secure landing spots. So, your materials should attempt to portray your organization as a safe harbor in which they may allow their second career to set sail. Also, to the extent that you can, consider tailoring these materials to each specific stakeholder group. For example, you would call out successful Army hire case studies if you were targeting Army personnel, or you might add subtle patriotic color schemes in recruiting materials to help endear your audience to your message.

As you construct your materials, you might consider examples from the military-related career websites of these leading organizations:

- ADP
- Amazon
- JPMorgan Chase
- Performance Contractors
- Procter & Gamble
- Prudential
- Schlumberger
- Tesla
- USAA
- US Department of State
- Walmart
- Xavier University

We can now fashion a communications plan to set expectations internally and externally with these materials. This plan will address such questions as:

- What message gets sent to which stakeholder group, in what order, for what purpose, at what timing, and via what method?
- Who is responsible for communicating the message, and what is the status of each scheduled communication?

See Table 5-6 for a Communications Plan template and *sample content*. I provide a downloadable template in the Resources section of my website (*www.matthewjlouis.com*) for your use.

Stakeholder Group (To Whom)	Content (What)	Purpose (Why)	Timing (When)	Media (How)	Responsible (By Whom)	Status*
All Military (except Marines)	Organizational value proposition; veteran hiring program details (several waves of content that build upon one another)	Recruit for general needs.	1st of next month	Email	Veteran Hiring Team Member	Planned
Marines		Recruit for specific skills.	1st of next month	Email		Planned
Transition Support Units		Awareness	Next week	In-person	Veterans Support Program Emissary	In progress
Local Media		Awareness	Next week	Phone, email		Complete
Spouses		Recruit for general needs.	Two weeks out	Phone	Veteran Hiring Team Member	Complete
City Chamber of Commerce	Marketing piece that highlights organization's veteran support program	Encourage awareness, support, and coordination.	Annual; March 1st	Email, website	Veteran Program Leader	Planned
State ESGR						Planned
County Government						Planned
Veteran Collaborative						Planned
Community College						Planned
County Veteran Service Officer						Planned
Industry Trade Group	Applicable details of veteran support program	Understand opportunities and benefits of program.	Annual; Sept. 1st	Email, sponsorships	Marketing, w/ Vet Program Lead	Complete
Suppliers			Biannual	Email, website	Purchasing, w/ Vet Program Lead	In progress
Customers			Monthly	Email, website, adverts	Marketing, w/ Vet Program Lead	In progress

Table 5-6: Communications Plan Template

Stakeholder Group (To Whom)	Content (What)	Purpose (Why)	Timing (When)	Media (How)	Responsible (By Whom)	Status*
Employee Civilian Peers	Documentation of all program details, training materials, expectations, roles & responsibilities	Understand and comply with program expectations.	Annual	Email; intranet site	Veteran Talent Translator, Veteran Support Program lead	Complete
Fellow Veteran Employees			Biannual			In-progress
Employee Managers			Annual			Complete
Employee Trainers			Annual			Complete
Employee Recruiters			Biannual			In-progress

*Status: Planned, In Progress, Complete

Table 5-6 *(continued)*

You begin to put this communications plan to use in the next chapter, as you start engaging with veteran candidates while maintaining expectations with external stakeholders.

KEYS TO SUCCESS

◆ Proactively identify internal and external stakeholders.

　◇ Internally, this is more than just HR's role. Every business function can—and should—play a role.

　◇ Externally, this may involve interfacing with individuals and organizations that are an extension of your existing network. Leverage those connections to build relationships.

◆ Define how your organization can be military-friendly and enroll internal stakeholders in making it so.

◆ Thoughtfully plan how you will influence internal and external stakeholder groups to support your program.

◆ Purposefully consider the selection criteria for veteran applicants and share them with those applicants.

◆ Conduct a stakeholder analysis before updating recruiting and marketing materials.

◆ Compose a communications plan before engaging with stakeholder audiences.

CHAPTER 6

IDENTIFY AND RECRUIT CANDIDATES

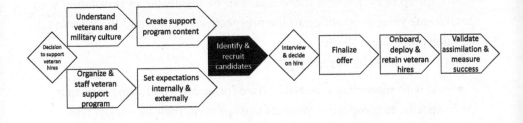

"I think I'd be a better president because I was in combat."

—George H. W. Bush[1]

A veteran himself, President Bush implicitly understood the value his experiences brought to the highest office in the land. As an employer, that same value can be yours, but you must first understand where to find veteran talent and how to attract it to your organization. Those locations will be different and more varied than your typical sources off campuses elsewhere in the market. Moreover, the standard recruiting approaches that civilian recruiters unfamiliar with veteran culture use will not succeed.

This chapter will portray an alternate approach whose implementation will position you for success. By the end of this chapter, you should understand how to:

- Augment established recruiting processes.

- Identify sources of veteran talent.

- Translate role descriptions.

- Establish or update outreach platforms.

- Vet and prioritize candidates.

AUGMENT ESTABLISHED RECRUITING PROCESSES

To overcome the cultural differences inherent in the civil-military divide and connect with veteran talent, you would be wise to start staffing your recruiting team with experienced veterans from your veteran support program or business resource group (BRG). These individuals can be invaluable in translating your organization's value proposition to the prospective veterans and the veteran talent's value proposition to you.

In parallel, consider addressing these items:

- As with marketing materials, create (or update) recruiting materials specific to prospective veterans and appeal to their views. Use translated terminology that would resonate with them. Use patriotic color schemes. Portray wounded warriors and men and women of different races in and out of uniform; doing so will appeal to the diverse audience you want to recruit. Review any stock photography used for accuracy; many media outlets (including major motion pictures) get this wrong.

- Ensure that your recruiting materials and website clearly articulate your organization's values. As noted in Chapter 1, military culture is big on values. Overtly relating how your organization's values match with military values will tend to resonate with veteran talent.

- If your organization has one, educate applicants with military backgrounds on how to overcome the challenges associated with Applicant Tracking Systems (ATS), which have historically been the bane of such applicants. While they exist to provide employers an automated way to keep track of applicants and support compliance with applicable regulations, an unspoken part of their purpose is to screen out candidates. They do so by focusing on keywords in résumés. If a résumé does not contain the words or combination of words sought by the employer, the ATS may reject it before being read by a human being. To help service members overcome the ATS, teach them to:

◇ Identify the keywords used in the job description. Tailor their résumé to include those keywords multiple times throughout the document.

◇ Submit a cover letter (see the Resources section of my website [*www.matthewjlouis.com*] for a sample) and résumé that likewise leverages the keyword approach.

◇ Use both the long-form and acronym version of keywords (e.g., "Master of Business Administration [MBA]" or "Search Engine Optimization [SEO]").

◇ Use a chronological or hybrid résumé format; avoid the functional résumé format.[2]

◇ Not use tables or columns as they often cause significant parsing errors.[3]

◇ Use a traditional résumé font like Helvetica, Garamond, or Georgia.[4]

◇ Not use headers or footers as the information might cause a parsing error.

◇ Use standard résumé section headings like "Work Experience" rather than being cute or clever (e.g., "Where I've Been").[5]

◇ Save their file as a .docx if possible, as this format is parsed most accurately.

Again, leverage your experienced in-house veterans in executing these approaches. They will inherently understand what will resonate with your intended targets and thus make your overtures more effective and your results more productive.

IDENTIFY SOURCES OF VETERAN TALENT

Many organizations struggle with where to find veterans. The geographic location of veterans varies, depending on whether you target all veterans or those veterans who have recently left the military. If you are open to considering all veterans, they are more prevalent in some states, as Table 6-1 shows.

States with Highest Percentage of Veterans Per Capita		States with Highest Number of Veterans	
Alaska	9.2%	California	1,789,862
Maine	9.0%	Texas	1,603,328
Montana	9.0%	Florida	1,594,218
Washington	8.7%	Pennsylvania	872,301
New Hampshire	8.3%	New York	838,129

States with Highest Percentage of Women Veterans Per Capita		States with Highest Number of Women Veterans	
District of Columbia	14.0%	Texas	168,967
Virginia	13.6%	California	142,904
Alaska	13.3%	Florida	142,193
Maryland	12.6%	Virginia	99,399
Georgia	12.1%	Georgia	84,894

States with Highest Percentage of Minority Veterans Per Capita		States with Highest Number of Minority Veterans	
Puerto Rico	98.7%	California	628,963
District of Columbia	63.7%	Texas	564,675
Hawaii	63.7%	Florida	347,821
New Mexico	41.0%	Georgia	265,255
Maryland	38.3%	Virginia	219,961

Table 6-1: Geographic Profile of Veterans[6]

COMPANIES IN THE COCKPIT

"Throughout the hiring process, we focus a lot on education. We visit military bases and bring our Human Resource personnel along. In doing so, we conduct seminars that effectively pick up where SFL-TAP [Soldier for Life—Transition Assistance Program; the military's transition course] left off. Since the résumés we tend to see from TAP graduates lack specifics needed for the oil and gas industry, we will train these veterans how to produce résumés that will resonate with HR professionals in our industry. We also facilitate shadow days for aspiring veteran hires."

Nick B. Tran, Manager, Community and Veteran Affairs at Schlumberger

If you are open to considering only veterans who recently departed from the service, those geographic locations paint a slightly different picture. As the table below indicates, more than 80 percent of active-duty service members reside in sixteen states. Having a presence at duty stations within those states could be a productive approach. About half of veterans do not return to their home of record, the geographic location from which they originated their service. The transition centers at those locations will be your primary points of contact. For a list of the precise locations of military installations by state, please see the Resources section of my website (*www.matthewjlouis.com*).

Rank	State	Number of Active Duty	Percentage of Total US Active Duty	Cumulative Percentage
1	California	162,936	14.0%	14.0%
2	Virginia	125,665	10.8%	24.7%
3	Texas	115,574	9.9%	34.7%
4	North Carolina	100,055	8.6%	43.2%
5	Georgia	68,276	5.9%	49.1%
6	Florida	62,735	5.4%	54.5%
7	Washington	57,645	4.9%	59.4%
8	Hawaii	40,495	3.5%	62.9%
9	South Carolina	39,573	3.4%	66.3%
10	Colorado	37,274	3.2%	69.5%
11	Kentucky	33,759	2.9%	72.4%
12	Maryland	28,906	2.5%	74.8%
13	Illinois	26,375	2.3%	77.1%
14	Kansas	21,859	1.9%	79.0%
15	Oklahoma	21,714	1.9%	80.8%

Table 6-2: Geographic Profile of Active-Duty Service Members[7]

COMPANIES IN THE COCKPIT

"From a recruiting standpoint, we find the best results occur when we are active on military bases and at career fairs. Success doesn't come easy, however. You have to be committed to recruiting these deserving veterans. You need to walk the talk through each stage of the employment life cycle."

Chris Newton, Workforce Development Manager at Cajun Industries

Aside from military installations, there are many sources of veteran talent. As you'll see, the only excuse for not finding veteran talent is not looking. Consider the following:

- Internal referrals. Perhaps the most reliable source of leads will come from veterans within your organization. A tight-knit community, most veterans are anxious to help their peers and have more transitioning veterans working side-by-side with them in the workplace. Amazon notes that they tend to have many applicants due to a large and growing referral network.[8]

COMPANIES IN THE COCKPIT

"Actually getting out on the job site to remind veterans about our hiring program, what it does, and our open opportunities has been the best advertising—and it costs almost nothing."

David Theriot, Military Workforce Development at Performance Contractors

- Veteran collaboratives. Those with locations in cities with a veteran collaborative enjoy an advantage. These collaboratives act as an in-processing center for all veterans settling in that geographic area. They can act as a single point of contact for transitioning veterans seeking employment in that area. See "Veteran Collaboratives" on page 109 for details.

Veteran Collaboratives

Veteran collaboratives are organizations (usually private, nonprofit) that bring veterans, agencies, organizations, and community members together locally in an atmosphere of mutual support to solve issues systemically that each could not address alone. Most offer support in employment, education, healthcare, housing, wellness, and family support. They exist in recognition of the fact that federal support for helping veterans effectively settle in local areas is lacking, and there is either 1) a lack of support resources in some communities or 2) an overabundance of support resources in some communities (referred to as the "sea of goodwill"), leading to confusion, apathy, and unsought support. When veterans in-processed in the military, they did so through a military one-stop processing center that cared for all their needs (e.g., ID cards, benefits, housing, finance, transportation, and travel claims). Those in-processing centers did it all. Think of these veteran collaboratives as a veteran's one-stop in-processing center in their new community. Ideally, collaboratives are some of the first resources veterans seek out in their local area. They can be beneficial to employers as well.

For example, Houston (home to 270,000+ veterans) contains hundreds of nonprofit organizations with the word *veteran* in their mission or vision statements. Neither veterans nor your organization has the time or patience to navigate all of those on your own. Combined Arms, a collaborative in Houston, is your one-stop shop. They will help organize all the support veterans need from the best local agencies. From your organization's standpoint, *the collaborative acts as your single point of contact for identifying veterans relocating from the military to your local area.*

Some other examples from around the country include (see the Resources section of my website [*www.matthewjlouis.com*] for hyperlinks):

◆   Combined Arms in Houston, Texas.

◆   Mount Carmel Veterans Service Center in Colorado Springs, Colorado.

◆   San Diego Military Family Collaborative.

◆   Still Serving Veterans in Alabama.

◆   Illinois Joining Forces in Chicago and Springfield, Illinois.

◆   Oklahoma Veterans Alliance.

◆   The Veterans Collaborative in Boston.

◆   Operation Stand Down Tennessee in Nashville.

◆   Upstate Warrior Solution in South Carolina.

◆   Veterans Bridge Home in Charlotte, North Carolina.

◆   The Warrior Alliance in Atlanta.

◆   Arizona Coalition for Military Families in Phoenix.

◆   Los Angeles Veterans Collaborative.

◆   The Veterans Community Action Teams in Michigan.

- AmericaServes affiliates in several regions of the United States: New York City; Upstate New York; Charlotte, North Carolina; Coastal North Carolina (Jacksonville); RDU/Fayetteville, North Carolina; Asheville, North Carolina; Lowcountry, South Carolina; Pittsburgh; Greater Puget Sound in Washington State; Rhode Island; North Texas; San Antonio, Texas; Rio Grande Valley; San Diego, California; Tulsa, Oklahoma; Norfolk, Virginia; and Washington DC.

- America's Warrior Partnership affiliates and Community Branches in Alaska, Permian Basin, Northwest Florida, Central Indiana, and the Navajo Nation.

- Bob Woodruff Foundation Local Partner Network.

- United Way's Mission United.

- Code of Support Foundation.

Call your local chamber of commerce to research the existence of a collaborative there.

- College campuses. Studies show that about 4 percent of transitioning veterans use college or graduate school as a transition vehicle.[9] Assuming that transitioning veterans self-identify, career centers at many schools offer veteran-specific programs, services, and training to enable their successful educational experience. Veteran support offices at such schools can be a great source of newly up-skilled veteran talent. (For colleges considering such programs, please see "Becoming a Military-Friendly Academic Institution" on page 111.) *US News & World Report* maintains an annual ranking of best colleges for veterans.[10] Other notable schools that maintain veteran-specific programs include:

  ◇ Butler University.

  ◇ Columbia University.

  ◇ De Anza College.

  ◇ Grantham University.

  ◇ Vanderbilt University.

  ◇ Xavier University.

  ◇ University of Wyoming.

- Veteran student support groups. Some veteran-related organizations may exist on college campuses that pose yet another avenue for identifying qualifying talent:

◇ Student Veterans of America.[11] Veteran student support organization with 1,500 on-campus chapters in all fifty states and four countries representing more than 750,000 student veterans.

◇ MBA Veterans Network

Becoming a Military-Friendly Academic Institution[12]

"Military-friendly" on college campuses entails more than we've previously discussed. In addition to our earlier definition, the idea is to build a campus climate geared toward supporting veterans' holistic success in higher education and engaging them in their growth toward a new career in civilian life. Consider implementing these programmatic steps to build a "military-friendly" campus climate:

◆ **Military cultural competency training.** Implement military cultural competency training campus-wide, particularly for those responsible for teaching and advising activities. Instructors and advisors must learn how to effectively educate veterans and make thoughtful referrals to supportive resources as needed.

◆ **Academic outreach.** Provide veterans with sufficient information to know how their military education will be credited and understand the remaining requirements for graduation. A good resource is NASPA's annual Symposium on Military-Connected Students.[13] Information might include credit for American Council on Education (ACE)-evaluated military courses or experience, the CLEP exam, or the DSST exam.[14]

◆ **Career services outreach and staff training.** Because veterans may not be aware of career services assistance, career services representatives might proactively initiate contact with them before and during their presence on campus. Columbia University offers online courses that veterans may take before attending and provides voluminous support while on campus.[15]

◆ **Integrated counseling, disability services, and student health.** Veterans in higher education need information about resources to address mental health, disability, and health challenges unique to their experience in the military.

◆ **Financial aid and business services.** Financial aid representatives should be prepared to fully explain the financial aid options available and the actual cost of education, in addition to helping veterans understand their education benefits. Columbia University offers an example of a robust website for this purpose.[16] Beyond federal benefits, some aid options might include in-state residency recognition for tuition purposes, willingness to accept military tuition assistance (TA) payments, the presence of scholarships for members of the military, or reduced tuition for the same.

- **Involvement in federal programs.**[17] Consider participating in several of the following programs: Yellow Ribbon GI Education Enhancement Program (provision of the Post-9/11 GI Bill),[18] official commitment to the Eight Keys to Veterans' Success,[19] VA's Principles of Excellence,[20] The College Financing Plan,[21] Armed Forces Tuition Assistance (TA) Funding,[22] DoD Voluntary Education Partnership Memorandum of Understanding (MOU) for Tuition Assistance,[23] the Veteran Success on Campus (VSOC) Program,[24] and the Workforce Recruitment Program (see below). Also, the US Department of Veterans Affairs offers a Campus Toolkit for faculty, staff, and administrators to support veterans.[25]

- **Support group presence.** The presence of a Student Veterans of America chapter or the MBA Veterans Network is also an indicator of veteran community support.

Please see the free Toolkit for Veteran Friendly Institutions that the American Council on Education created for additional guidance.[26]

- Workforce Recruitment Program, a Department of Labor and Department of Defense program for college students (including veterans returning to school) with disabilities helps them find summer or permanent jobs.[27]

- Military scholars fellowships. These programs run the range from scholarships to experiential development opportunities. At a minimum, they result in better trained, more worldly, experienced veteran talent. Some even produce new college graduates. All may be good sources for newly up-skilled veterans. Many also offer the opportunity to sponsor a fellowship.

  ◇ Tillman Scholars Program.[28] This program supports active-duty service members, veterans, and their spouses with academic scholarships, a national network, and professional development opportunities in medicine, law, business, policy, technology, education, and the arts.

  ◇ Bass Military Scholars Program.[29] Vanderbilt University awards ten to fifteen scholarships annually to veterans pursuing graduate and professional degrees across five Vanderbilt schools:

    - Law School (JD)

    - School of Medicine (MD)

    - School of Nursing (MSN)

- Owen Graduate School of Management (MBA)

- Peabody College of Education and Human Development (MEd, MPP)

◇ Veterans in Global Leadership Fellowship.[30] This program offers a twelve-month leadership fellowship for student veterans (enlisted and JMOs) who aspire to global leadership positions.

◇ Mission Continues Veteran Leadership Accelerator.[31] Enables post–9/11 veterans, Guardsmen, and Reservists to deliver volunteer services in their local communities in exchange for mentoring, professional development, and personal growth experiences.

◇ ServiceCorps Fellowship.[32] Fellows receive leadership development training and living stipends that cover 100 percent of student loan payments to become a leader serving in the nonprofit and public sectors.

◇ Governmental entities may have an interest in graduates of the following programs:

- Council on Foreign Relations (CFR) Military Fellowship

- White House Fellowship

- Veterans of Foreign Wars (VFW)-Student Veterans of America (SVA) Legislative Fellowship

- Anna Sobol Levy Foundation Fellowships

- Department of Homeland Security's Secretary's Honors Program

- The Smith Richardson Foundation Strategy and Policy Fellows Program

- Hertog War Studies Program

- Belfer Center Fellowships

- Graduating recipients of one of many military-themed scholarships.

◇ American Veterans (AMVETS) scholarships[33]

◇ Armed Forces Communications and Electronics Association scholarships[34]

◇ Army Women's Foundation Scholarship Program[35]

◇ Divine Mercy University's Patriot Scholarship[36]

◇ Liberty University's Heroes Fund Scholarship[37]

◇ Lunacap Foundation scholarships[38]

◇ Military Order of the Purple Heart Scholarship Program[39]

◇ Military spouse tuition assistance programs:
  ◆ Air Force Aid Society[40]
  ◆ Army Emergency Relief Scholarships[41]
  ◆ Army Scholarship Foundation[42]
  ◆ Chief Petty Officer Scholarship Fund[43]
  ◆ Coast Guard Foundation[44]
  ◆ Folds of Honor Scholarships[45]
  ◆ Hope for the Warriors Scholarships[46]
  ◆ Marine Corps League Scholarship Program[47]
  ◆ National Military Family Association Scholarships[48]
  ◆ Navy-Marine Corps Relief Society Education Programs[49]
  ◆ ThanksUSA Scholarship Program[50]
  ◆ Wings Over America Administered Scholarships[51]

◇ National Ranger Memorial Foundation Scholarship[52]

◇ National Veterans Leadership Foundation, a nonprofit that supports military-connected students attending America's universities[53]

◇ Paralyzed Veterans of America Scholarship Program[54]

◇ The Posse Veterans Program, a nonprofit that identifies, trains, and supports veterans interested in pursuing bachelor's degrees at partner universities (University of Virginia, Vassar College, and Wesleyan University)[55]

◇ Veterans of Foreign Wars (VFW) scholarships[56]

◇ Warrior-Scholar Project, a nonprofit focused on ensuring every degree-seeking enlisted veteran and transitioning service member succeeds in higher education and beyond, can connect you with their program alumni, who complete academic boot camps conducted by their partner universities:[57]

- Yale University
- Georgetown University
- Princeton University
- University of Southern California
- University of Pennsylvania
- Texas A&M University
- University of Michigan
- Massachusetts Institute of Technology
- University of Notre Dame
- Harvard University

- Cornell University
- University of North Carolina
- University of Arizona
- Syracuse University
- Columbia University
- Amherst College
- University of Chicago
- University of California, Irvine
- California Institute of Technology
- Williams College
- Pomona College

COLLEGES IN THE COCKPIT

"We recognize that when veterans transition out of the military and succeed, our communities succeed. Higher education can be a transformative experience for veterans, utilizing their existing leadership ability, skill sets, and strengths and providing them with a new career path. A military-friendly campus is one in which the institution makes a commitment to support veterans throughout their higher education transition, with services and programs that fit the veteran and not the other way around. All too often, campuses try to fit veterans into existing resources that are designed for traditionally experienced students; and that typically doesn't work. The most important pieces are having an actual center for student veterans, dedicated staff with that center, and money to support programs and services. If you have all three, a cultural shift can happen on any campus."

Brad Fittes, former Xavier University Student Veterans Center Director

♦ Career fairs (virtual and in-person):

  ◇ National Labor Exchange Career Events[58]—enables access to all state job banks and all state workforce agencies

  ◇ VA for Vets hiring events[59]—includes Hiring Our Heroes and Disabled American Veterans (DAV) events

  ◇ US Department of Defense Civilian Employment job fairs[60]

  ◇ Service Academy Career Conferences[61]

  ◇ Soldier for Life—Transition Assistance Program job fairs[62]—includes the MEGA Career Fair at Fort Hood, Texas

  ◇ The American Legion veterans career fairs[63]

  ◇ Military Officers Association of America (MOAA) career and education events[64]

  ◇ RecruitMilitary veteran job fairs[65]

  ◇ Corporate Gray job fairs[66]

  ◇ Cleared Jobs job fairs[67]

  ◇ Job Zone job fairs[68]

  ◇ Military.com job fairs[69]

  ◇ Veteran Recruiting job fairs[70]

- National veteran-related conferences:
  - Elite Meet conferences[71]
  - Women Veterans Alliance Unconference[72]
  - Student Veterans of America National Conference (NatCon)[73]
  - MBA Veterans Conference[74]
  - National Association of State Workforce Agencies Veterans Conference[75]
  - American Veterans Center Annual Conference[76]
  - Academy Women's Officer Women Leadership Symposium (OWLS)[77]

Vetting Career Fairs and Hiring Conferences

As a prospective employer, you have many options for accessing veteran talent via career fairs or hiring conferences. To select those that are best for your organization, consider those that:

- Have a strong track record of attendance, with database documentation of the rank, service, and occupational specialty of all candidates.
- Allow for virtual participation.
- See a robust list of interested employers in attendance and allow for sponsorship opportunities.
- Demonstrate broad promotion and marketing campaigns.

- Hire Heroes USA. Hire Heroes USA is a nonprofit that provides free job search assistance to US military members, veterans, and military spouses and helps companies hire them. They provide employers services such as job board postings, employment training, virtual career fairs, and talent sourcing.[78]

- American Job Centers. Consider using the resources provided by one of the nearly 2,500 American Job Centers (AJCs).[79] Most AJCs have Business Service Representatives and Veterans Service Representatives. They offer a robust set of resources, support, and training through their Business Centers,[80] including:

- ◇ Recruiting and hiring.
  - ◆ Identifying your hiring needs
  - ◆ Where to find candidates
  - ◆ Interviewing and hiring
  - ◆ Hiring a diverse workforce
- ◇ Training and retaining.
  - ▪ Identifying employee skill needs
  - ▪ Training options
  - ▪ Funding employee training
  - ▪ Managing and retaining employees
- ◇ Toolkit.
  - ▪ American Job Center finder
  - ▪ Available workforce (a workforce profiler)
  - ▪ Salary finder
  - ▪ Military-to-Civilian occupation translator
  - ▪ Occupation comparison tool
  - ▪ Certification finder
  - ▪ Local training finder
  - ▪ Professional association finder
  - ▪ State resource finder
  - ▪ Job description writer
  - ▪ Competency model clearinghouse

◆ Other organizations' HR representatives. It is wise to maintain a network of peers across other organizations—even competing organizations. While the competition for the best talent is fierce, it can only be productive when and where a proper fit exists. And if the fit in a sister organization doesn't come to fruition, that organization's HR representative may be willing to pass those potential veteran hires your way.

- Federal apprenticeship programs. The federal government sponsors several of these, which represent an opportunity for your organization to support an apprenticeship and take advantage of their newly up-skilled products. Think of this as your "try before you buy" option. (See Appendix E for guidance on establishing your Registered Apprenticeship Program.)
  - Various Department of Labor apprenticeships[81]
  - The US Chamber of Commerce Foundation Fellows program, also known as the Hiring Our Heroes Corporate Fellowship Program[82]
  - Department of Defense SkillBridge Program[83]
  - Army Career Skills Program, whose participating companies are unique to each Army post[84]
  - The State Department's Veterans Innovation Partnership (VIP) Fellowship[85]
  - The Department of Energy's Veterans Programs[86]
  - Office of the Secretary of Defense Fellows program[87]
  - United Services Military Apprenticeship Program (USMAP). Allows service members to complete an apprenticeship while on active duty.[88]
  - Also, the VA provides benefits that cover costs associated with on-the-job training and apprenticeships[89]
- Civilian apprenticeship programs. Civilian organizations sponsor hundreds of these, all of which produce up-skilled veterans ripe for the picking.
  - Fastport's national apprenticeship program, in partnership with the Department of Labor.[90]
  - ForgeNow runs an eight-week basic training program for HVAC and electrical trades.[91]
  - Helmets to Hardhats.[92] National nonprofit program that connects veterans and military service members with training and career opportunities in the construction industry.

◇ Operation Socrates.[93] Nonprofit that mentors active-duty military and veterans desiring to become a teacher and links them to employment opportunities.

◇ The Painters and Allied Trades Veterans Program.[94]

◇ Purdue University's Cyber Apprenticeship Program.[95]

◇ Shift.org facilitates several programs that serve veterans, transitioning service members, and their prospective employers.[96]

◇ Soldiers to Sidelines.[97] Nonprofit that provides training and certification opportunities for aspiring coaches, many of whom also become teachers.

◇ Explore the Trades.[98] Nonprofit that provides veterans employment opportunities within the plumbing, HVAC, and electrical services industries.

◇ United Association Veterans in Piping Program.[99]

◇ The US Department of Veterans Affairs maintains a list of employers that offer apprenticeships.[100] (At the top of the page in Search Filters, select Program Type "On-the-Job-Training/Apprenticeship," then select your state on the map.)

◇ Workshops for Warriors.[101] Nonprofit that provides training and education for veterans interested in an advanced manufacturing career field.

◇ Graduates of any vocational, trade, or technical programs featured on the Real Work Matters website.[102]

◆ VetsInTech. A multidimensional resource for veteran talent in the technology industry, VetsInTech supports veterans with reintegration services focused on education, entrepreneurship, and employment. Their support of prospective employers includes a job board and a résumé database.[103]

◆ Department of Labor's Veteran Employment and Training Service (VETS). VETS provides employers with assistance in finding qualified transitioning service members and veterans in their local area.[104] Check out the partners participating in their Employment Navigator & Partnership Pilot (ENPP) program.[105] Also, VETS offers employment and training services to eligible veterans through two principal programs, noted below. Both may be useful in providing funding and resources for veterans in your organization and acting as a source of newly skilled veteran talent.

◊ Disabled Veterans' Outreach Program (DVOP).[106] DVOP provides job and training opportunities for veterans with service-connected disabilities, including apprenticeships and on-the-job training, enabling them to be more competitive in the labor market. DVOP specialists work with employers, veteran service organizations, the Departments of Veterans Affairs and Defense, and other community-based organizations to link veterans with appropriate jobs and training opportunities, such as the federally funded VA Vocational Rehabilitation program.[107]

◊ Local Veterans' Employment Representatives (LVERs) Program.[108] LVERs are state employees located in state employment offices that provide the following types of assistance to veterans:

   ◆ Supervise the provision of all state employment services, including counseling, testing, and identifying training and employment opportunities.

   ◆ Monitor job listings from federal contractors to ensure eligible veterans get priority referrals to these jobs.

   ◆ Monitor federal department and agency vacancies listed at local state employment service offices.

   ◆ Process complaints from veterans about the observance of veterans' preference by federal employers.

   ◆ Promote and monitor the participation of veterans in federally funded employment and training programs.

   ◆ Cooperate with the Department of Veterans Affairs to identify and aid veterans who need work-specific prosthetic devices, sensory aids, or other special equipment to improve their employability.

   ▪ Contact community leaders, employers, unions, training programs, and veteran service organizations to ensure eligible veterans get the services to which they are entitled.

- The Department of Defense's Military Spouse Employment Partnership is a program that connects military spouses with partner employers who have committed to recruit, hire, promote, and retain military spouses.[109]

- Corporate internship or rotational programs. Some larger organizations have designed internships or rotational programs that expose transitioning veterans to several functions over the program. These programs tend to be geared toward junior military officers (JMOs) or non-commissioned officers (NCOs) with at least a bachelor's degree. Upon completing these programs, some veterans may decide that the sponsoring organization is not a fit. That, in turn, may present an opportunity for you.

- Federal agency internships. Several federal agencies have initiated internship programs for veterans. Participants in these programs would be possible acquisition targets for commercial and governmental organizations.

  ◇ The Department of Defense's Operation Warfighter. This internship program matches qualified wounded, ill, and injured service members with non-funded federal internships so they may gain work experience during their recovery and rehabilitation.[110]

  ◇ Pathways.[111] These programs offer federal internships for students from high school through postgraduate school and clear paths to federal careers for recent graduates.

    - Internship Program: Offers currently enrolled students paid opportunities to work in agencies and explore federal careers while still in school.

    - Recent Graduates Program: Offers recent graduates of qualifying educational institutions a career development program with training and mentoring.

    - Presidential Management Fellows Program: The federal government's premier leadership development program for advanced degree candidates.

◇ Department of Veterans Affairs Intern Programs[112]

- Non-Paid Work Experience (NPWE): Provides eligible veterans with the opportunity to obtain training and practical job experience by working in a federal, state, or local government agency.

- On-the-Job Training (OJT) Program: Provides eligible veterans an opportunity to obtain training and practical hands-on experience at federal agencies.

◆ Federal agency hiring programs.[113]

◇ Vets-to-Feds (V2F) Program. Career development program sponsored by the Interagency Council on Veterans Employment and designed to recruit and support the development of veterans for careers with the federal government.

◇ Reintegration of Guard and Reserve Members. The government-wide Reintegration Framework outlines a systematic approach to reintegrating federal employees who are Guard or Reserve members. See Appendix I for more detail.

◇ Disabled Veterans Affirmative Action Program. Under Title 5 of the Code of Federal Regulations, part 720, subpart C, and 38 United States Code, section 4214, all agencies are responsible for developing annual Disabled Veterans Affirmative Action Program (DVAAP) Plans.

◇ Women Veterans Hiring Initiative. While not yet a formal program, federal agencies might consider the Council on Veterans Employment's Women Veterans Initiative findings.[114]

Women veterans represent a small (approximately 17 percent) but growing portion of the veteran population. Combined with their evolving roles in the military, that tends to result in a transition from the military that is remarkably different from their male counterparts. According to a DAV report on the topic, "Our nation does not yet adequately recognize and celebrate the contributions of women in military service, treat them with dignity and respect, or promote their successful transition to civilian life."[115] Now is your organization's chance to do so. Women are no strangers to hurdles and overcoming barriers, as many dealt with this routinely while serving in a male-dominated profession. Moreover, they are strong, intelligent, and driven. Many companies desire to leverage these skill sets and build on a diverse employee base. Several organizations stand ready to assist your efforts in doing so. Among them are:

- Academy Women.
- Foundation for Women Warriors.
- LeanIn Women Veterans.
- National Association of State Women Coordinators.
- Service Women's Action Network (SWAN).
- Veteran Women Igniting the Spirit of Entrepreneurship (V-WISE).
- Women Veterans Alliance.
- Women Veterans Interactive.
- Women Veterans ROCK.
- Women Vets USA.

- Education and Employment Initiative.[116] This US Department of Defense program matches wounded or injured service members with education and career opportunities that will help them transition successfully to civilian life. The program's regional coordinators maintain relationships with public, private, and nonprofit employers interested in hiring wounded or injured service members.

- Corporate transition programs. Many organizations, for-profit and nonprofit, sponsor transition programs for military service members. Most have a diligent vetting process; their graduates would have already met specific standards.[117]

  ◇ American Corporate Partners (ACP). ACP is a national nonprofit organization that helps returning veterans and active-duty spouses find subsequent careers through one-on-one mentoring, networking, and online career advice. Its website provides opportunities to become an ACP partner and sponsor mentorships.[118]

- BreakLine.[119] BreakLine is an immersive educational program for veterans transitioning into new careers.

- Deloitte's Career Opportunity Redefinition & Exploration (CORE) Leadership Program.[120] This program helps veterans and armed forces members:

  - Define their personal brand, identify their strengths, and tell their own story.

  - Learn networking strategies and communication techniques, including best practices in using social media, through employment simulations.

  - Interact and network with professionals from both the public and private sectors.

  - Gain access to other alumni of the CORE Leadership Program.

- FourBlock conducts a career readiness transition program for active-duty military personnel. It offers employers several ways to get involved.[121]

- Microsoft's Software and Systems Academy (MSSA). MSSA is a full-time, seventeen-week technical training program for careers in cloud development, cloud administration, and related fields for veterans and service members.[122]

- Onward to Opportunity (O2O). O2O is a collaboration between the Department of Defense, the Schultz Family Foundation, and the Institute for Veterans and Military Families at Syracuse University to bring no-cost civilian career training to eligible military members and their spouses.[123]

- Military recruiting firms. These for-profit "headhunters" tend to refer candidates on a contingency basis and focus on transitioning service members that are either Junior Military Officers (JMOs) or Non-Commissioned Officers (NCOs) with at least a bachelor's degree. Many also place transitioned veterans considering a career change. Here are some examples:

⋄ Alliance—specializes in JMO recruiting

⋄ Cameron-Brooks—specializes in JMO recruiting

⋄ Orion Talent—includes opportunities for technicians

⋄ Lucas Group—scope ranges from technicians to retirees

⋄ Bradley-Morris—has opportunities for technicians

⋄ Military-Civilian.com—scope includes military spouses, dependents, DoD employees and contractors, retirees, and National Guard

⋄ Hire Velocity

⋄ Robert Half—maintains a veterans initiative that includes military spouses

⋄ 7 Eagle Group

⋄ SHRM HireVets—monthly subscription service that offers access to a nationwide veteran database and a military skills translator[124]

◆ Veteran job boards, including:

⋄ Fastport

⋄ FedsHireVets

⋄ GI Jobs

⋄ HireMilitary

⋄ Hire Purpose

⋄ Hire Veterans

⋄ HotJobs.vet

⋄ Military.com

⋄ Military Hire

⋄ Military Times

◇ RallyPoint

◇ RecruitMilitary

◆ Job-matching sites. While applying veterans would need to self-identify, you can readily find veteran talent among these platforms:

◇ CareerBuilder

◇ Indeed

◇ Monster

◇ Purepost

◇ ZipRecruiter

◆ Select nationwide veteran service organizations (VSOs). Some larger VSOs provide career training and placement services for transitioning veterans.

◇ The USO's Pathfinder program, through its transition support efforts, produces veterans prepared to join your organization.[125]

◇ VetJobs, sponsored by Corporate America Supports You (CASY), offers an online job board for veterans.[126]

◇ The Wounded Warrior Project's Warriors to Work program provides employers direct access to a pool of available veterans that completed the organization's programs and services.[127]

◇ National Veterans Foundation provides a job board for employers looking to hire veterans and a toll-free, vet-to-vet helpline.[128]

◇ Military Spouse Jobs offers career development for military spouses and connects employers with job seekers.[129]

◇ Green Beret Foundation (GBF). GBF's The Next Ridgeline program is for Army special operations professionals.[130]

◇ The Honor Foundation (THF) sponsors a transition program for military special operations professionals.[131]

◇ Vets2Industry Foundation. V2I acts as a free resource library for the military community and lists companies with opportunities for veterans, those with specific military hiring programs,

"Military Friendly" companies, and those that provide mentors via their ACP affiliation.[132]

- Organizations supporting the employment of veterans with disabilities. In addition to those services noted in Chapter 2, consider the following:

  ◇ Centers for Independent Living (CILs). These community-based nonprofit agencies are run by and for people with disabilities and provide employment-related services. They help employers find qualified candidates with disabilities and provide advice on employment support that may impact an employer's ability to hire, retain, and advance veterans with disabilities.[133]

  ◇ Employment Networks (ENs). ENs are private organizations or public agencies that have agreed to provide employment and vocational rehabilitation services to beneficiaries with disabilities under the Social Security Administration's Ticket to Work Program. Employers may contact ENs in their area to express interest in employing people with disabilities.[134]

  ◇ Council of State Administrators of Vocational Rehabilitation/ National Employment Team (NET). Nationwide network of business consultants that serves as employers' point of contact for vocational rehabilitation (VR) and ensures the workforce needs of VR agencies' business customers are met.[135]

  ◇ State vocational rehabilitation agencies. Organizations that provide state and federally funded programs to help disabled veterans find, secure, and retain employment and accept job postings from employers interested in hiring them.[136]

  ◇ Employment Referral Resource Directory. Maintained by the US Department of Labor's Office of Federal Contract Compliance Programs (OFCCP), this directory lists not-for-profit organizations that assist in hiring qualified applicants and programs providing job referral services to veterans, individuals with disabilities, women, and minority groups.[137]

- Job boards connecting employers with disabled veterans. These include:
  - American Association of People with Disabilities (AAPD) Career Center. Job board for companies of all sizes seeking qualified disabled job candidates.[138]
  - Association of University Centers on Disability (AUCD). Membership organization that supports a national network of university-based programs for people with disabilities and offers a free job board for employers interested in hiring people with disabilities.[139]
  - Workforce Recruitment Program (WRP). Free job board for employers interested in hiring students and recent graduates that previously participated in the Federal Government's Workforce Recruitment Program (WRP).[140]
  - abilityJOBS[141]
  - AbilityLinks. Free job board for employers and disabled candidates.[142]
  - disABLEDperson Inc.
  - Diversity Jobs
  - Getting Hired
  - OurAbility Connect
  - RecruitDisability.org
  - Job Opportunities for Disabled Veterans (JOFDAV)
- Entrepreneurship programs. Franchise organizations may find a ready talent pool in these programs.
  - Boots to Business
  - Bunker Labs
  - Entrepreneurship Bootcamp for Veterans
  - National Veterans Entrepreneurship Program (VEP)
  - Patriot Boot Camp

- ◇ PenFed Foundation Veteran Entrepreneur Investment Program

- ◇ VETRN

- ◇ VetFran

- ◇ Veteran Business Outreach Centers (VBOCs) of the US Small Business Administration

- ◇ Veteran Institute for Procurement

- ◇ The Rosie Network's Service2CEO Program

- ◇ Greater Philadelphia Veteran Network (GPVN)

- ◆ Employer Support of the Guard and Reserve (ESGR). ESGR is an organization that acts as an advocate for employers within the Department of Defense and facilitates initiatives to foster employer support for members of the National Guard and Reserve. Local ESGR representatives may have leads on available veteran talent.[143] See Chapter 8 for more detail on ESGR.

- ◆ County Veteran Service Officers (CVSOs). CVSOs help veterans, their families, and caregivers access government benefits and community support services they need. They exist in most, but not all, states. The National Association of County Veterans Service Officers (NACVSO) offers a directory to locate the one nearest you.[144]

- ◆ Chambers of commerce. The Association of Chamber of Commerce Executives (ACCE) defines a chamber of commerce as "an organization of businesses seeking to further their collective interests while advancing their community, region, state or nation. Business owners in towns, cities, and other territories voluntarily form these local societies/networks to advocate on behalf of the community at large, economic prosperity, and business interests."[145] There are three types of chambers that might act as helpful resources and purveyors of available veteran talent. National and regional veterans chambers of commerce assist transitioning wounded, ill, and injured service members, families, and caregivers. Local chambers, when partnered with local or regional veteran collaboratives, may also provide both a conduit to veteran talent and programmatic support for hiring or BRG activities.[146] And specialized chambers, such as the Military Spouse Chamber of Commerce, offer much of the above for specific clientele.[147]

- Social media. Most veterans interact on some of the typical platforms where they will find job opportunities. Consider posting your organization's job opportunities to the following sites:

  ◇ LinkedIn

  ◇ Facebook

  ◇ Twitter

  For example, the US State Department advertises on LinkedIn and Facebook to recruit veterans and people with disabilities for various Foreign Service Specialist positions.

- Classifieds/want ads. While seemingly outdated, this approach may work for smaller organizations seeking local veteran talent. The websites of local newspapers or periodicals would have links to the information needed to advertise. On a national and international basis, consider promoting employment opportunities in the *Military Times* or its service-specific publications (e.g., *Army Times*, *Marine Corps Times*, *Navy Times*, *Air Force Times*).[148] For the same geographic scope, consider advertising jobs in *Stars and Stripes*.[149]

TRANSLATE ROLE DESCRIPTIONS

Reaching veterans in a language that they can understand has proven to be one of employers' most significant challenges in hiring veterans. The good news is that there are tools to enable effective communication. The Department of Labor has produced competency models that define the skills and competencies needed to succeed in many industries.[150] These models provide a common framework that:

- Identifies specific employer skill needs.

- Develops competency-based curricula and training models.

- Develops industry-defined performance indicators, skill standards, and certifications.

- Develops resources for career exploration and guidance.

These models help veterans identify the knowledge, skills, and abilities they gained during their time in the military and how to translate them into the civilian world. They also help determine the additional knowledge, skills, or abilities veterans may need to acquire to succeed in a specific industry or sector. As an employer, you might leverage these models as a common platform to define the requirements of available roles that you desire veterans to fill. They enable an apples-to-apples way to communicate your employment needs and, as such, allow a transparent form of relaying those needs in a language veterans understand.

Figure 6-1 shows the generic building blocks competency model. Competency models for specific industries will have content in the various blocks of the model specific to that industry or sector's needs. Each competency model comes with worksheets to help you fashion the required competencies for roles within your industry and your internal training curricula.[151] There are helpful gap analysis

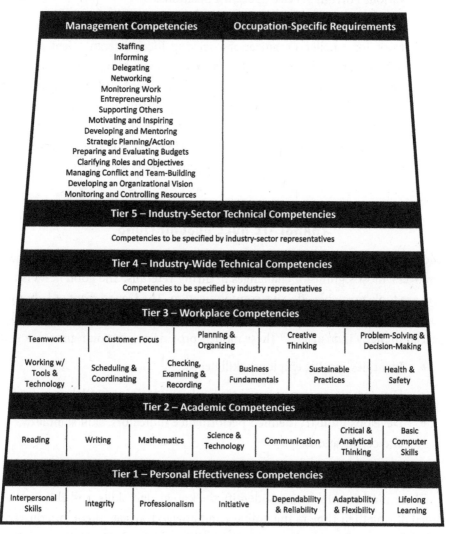

Figure 6-1. Generic Building Blocks Competency Model[152]

worksheets available at the same link for veteran applicants to help identify specific knowledge, skill, or ability gaps they may have. You might refer veterans interested in roles within your organization to these.

Consider leveraging experienced veterans within your organization to draft these descriptions, overlaying their military experience with the content of the above competency models. That combined approach holds the most potential for effectively reaching the veteran applicant.

In addition to competency models, those crafting role descriptions might also benefit from one of a few broadly available tools:

♦ CareerOneStop's Civilian-to-Military Occupational Translator helps identify which military occupations (including Military Occupation Specialty, or MOS and MOC codes) best match civilian roles based on education, training, skills, and experience.[153]

♦ O*Net Online provides a handy military crosswalk that will produce a civilian-friendly reading of the knowledge, skills, abilities, and other details related to that role upon entering a military occupational classification.[154]

♦ The skills translator at Military.com[155] matches military experience to possible civilian job openings. Upon entering a branch of service and military occupational specialty, a list of related civilian positions and job openings appears.

♦ Purepost's Passport provides a comprehensive competency model for transitioning veterans to use as a pathway to growth and a successful career outcome. Purepost's Skills Strataplex and Cross-Industry Translation Framework translate military experience of all services into language and competencies that civilian employers can easily comprehend.[156]

♦ Several large corporations, including Google, have developed skills translators.[157] Some of these tools are tailored for their organization's purposes, whereas others are more widely applicable. An internet search for "military skills translator" will reveal several.

ESTABLISH OR UPDATE OUTREACH PLATFORMS

Earlier, you updated your marketing and recruiting materials. You now need to establish (or refresh) the conduits to best reach veteran talent in distributing these materials—your marketing or outreach platforms. Your aim in updating them should be to influence word-of-mouth within the military community. Why?

♦ 76 percent of the military community say they learn about opportunities from word of mouth. (The second-highest-ranking medium is print ads at only 30 percent.)[158]

♦ Members of the military community have strong bonds and trust each other's opinions; they can be suspicious of outside offers. When marketing to the military, your offers and promotions must be thoughtful, generous, and transparent.

And so, as with all of these tasks, leverage your in-house veteran network to assist in this effort. They will not only have insight into how best to complete the updates, but they also can help by connecting with their extended military networks. It's a win-win.

There are several platforms you should consider using (ideally, in combination):

♦ Clearly, your website will be one of those avenues. Here's how to utilize it:

◇ Prominently feature your commitment to hiring veterans on your website. Typical places organizations feature this is on their "About" page and their "Careers" page. For example, consider including ESGR's Statement of Support.[159] As with your recruiting materials, use translated terminology that would resonate with veterans, use patriotic images and icons, portray both men and women of different races in and out of uniform in addition to wounded warriors, and review any stock photography used for accuracy.

◇ You might also consider having a separate page devoted to content addressing military-connected job seekers. You might list information about benefit programs, business resource groups, and the kinds of activities that they might expect after being hired.

◇ Finally, consider updating job descriptions to portray how military skills might relate to required organizational skills. Consider a simple two-column grid that makes it easy for job seekers to identify which opportunities might be the best fit for them.

- ◆ Social media. Most veterans maintain a presence on one or more social media platforms. Consider a proactive campaign through one or more of these channels. Ranked by popularity, the social media platforms with the largest military community are:

  - ◇ Facebook

  - ◇ Snapchat

  - ◇ Instagram

  - ◇ Twitter

  - ◇ LinkedIn

  - ◇ WhatsApp[160]

- ◆ In addition to mainstream social media sites and blogs, the military community uses military-specific online resources to seek information and connect with others. Currently, the top three military resources are:

  - ◇ Military.com

  - ◇ Military Times

  - ◇ Military OneSource[161]

In timing your outreach to veteran audiences, consider timing your push before a "military" holiday. Understanding the importance of word-of-mouth referrals in this community and the focus on military issues around Veterans Day, Memorial Day, and Independence Day (also, May is Military Appreciation month) make these celebrations great times to announce a military-related initiative.

COMPANIES IN THE COCKPIT

"Our communications and engagement pillar includes a focus on social media. We mostly leverage LinkedIn and internal newsletters. Our affinity group also sends an introductory message to the managers and senior managers of newly hired veterans upon their arrival."

John Myers, Procter & Gamble Veterans Affinity Group Lead

VET AND PRIORITIZE CANDIDATES

Once your talent targets begin to respond to your updated recruiting channels, you will face the challenge of identifying which candidates should advance to the interview stage. This task requires a complete understanding of each candidate's underlying skills and competencies, historically the bane of human resource professionals struggling to make sense of the military blather found in most veteran résumés. To do so, I would recommend taking advantage of your veteran affinity group members. Why?

1. Fellow veterans will quickly translate the military jargon many of these résumés will contain.

2. They will act as tutors for non veterans struggling to understand the intricacies of an applicant's Verification of Military Experience and Training (VMET, DD Form 2586), their Joint Services Transcript (JST), and their military awards—which they all possess.

3. They will recommend which applicants might proceed to the interview stage based on the materials provided.

You can then decide whom you should interview with input from your veterans or their trained counterparts. Here, you will leverage the previously identified criteria with your inputs to Table 5-4 and a simple prioritization matrix (see below). You can download a free version of this matrix from the Resources section of my website (*www.matthewjlouis.com*).

Prioritization Matrix

To narrow your slate of interviewees, try this:

- List the criteria by which you will judge each applicant from Table 5-4, ranking the criteria on a 1–5 scale (1 = less important, 5 = most important).

- List the applicants on the horizontal axis and score them using the following scale (1 = not a good fit, 3 = good fit, 9 = best fit).

- Define a "floor" ranking below which you will not interview applicants.

- The cross-multiplication will produce an emotionless outcome. In Figure 6-2, Applicant C would not be interviewed in the figure below if our "floor" ranking were 250.

Criteria from Table 5-4	Ranking	Applicants			
		Applicant A	Applicant B	Applicant C	Applicant D
Cultural match	5	3	9	9	1
Education & training	3	3	3	1	3
Certifications	4	9	9	3	9
Work Experience	2	1	3	9	1
Technical skills	5	3	9	1	3
Supervisory skills	4	9	9	3	9
Leadership skills	5	3	9	9	1
Interpersonal skills	3	3	3	1	3
Problem-solving skills	4	9	9	3	9
Teamwork skills	2	1	3	9	1
Time-management skills	5	3	9	1	3
Customer-service orientation	4	9	9	3	9
Personal motivation	5	3	9	1	3
Compensation and benefits expectations	4	9	9	3	9
Etc.					
	Outcome	277	435	207	257

Figure 6-2. Sample Prioritization Matrix

Alternately, you can shortcut the vetting process using Purepost's Sonar application. For a fee, an organization's job requisitions instantly match with applicants who complete a Passport (a translated online profile) based on their underlying skills and competencies. Applicants who are a match for a given opportunity are ranked based on their fit for each role as determined by the organization's ranking of specific criteria.

So, with your processes and platforms in place to identify, recruit, and prioritize veterans, you must now conduct the interviews required to validate their potential fit within your organization. That is the subject of the next chapter.

KEYS TO SUCCESS

- Take advantage of all relevant sources of veteran talent.

- Allocate recruiting resources strategically to the most productive of those sources.

- Translate role descriptions into language veterans can implicitly understand.

- Leverage your in-house veterans in performing these tasks.

- Update your recruiting processes to resonate with today's veterans and establish or update the outlets you use to connect with them.

- Educate applicants on overcoming typical challenges posed by ATSes.

- Utilize Purepost applications to simplify applicant vetting and prioritization.

CHAPTER 7

INTERVIEW CANDIDATES AND INITIATE OFFERS

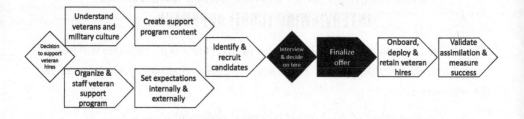

"Patriotism is easy to understand in America. It means looking out for yourself by looking out for your country."

—Calvin Coolidge[1]

Though you may not have undertaken this effort with patriotism in the forefront of your mind, you are helping veterans achieve full employment in their chosen career fields, which benefits the country. As veterans help your organization succeed, the nation's economy and its military benefit. Once again, good goes around. If you're not already trumpeting this in your marketing materials to internal and external stakeholders, I suggest you consider doing so.

Now that you have identified and recruited potential veteran hires, you must proceed with the next step in the hiring life cycle—conducting interviews. Your standard approach to conducting these interviews may require an adjustment to convert veteran talent successfully. Also needed are detailed attention to the types of questions asked, the appropriate translation of the questions asked, and additional education on the implications for choosing to work for your organization.

By the end of this chapter, you should understand how to:

- Structure a Competency-Based Behavioral Interviewing (CBBI) approach

- Ask appropriate questions of veterans.

- Translate job offer components.

- Help veterans understand your culture and organizational expectations.

- Support the veteran decision-making process.

STRUCTURING A COMPETENCY-BASED BEHAVIORAL INTERVIEWING (CBBI) APPROACH

Why do we conduct interviews? We do so to determine if a candidate will be successful in their considered role. There are three areas that we try to assess during the interview:

- Confirmation of the needed technical skills and knowledge

- Confirmation of the needed functional skills and abilities

- Demonstration of the position's competencies (and the values underlying them)[2]

Most interviews tend to focus on the first two. Many fail to consider the third, which is precisely where veteran talent shines. *Competencies are behaviors that describe the expected performance in a particular work context.* They are different from technical skills, functional skills, knowledge, education, and experience. Asking veterans about competencies gets at your core need and will better align with their experience in the military. For example, asking veterans whether they have had four years of management experience is insufficient. Its lack of clarity may confuse a veteran fresh off active duty. However, asking a veteran whether they had four years of experience managing diverse teams invites a demonstration of the required competency of valuing diversity—an area in which all veterans excel.

Broad implementation of this approach results in a structured interviewing process called Competency-Based Behavioral Interviewing (CBBI). It examines competencies with the premise that:

◆ The best predictor of future performance is past performance.

◆ The more recent the performance, the more likely it is to be repeated.[3]

Research demonstrates that CBBI is three to five times more accurate in predicting a person's potential than traditional interviews.[4] Because CBBI focuses on actual past behavior, it is more likely to result in a successful hire, which in turn results in:

◆ Greater productivity.

◆ Lower turnover.

◆ Higher morale.

◆ Better quality.

◆ Improved customer service.

Moreover, because it is a structured process and helps interviewers stay on track, CBBI minimizes the possibility of asking illegal or inappropriate questions. Thus, it provides you with a legally defensible interview process. Once implemented and considering its results, you may desire to adopt this approach as your standard for *all* candidates!

So how does one go about generating a CBBI approach? You will find the details in Victoria Hoevemeyer's book *High Impact Interview Questions (Second Edition),* but I summarize the process here. Throughout this process, I highly recommend leveraging the support of your in-house veteran affinity group in structuring the questions, training interviewers on their implementation, and participating in interviews themselves. Doing so will help ensure that nothing gets lost in translation throughout the interview process.

1. Determine the structure of the competency model, which will be unique to every organization. There is no singular "best" way. Options include:

    a. Organization-wide. A set of competencies tied to the organization's strategy and applied to everyone in the organization.

b. Corporate build. Sets of competencies that apply to every individual in the organization. Additional competencies are added for incremental levels individuals assume. (This is the least time-consuming approach.)

c. By level. Unique competencies apply to each level in the organization:

    i. Hourly

    ii. Professional

    iii. Supervisor

    iv. Management

    v. Executive

d. By function or department. Each function has a unique set of competencies applicable to every person, regardless of position.

e. By position. Competencies are established for each position in the organization. (This is the most time-consuming but most complete approach.)

2. Determine and define the competencies. Focus on those critical to the success of the individual and the organization.

3. Determine the interview questions. (See the next section.)

4. Develop the rating scale.

5. Design the organization's interview formats (e.g., screening, face-to-face, virtual).

6. Provide training to all interviewers. Include the following topics:

a. How much time to spend on each part of the interview

b. Developing and presenting consistent messages about the role and the organization

c. Using rating scales

d. How to ask questions and listen for STAR (Situation, Task, Action, Results) answers

e. How to use interview forms and take notes

f.   Probing for additional information and evidence of critical thinking skills

g.   Legal and illegal queries

h.   Discussing candidates and making a hiring decision[5]

ASK APPROPRIATE QUESTIONS OF VETERANS

B. H. Liddell Hart wrote, "If you want peace, understand war."[6] Likewise, if you want to hire veterans, you have to make extra effort to understand their background and what that will mean in coming to work for your organization. That understanding must translate into the kinds of interview questions you ask. It will be a different task for most of those conducting interviews (recall that more than 99.5 percent have never served). It will require training. Many civilians are curious about veterans and what they have done. Most of their views are shaped by what they see on television, in feature films, or on other media—a good portion of which is neither realistic nor accurate. The ensuing stereotypes influence many. I've attempted to debunk several of these in Appendix H; I suggest you incorporate these details into any interviewer training. To offset these stereotypes, I strongly recommend you include a member of your veteran affinity group in all interviews of veterans.

COMPANIES IN THE COCKPIT

"We leverage our dedicated military recruiting team to identify and prep veteran talent for the interview process within the firm. Our veteran recruiting team finds that if we can get the veteran candidate on the slate for the interview, they tend to perform well and have a high conversion rate concerning job offers."

Rhett Jeppson, JPMorgan Chase Military and Veterans Affairs Team

Let's start by contrasting two sets of questions: those you should ask veterans and those you should not.

Questions to Ask Veterans	Questions *Not* to Ask Veterans
◆ What did you do in the military?	◆ What kind of discharge did you get from the military?
◆ Which of your military experiences will translate to this job?	◆ When will you get deployed again?
	◆ Have you ever killed anyone?
◆ Will you be able to perform the duties in the job description with reasonable accommodation?	◆ Were you ever injured in combat?
	◆ Will you have to miss much work for your National Guard or Reserve military service?

Table 7-1: Questions for Veterans

How would you characterize their differences?

◆ The first list is open-ended and open to possibilities. It invites the veteran to demonstrate how the competencies learned in the military will translate into this potential role.

◆ The second list is not only closed in nature but outright illegal. They may be violations of either Title VII of the Civil Rights Act of 1964 or Title I of the Americans with Disabilities Act. Such questions are discriminatory and reveal nothing about the veteran's ability to demonstrate the competencies required for the role in question satisfactorily.

So, how do you avoid venturing into illegal territory?

◆ Ask only job-related questions. Focus on competencies, skills, and behaviors directly related to the job description.

◆ Ask questions directly. Veterans appreciate and respond to clarity and direct approaches. Don't beat around the bush, play games, or expect them to read between the lines.

◆ Ask questions that involve work scenarios, not personal issues. You are there to assess the candidate's fit, not develop a personal relationship.[7]

Let's now consider converting traditional interview questions into CBBI-type questions to enable veterans to demonstrate their competencies. Here are some examples:

Traditional Question	CBBI Question	Competency Tested
How well do you work under pressure? Do you handle pressure well?	Tell me about a time you faced stressors at work that tested your coping skills. Tell me about a time you did not handle a high-pressure situation well.	◆ Stress management ◆ Taking charge ◆ Planning/Priority setting
How would you rate your communication skills? What have you done to improve them?	Give me an example of when you were not as successful in your oral communication as you would have liked to have been. What did you learn from that situation to improve your communication skills?	◆ Oral communication ◆ Learning ◆ Listening
With what kind of people do you like to work? With what kind of people do you have difficulty working?	Describe how you handled a situation involving others with different values, beliefs, or ideas.	◆ Valuing/Encouraging diversity ◆ Respect for others ◆ Teamwork
What motivates you to put forth your best effort?	We all get assignments we would prefer not to do. Give me an example of when that happened to you and how you managed to get it done.	◆ Motivation ◆ Flexibility/Adaptability ◆ Perseverance
How do you make a sale to a demanding customer?	Tell me about your most challenging customers. How were you able to work with them?	◆ Sales ◆ Understanding others ◆ Political awareness/Savvy
What process do you use to solve problems?	Give me an example of a difficult problem you faced and how you went about solving it.	◆ Creativity/Innovation ◆ Problem-solving ◆ Results orientation
What are your strengths?	Describe a time when one of your strengths enabled you to be successful. What did you learn from that situation?	◆ Self-awareness ◆ Personal growth ◆ Perspective

Table 7-2: Traditional vs. CBBI Questions[8]

Much as you do with the questions themselves, you may also want to update the forms you use to screen and interview veterans to be more aligned with the CBBI intent. These should be the identical forms you use to interview *all* individuals applying for the same role to avoid straying into illegal territory. Their use will parallel their typical sequence: a screening interview followed by an in-person interview.

SCREENING INTERVIEW FORM

The screening interview—regardless of the format used (telephone, video)—should address several items (see Figure 7-1 on page 147 for an example form):

- Competencies required for the role

- Candidate qualifications (Do they match the required competencies, and is the candidate willing to meet specific requirements of the role?)

- Motivation for change (Why does the candidate seek this career field, and what are their goals within it?)

- Compensation expectations

- Availability for an in-person interview and beginning work

Figure 7-1 is a template that enables you to capture the necessary data to decide to move to the next stage of an in-person interview. To help veterans understand their compensation expectations, please direct them to the financial exercises in the Resources section of my website (*www.matthewjlouis.com*).

IN-PERSON INTERVIEW FORM

The in-person interview, whether formal or informal, should contain at least three sections (see Figure 7-2 on page 148 for an example form):

- Technical skills (specific requirements, as above, to include certifications or licenses)

- Competencies (probed via CBBI questions, as above)

- Overall summary with a recommendation

Use a rating scale in all three areas to judge the candidate's fit for the role and organization. Your organization's culture would inform this scale as a means to differentiate between multiple candidates for the same position

	Outstanding	Meets the Requirement	Does Not Meet the Requirement
Candidate Name: _____ Date: _____ Interviewer: _____ Required Competencies (to be populated ahead of the interview) ♦ Competency A ♦ Competency B ♦ Competency C Role Requirements (to be populated ahead of the interview) ♦ Requirement A ♦ Requirement B ♦ Requirement C			
Candidate Qualifications			
♦ Question about Competency A (use CBBI questions per above)			
♦ Question about Competency B (use CBBI questions per above)			
♦ Question about Competency C (use CBBI questions per above)			

Some roles may require candidates to meet specific expectations (e.g., able to lift X pounds, willing to work in Y conditions, wear specific equipment, willing to work particular shifts)—with or without reasonable accommodation. The answers are binomial.	Willing / Able?	
	YES	NO
♦ Requirement A		
♦ Requirement B		
♦ Requirement C		

Motivation for Change	Answer/comment
♦ Why are you seeking this <u>career field</u> (not this job)?	
♦ What goals do you have as you enter this profession?	
Compensation Expectations*	

♦ What is your desired salary?
  ♦ Base
  ♦ Variable component
  ♦ Deferred compensation / long-term incentives, etc.	

Availability for an in-person interview and beginning work	
♦ Availability to interview	
♦ Availability to begin work	
Overall Assessment	
♦ Comment 1 ♦ Comment 2 ♦ Comment 3	

* Ensure the questions you ask in this section comply with state and local law.

Figure 7-1. Screening Interview Form[9]

	Does not meet the requirement	Meets the requirement	Exceeds the requirement	Far exceeds the requirement
Candidate Name: _____ Date: _____ Interviewer: _____				
Technical Skills				
◆ Requirement 1				
◆ Requirement 2				
Competencies				
◆ Competency 1 　◆ Lead question: 　◆ Response: 　◆ Follow-up question & response:				
◆ Competency 2 　◆ Lead question: 　◆ Response: 　◆ Follow-up question & response:				
Summary				
◆ Knowledge				
◆ Skills				
◆ Abilities				
◆ Organizational / cultural fit				
Overall comments				
Recommendation				
◆ Make offer				
◆ Do not make an offer				

Figure 7-2. In-Person Interview Form[10]

When conducting any interview, remember this may be the first time veteran candidates have had to interview for a role. They will be nervous. They may not know what to expect. They may struggle with translating what they've done in the military, may still use military acronyms and courtesies, and may struggle with relating their accomplishments in the first person. In light of this, consider a few tactics proven to be successful:

♦ Include a member of your veteran affinity group when conducting all interviews.

♦ Acknowledge and show respect for their service. A simple thank-you will do the job.

♦ Be transparent; describe the interview process for this specific interview and the overall series of interviews to set expectations.

♦ Use ice-breakers and make them feel comfortable. Do you know someone who is or was in the military? Say so.

♦ Describe your organization's support of veteran efforts and programs designed to support their successful acclimation and assimilation. Make sure to highlight any programs that support veteran spouses.

♦ Describe how your organization's values align with those of the military.

♦ Use a similar approach in interviewing military spouses.

♦ Avoid judgments regarding the frequency of job changes and relocations. Military members and their spouses follow orders for a good reason, and those orders are almost always outside their control.

COMPANIES IN THE COCKPIT

"For veterans, Tesla takes the time to provide additional instruction for those that conduct interviews. They choose to do this on the ground and in-person to ensure those personnel know how to interface with veterans and translate their varied terms."

Dustin Whidden, former Tesla Veterans Program Manager

Despite your best efforts, you may encounter employees (normally non veterans) who struggle to support the program. The reasons are numerous. Change is always hard, and changing your recruiting focus to include a veteran hiring initiative is no different. Understand that beyond the additional training you will provide and beyond the logic underlying the business case for hiring vets, you may need to provide additional incentives or motivations to civilian hiring managers to encourage support. As Dustin Whidden said, "Some service managers are slow to get on board with hiring vets. It's hard for them to overcome their traditional thinking and [instead] defer to bringing in their old Silicon Valley buddies. They need to get OK with taking a chance on an unknown talent that has a ton of upside if properly onboarded and trained."[11]

TRANSLATE JOB OFFER COMPONENTS

Veterans are not used to considering all aspects of a compensation package. While on active duty, they tend to be blissfully unaware of some of their benefits, many of which the government automatically provides. The military provides healthcare and housing. It provides meals and uniforms to enlisted members. If service members live off the installation, it provides housing and subsistence allowances tax-free. Incentive pay for pilots or individuals in combat zones is likewise tax-free. Life insurance, while provided at marginal cost, is easy to obtain. In short, service members may have never considered the quantifiable impact their many valuable benefits from military service had on their total compensation. And they have little understanding of what a comprehensive compensation package might look like outside the military.

Assuming you want to decrease the number of declinations you realize from veterans and increase their retention rates, I would strongly suggest you help them identify, quantify, and qualify the differences in the components of your offer and their total compensation in the military. To do so, I would recommend that you do two exercises with your veteran candidates, which—due to space limitations in this book—you will find in the Resources section of my website (*www.matthewjlouis.com*). The first of these compares military and civilian compensation package components and their relative values on an apples-to-apples basis. After identifying which of these apply to a given candidate, the second exercise allows you to summarize this comparison and use it as a basis for comparison with any other offers the candidate may have in play.

In having your candidates review the output of these exercises, you might emphasize a couple of points where applicable:

- On par, the amount and value of benefits they received both while serving and afterward are significantly more than they may realize.

- Compensation packages include many benefits. They are much more than just salary, and benefits that are part of the package have value—sometimes significant value.

- Items outlined in your offer represent a starting point. Given the potential opportunities to progress in your organization, the quantity and quality of compensation and benefits will correspondingly increase.

COMPANIES IN THE COCKPIT

"Sell the veteran candidate on the opportunity to progress in the organization when certain goals are met, especially if the starting salary is less than they might expect."

Chris Newton, Workforce Development Manager at Cajun Industries

If your candidates are struggling with understanding what salary they will need or how much they will need to save to retire from the workplace, please direct them to the financial exercises in the Resources section of my website (*www.matthewjlouis.com*).

HELP VETERANS UNDERSTAND YOUR CULTURE AND ORGANIZATIONAL EXPECTATIONS

In Chapter 1, you defined your company culture and compared it to that in which military personnel have been working for most of their adult lives. They will likely not have worked in many other environments and thus be unfamiliar with the differences between the military's way of doing things and yours. While in my first book I strongly advocated for them to research the culture of organizations in which they have an interest, the reality is that the nuances of an organization's culture are challenging to assess accurately. Thus, it would benefit you to inform these recruits how they may experience each of the cultural dimensions noted in Chapter 1 in your organization vis-à-vis their time in service. Providing a summary chart of differences in cultural dimensions (similar to Table 1-3) and facilitating a discussion on the topic with one of your veteran affinity group members would go a long way to making this clear to candidates.

In Chapter 9, we talk about some cultural assessments that you might incorporate into your program following onboarding to optimize the success of your assimilation process.

COMPANIES IN THE COCKPIT

"Amazon's leadership principles are the ties that bind all Amazonians together. We use our leadership principles every day, whether discussing ideas for new projects or deciding on the best approach to solving a problem. All candidates are evaluated based on our leadership principles, and we look to see how veterans emulate our leadership principles in their military careers."

Beau Higgins, Senior Manager, Amazon Military Recruiting Center of Excellence | Worldwide Operations Talent Acquisition

SUPPORT THE VETERAN DECISION-MAKING PROCESS

It may be the first time your veteran candidate has faced this many considerations in deciding on their career. Pondering the many avenues their future holds tends to cause them and their spouses significant undue stress. You can help intervene in this crisis-like environment by providing a means to help them arrive at their decision in a way that minimizes the emotion involved. In doing so, you will likely earn some goodwill that may sway the candidate your way. Worst case, the provision of the Prioritization Matrix below will result in a faster decision that will enable you to allocate your limited bandwidth to other viable candidates and tasks. You will find a downloadable template of the Prioritization Matrix in the Resources section of my website (*www.matthewjlouis.com*).

In addition, consider making members of your staff available (especially fellow veterans and members of the organization's veteran affinity group) to answer any questions the candidate or their family might have at any point in their decision-making process. Making their contact information available via an application portal and providing a thorough list of answers to frequently asked questions (FAQs) are also helpful. In doing so, emphasize what the future could hold within your organization beyond the role for which they are applying. Help the candidate see themselves as a successful hire and what that could entail for them down the road.

COMPANIES IN THE COCKPIT

"Take the time to explain to them what life could be like. Show them the possibilities. Show them how a career path can evolve. Provide real-world examples; make it real for them. Be positive in what your organization can do for the veteran, not vice versa. Help them understand how their skills translate into your organization. Let's say you are interviewing a veteran with skills as an electrician, but you're not currently in the market for electricians. You should help that veteran understand through the interview process how the translatable aspects of those skills would apply to other parts of the organization or in other areas of the country."

Chris Newton, Workforce Development Manager at Cajun Industries

Prioritization Matrix

If your veteran candidate is considering multiple employment options, suggest trying this to narrow their choices. Have them:

♦ Make a list of criteria by which they would judge their employment options, ranking the criteria on a 1–5 scale (1 = less important, 5 = most important).

♦ List their employment options on the horizontal axis and score them using the following scale (1 = not a good fit, 3 = good fit, 9 = best fit) with input from their family.

♦ The cross-multiplication will produce an emotionless direction for them. In theory, the highest-scored option will best match the relative importance of their stated criteria. In Figure 7-3, Option B is the clear winner.

		Employer Options			
Criteria	Ranking	Employer A	Employer B	Employer C	Employer D
Career Field Match	5	3	9	9	1
Leadership Potential	3	3	3	1	3
Compensation	4	9	9	3	9
Travel Requirements	2	1	3	9	1
Culture Match	5	3	9	1	3
Benefits Package	4	9	9	3	9
Etc.					
	Outcome	113	177	95	103

Figure 7-3. Sample Prioritization Matrix

Assuming the candidate has positively responded to all your hard work and decided to join your organization, you now face the challenge of effectively onboarding and training these resources to ensure their retention. Lest you think otherwise, your work in successfully acclimating and assimilating these new hires to your organization has only just begun.

That is the subject of the next chapter.

KEYS TO SUCCESS

- Ensure a member of the organization's veteran affinity group participates in all interviews of veterans.

- Ensure all interviewers are trained on how to conduct interviews with veterans, what questions to ask, and what questions not to ask of veteran candidates.

- Use competency-based behavioral interviewing (CBBI) questions when interviewing veterans.

- Use standard interviewing forms that leverage a CBBI approach.

- When conducting interviews, make veterans feel comfortable by acknowledging their service, being transparent, using ice-breakers, and relating your organization's support for veterans' efforts.

- To set expectations, veteran candidate interviews and offers will require more detail than a typical new hire.

- Ensure veterans understand the components of your compensation package on an apples-to-apples basis.

- Make the culture of your organization transparent to veteran candidates.

- Help veterans take the emotion out of deciding on your offer.

CHAPTER 8

ONBOARD, TRAIN, AND RETAIN VETERAN HIRES

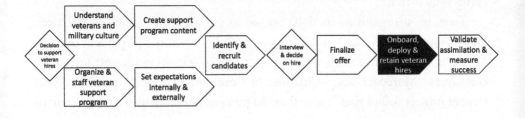

"I've experienced a lot of grateful behavior by potential employers. Many seemed to really like the idea of hiring veterans, but they didn't know what to do with them once they were in the door."

—Former Army Colonel

Unfortunately, this colonel's experience is more typical than not. Implementing the contents of this chapter will enable your organization to rise above this less-than-ideal outcome. From the minute that a veteran candidate has accepted your offer, this newly hired employee will be judging your organization on several fronts. Their judgments will directly impact their view on whether—and how long—to remain in your organization. In short, your retention challenge now begins. This chapter will enable you to welcome these new hires successfully and offset those potentially adverse outcomes. By the end of this chapter, you should know how to successfully:

♦ Welcome, onboard, and train new veteran hires, and facilitate integration with the rest of the employee base.

♦ Deploy and develop veterans.

♦ Facilitate veteran business resource groups and mentoring programs.

♦ Manage members of the Guard and Reserve.

♦ Utilize tactics to improve retention rates.

There is much on the line here—for both you and the new veteran hire. The future productivity and incremental revenue of your organization are at stake. As shown throughout the book, veterans can be significant contributors to this growth. But success for many organizations has been a struggle due to the inability to retain new veteran hires successfully. The root causes of many reasons for veteran hire departures appear at this stage of the employment life cycle. Why is that?

First, most organizations don't bother to onboard their new veteran hires. Recall from the Introduction a Korn Ferry study that noted 52 percent of organizations surveyed did not provide onboarding or transition support to veteran employees.[1] Moreover, a US Chamber of Commerce Foundation's Hiring Our Heroes project found that "more than 80 percent of companies lack specialized training to help civilian employees and staff relate to veterans."[2] Whether or not the organization had an onboarding program or trained their non veteran employees, several additional reasons explain why veterans quickly leave their roles. The Institute for Veterans and Military Families (IVMF) at Syracuse University identified the reasons veterans most frequently cited for leaving their first post-military role:

♦ Lack of career development

♦ Lack of meaningful or challenging work

♦ Inadequate professional development[3]

Transparently addressing these points in your onboarding program will go a long way.

WELCOME, ONBOARD, AND TRAIN NEW VETERAN HIRES

Let's revisit Figure 4-2 (retitled here as Figure 8-1), a sample scenario of sequencing and tailoring the welcoming, onboarding, and training of new veteran hires. Regardless of the content of your program, appropriately sequencing and tailoring the delivery of that content will be critical for it to have an optimum impact on its intended audiences. So, let's walk through the nature of each of these steps.

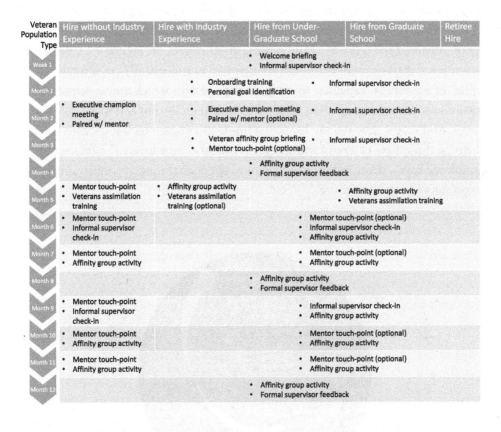

Veteran Population Type	Hire without Industry Experience	Hire with Industry Experience	Hire from Under-Graduate School	Hire from Graduate School	Retiree Hire
Week 1			• Welcome briefing • Informal supervisor check-in		
Month 1			• Onboarding training • Personal goal identification	• Informal supervisor check-in	
Month 2	• Executive champion meeting • Paired w/ mentor		• Executive champion meeting • Paired w/ mentor (optional)	• Informal supervisor check-in	
Month 3			• Veteran affinity group briefing • Mentor touch-point (optional)	• Informal supervisor check-in	
Month 4			• Affinity group activity • Formal supervisor feedback		
Month 5	• Mentor touch-point • Veterans assimilation training	• Affinity group activity • Veterans assimilation training (optional)	• Affinity group activity • Veterans assimilation training		
Month 6	• Mentor touch-point • Informal supervisor check-in		• Mentor touch-point (optional) • Informal supervisor check-in • Affinity group activity		
Month 7	• Mentor touch-point • Affinity group activity		• Mentor touch-point (optional) • Affinity group activity		
Month 8			• Affinity group activity • Formal supervisor feedback		
Month 9	• Mentor touch-point • Informal supervisor check-in		• Informal supervisor check-in • Affinity group activity		
Month 10	• Mentor touch-point • Affinity group activity		• Mentor touch-point (optional) • Affinity group activity		
Month 11	• Mentor touch-point • Affinity group activity		• Mentor touch-point (optional) • Affinity group activity		
Month 12			• Affinity group activity • Formal supervisor feedback		

Figure 8-1. Sample Timing of Program Content Delivery by Population Type

WELCOME

Welcoming newly hired veterans should be a momentous occasion. It should be something they will fondly recall. Ideally, the senior-most sponsor would make a personal appearance to welcome each new hire and take the opportunity to reinforce the organization's commitment to veteran inclusion, supporting resources available, and an expectation that new hires take advantage of all such support.

Consider inviting family members of the new hires to begin building a sense of community and tribal behavior. Then facilitate an introduction to the new hire's manager to relate expectations of the role and reinforce previous messages regarding career paths in the organization and requirements for being promoted or realizing pay raises. Finally, have the new hire meet their assigned mentor, the veteran affinity group leadership, and any other supportive networking contacts within the organization.

The idea is to quickly engage the new hire with a tribe of supporting resources. These resources will initiate the tribal behavior so crucial to retaining this talent pool. As noted in Figure 8-2 (and putting another spin on Figure 4-1), personal attention and frequent engagement are essential to successfully crossing the "last mile" of a veteran's transition journey. The speed with which a new veteran hire assimilates to an organization and its culture directly impacts their retention rates. And so, the new veteran hire's first line leaders bear much responsibility for helping those new veteran hires integrate with the "uneducated" balance of the employee base—those individuals who have not gone through formal training on veterans and veteran culture.

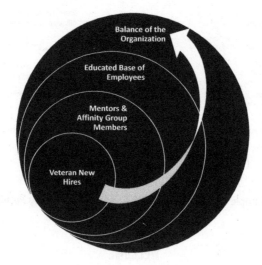

Figure 8-2. Assimilating with Employee Population Segments

COMPANIES IN THE COCKPIT

"In our Military Pathways program, we hire elite, transitioning veterans into a fast-track program within operations. The Pathways program was originally built solely for MBA students. Still, some of these candidates—while technically proficient—lacked some of the desired leadership skill sets to make an immediate impact. We appreciate that having a balance of both veterans and MBAs entering these programs is a successful model, as they can each leverage each other's skill sets."

Beau Higgins, Senior Manager, Amazon Military Recruiting Center
of Excellence | Worldwide Operations Talent Acquisition

ONBOARD

An onboarding program should rapidly follow the welcome and ideally includes the new hire's spouse. Military spouses are used to being engaged in benefit processes. Usually, that changes dramatically upon entering the workforce. As related in Chapter 1, most civilian organizations don't include spouses as part of ongoing business activities such as onboarding, and veterans may not share critical information gleaned from such meetings with their spouses. You can short-circuit those issues by simply including the spouse in such activities. In doing so, you may expose yourself to yet another underutilized talent pool. The Institute for Veterans and Military Affairs at Syracuse University outlines a business case for hiring military spouses below. To pursue this option, consider engaging the Military Spouse Employment Partnership, a Department of Defense initiative that links military spouses with employers committed to recruiting, hiring, promoting, and retaining them.[4]

Business Case for Hiring Military Spouses[5]

Here are ten abilities, attributes, and characteristics of military spouses that complement performance in any competitive business environment:

- ◆ **Resilient.** Military spouses face challenges, including family separations, frequent relocations, separation from friends and family, single parenting, and difficulty finding employment or finishing their education.

- ◆ **Adaptable.** Military families live with consistent uncertainty. Deployments can occur without warning; families often move unexpectedly; benefits and allowances frequently change. Healthcare, education, employment, childcare, and housing change when military families relocate. Military spouses adapt to their ever-changing circumstances and help their family members adjust. Some spouses reinvent their careers multiple times over a military career.

- **Educated.** The average military spouse is college-educated: 84 percent have some college education or higher, 25 percent have a bachelor's degree, and 10 percent have an advanced degree.[6]

- **Resourceful.** Military spouses learn to use the resources they have available to them. Often, they create unique and innovative solutions to problems despite obstacles.

- **Team-oriented.** Military spouses often live in remote locations or overseas, separated from friends, family, or familiar resources. When service members are deployed or away, at-home spouses must rely on each other for assistance and support.

- **Entrepreneurial.** Blue Star Families found that 23 percent of military spouse respondents have either been self-employed or operated their own business. Additionally, 48 percent indicated they are open to exploring entrepreneurship or small business ownership.[7]

- **Multitaskers.** Military spouses play multiple roles: part-time single parents, movers, event and social planners, employees, financial managers, and support group leaders.

- **Diverse.** Because the active military spouse community has a more significant proportion of ethnic and racial minorities than the broader civilian population, the inclusion of military spouses may enhance a corporate diversity strategy. In addition to racial and ethnic diversity, many military spouses have experience living or working overseas, may speak foreign languages, and may have experience working with various cultures.[8]

- **Civically engaged.** Military spouses are active community members. Blue Star Families found that 65 percent of survey respondents reported that they had volunteered in the past year,[9] significantly higher than the 24.9 percent of the general public who volunteered with an organization.[10]

- **Socially aware.** The military is diverse culturally, ethnically, and geographically. Because of this, military spouses often interact with people of different cultures, backgrounds, ages, and ethnicities. The military also has a rank structure that exposes spouses to various social situations. And finally, military spouses are often asked to maintain sensitive information for security reasons and therefore learn norms around operations security and safety.

Another onboarding standard is ensuring the identification of all new veteran hires from the outset. Some may have been missed in the interviewing phase or may not have self-identified. While you can't ask directly about a person's protected status, there is nothing wrong with asking whether someone has ever served in the military or simply asking the new hire to tell you about their background. In-house veterans are exceptionally skilled in facilitating such conversations, so please leverage them. Once identified, consider affording those veterans the same support systems noted on page 157 in the Welcome section. And, once identified, remember to complete all required affirmative action reporting.[11]

Initiate onboarding after identifying all military-related new hires. Utilize the content you produced in Chapter 4. Again, this activity consists of some critical elements:

- A formal onboarding session administered within the first ninety days of employment that addresses:

  ◇ Change in values and culture that veterans should expect.

  ◇ Change in leadership and communications styles that veterans should expect.

  ◇ Change in organizational structure that veterans should expect.

  ◇ Change in compensation and benefits, rewards and recognition systems, and expectations therein.

  ◇ Change in feedback systems, career planning processes, and expectations therein.

  ◇ Networking, influence, and the role of change itself in the organization.

- The assignment of peer-level sponsors to new veteran hires. Sponsors are ideally veteran employees who served in the same branch of service, separated at a similar rank, and have successfully made the transition (i.e., are high performers). A sponsor is not a mentor.

- The assignment of an executive-level mentor for at least twelve months. The mentor does not need to be a veteran; veterans new to Corporate America need to know how civilian leaders think, what made them successful, and organizational behavioral expectations.

- Candid conversations with their leaders about expectations in their first ninety days. They may find that all their boss wants them to do right away is learn. Whatever it is, it is probably different from their military experience.

COMPANIES IN THE COCKPIT

"Amazon is a great place to work for the military, where service members and spouses feel welcomed, appreciated, and enabled to thrive from the first day on the job. The Global Military Affairs team provides Amazon's military community a world-class customer experience across the employee life cycle—from onboarding to training and leadership learning—by delivering continued developmental support and encouraging long-term military retention. All veterans are also encouraged to join the Amazon Warrior Employee Resource Group, which enables camaraderie-building and esprit de corps."

Beau Higgins, Senior Manager, Amazon Military Recruiting Center
of Excellence | Worldwide Operations Talent Acquisition

For example, Procter & Gamble leverages its veteran affinity group to support onboarding practices they have shown to improve retention. They assign every new veteran hire a mentor. They also administer a "fast start" program, which provides veteran hires the "inside scoop" on succeeding at P&G. Finally, the group ensures all members understand how to complete their annual work plan reviews.[12]

COMPANIES IN THE COCKPIT

"Our onboarding best practices include our Find-a-Future program, our provision of mentors to incoming program members, and training programs available to veterans and military spouses that upskill/re-skill them and provide pathways consistent with their goals and aspirations."

Brynt Parmeter, Senior Director, Non-Traditional Talent
| Head of Walmart Military & Veterans Affairs

TRAIN

In Chapter 4, I suggest creating training programs for your new veteran hires and their civilian counterparts. After all, you can't close a civil-military gap if only one-half of the gap learns how to interact with the other. And so, consider educating the new veteran hire's management team on the following topics:

- Understanding veterans and the military
- Welcoming and onboarding military new hires

- Setting expectations for military new hires

- Communicating with military new hires

- Training military new hires

- Coaching/providing feedback to military new hires

COMPANIES IN THE COCKPIT

"We find that veterans enjoy an improved employee experience when they can partic-ipate in targeted training and acclimation programs designed exclusively with them in mind. At JPMorgan Chase, all newly hired, self-identified veterans undergo new hire training. Their managers participate in training that educates them on areas unique to leading veterans new to the corporate environment."

Rhett Jeppson, JPMorgan Chase Military and Veterans Affairs Team

As for the veterans themselves, ongoing training and engagement are critical aspects of supporting retention. Recall that career management and professional development are two primary reasons veterans leave their roles. You might con-sider focusing your training and development efforts on four key areas:

- Industry-specific skills and expertise relevant to the organization and its competitors

- Business-specific expertise regarding the organization's products or services

- Function-specific expertise that allows the individual to improve in their assigned role(s) continually

- Overall leadership abilities and their application in the above three areas

Consider conducting this training soon after the onboarding curriculum and with a blended audience of veterans and civilians. The goal is to gradually increase the levels of competence in all of these areas by periodic application of training designed to further increase skill levels in each. Ideally, such curricula exist for each level and role within the organization.

"Training within Schlumberger runs very much like the military. Incoming veteran hires go through a 'basic training' experience first. That is then followed by an advanced training experience that lasts anywhere from three to eight weeks, depending on the expertise of the role. Additional training takes place as needed throughout the course of their careers. The approach to the training—crawl, walk, run—also mimics what veteran hires experience in the military, which makes for an easier transition."

Nick B. Tran, Manager, Community and Veteran Affairs at Schlumberger

DEPLOY AND DEVELOP VETERANS

Paraphrasing, one of the military's leadership principles is to deploy your organization in accordance with its capabilities. Supervisors must deploy that talent in roles consistent with each individual's competencies to utilize their veteran talent optimally. In doing so, supervisors might consider some demographic details of—and trends within—the military population at our case study organizations. See Table 8-1 and Table 8-2.

Demographic Detail	Rank upon Exit from the Military	
	Enlisted (82% of the population)	Officers (18% of the population)
Educational profile	◆ Bachelor's degree (8%) ◆ High school diploma or equivalent (92%)	◆ Bachelor's degree (42%) ◆ Graduate degree (41%)
Typical strengths	◆ Supervisory skills ◆ Training facilitation ◆ Technical expertise	◆ Managerial skills ◆ Project management ◆ Leadership experience
Largest military occupational groups	◆ Engineering, science, and technical (15%) ◆ Combat specialty (14%) ◆ Vehicle and machinery mechanics (14%) ◆ Transportation and material-handling (12%) ◆ Electronic and electrical equipment repair (11%)	◆ Engineering, science, and technical (23%) ◆ Transportation (19%) ◆ Combat specialty (15%) ◆ Executive, administrative, and managerial (12%) ◆ Healthcare (11%)

Table 8-1: Veteran Population Demographic Details[13]

Exempt Hires	Non-exempt Hires	Both
◆ More likely to succeed at upper-level positions ◆ Greater geographic flexibility upon hire ◆ Less difficulty (compared to non veterans) adapting to larger companies ◆ Progressively less willing to relocate as they rise in the organization	◆ Less call-in absenteeism ◆ More likely to convert from part-time to full-time employment ◆ Higher exit rates; e.g., pursuing other opportunities or returning to school	◆ More promotions than non veteran peers ◆ Fewer disciplinary actions ◆ More willing to stay in roles for more extended periods

Table 8-2: Behavioral Trends of Exempt and Non-exempt Veteran Hires[14]

With that understanding, supervisors might consider the following strategies in deploying and developing new veteran hires:[15]

First, when deploying veterans, it is advantageous to assign them roles aligned with the organization's strategic goals and objectives. Doing so will allow them to see how the organization's purpose relates to their efforts.

Second, in making these assignments, directly reinforce the meaning and purpose of the role to each individual. Call out the obvious and help each person see their connection to the larger whole. Help them understand that what they do directly impacts organizational objectives. Tell them they are not mere cogs in what might seem to be an impersonal corporate "machine."

Third, ensure supervisors set challenging goals for veteran hires, incentivize vets to achieve them, and identify role models who have previously succeeded in similar capacities. Veterans tend to be task-oriented and have a high need for achievement. They are also very familiar with following role models, given the chain of command structure and unit histories in the military. Continually reinforcing this will likely have a significantly positive effect on your retention rates.

Fourth, service members receive immediate and regular feedback from direct supervisors in the military, which they view as having a direct impact on their personnel evaluation, promotion timing, and potential raises. And so, you should make it abundantly clear to veterans what to expect by way of feedback, appraisal or review cycles, reward systems, and career path expectations. Transparency is the best policy. That said, behavior and expectations don't shift overnight. You will want the new supervisors of these veterans (who ideally have already attended training on managing them) to provide some formal feedback to them within their first ninety days on the job. Furthermore, the supervisor should encourage the veteran to engage in the organization's veteran affinity group's activities and have regular conversations with their veteran peer sponsor and mentor.

Finally, be able to tell veteran hires what their potential career path looks like and what they need to do to make it to the next level (assuming that is their goal). Ideally, your organization utilizes career map and ladder constructs that plainly illustrate the required skills and competencies required for increasing levels within the organization. Such constructs appeal to veterans, as they mimic the constructs they experienced in the military. If you have yet to create such constructs, doing so will support your retention efforts. The US Department of Labor's Competency Model Clearinghouse offers several samples.[16] As mentioned, the best approach is clearly and transparently relating the requirements for maneuvering up a ladder or within a career map. But more than that, new veteran hires will need coaching on how to influence internal networks to achieve those requirements, as the typical promotion process in commercial entities varies widely from what they experienced in the military.

FACILITATE VETERAN BUSINESS RESOURCE GROUPS AND MENTORING PROGRAMS

Just because we have created a veteran support program, have executive-level support, and have started hiring doesn't mean we can set the effort on autopilot. It is in the ongoing execution of the program where the rubber hits the road and where the program will ultimately succeed or fail. There are two requirements to ensure that it succeeds.

The first is the thorough training of senior human resources managers to enable effective champions. These individuals must be fluent in all aspects of veteran benefits and be able to act as an in-house "one-stop": someone that a veteran employee can approach with questions about any issues they might face: healthcare (mental or physical), housing, finance, GI Bill questions,[17] VA services. These individuals need not be veterans, but they should be active stewards of their cause and advocate for them within the organization. Ideally, they are connected to and have relationships with both local and national veteran service organizations that could support their employees. You can find a good start to this list of resources at Military-Transition.org.[18]

The second requirement is that the veteran leadership of the affinity group proactively engage with the group, encourage participation, and enable regular meetings—a portion of which are in-person. Such activity results in the kind of tribal behavior that is the goal of such affinity groups and serves to benefit newcomers and old-timers alike, albeit in different ways. Newcomers acclimate and assimilate more quickly, and the old-timers benefit from strengthening existing bonds and trading best practices to further the group's aims. Such benchmarking is especially important—and works exceptionally well—in larger organizations with geographically dispersed locations, in which individuals do not meet frequently.

MANAGE MEMBERS OF THE GUARD AND RESERVE

A critical area that human resource champions must understand is how to manage members of the Guard and Reserve (collectively known as the Reserve Component). Chapter 2 spoke to the laws and regulations surrounding the Reserve Component. Let's call that the "science." The "art" of managing Guard and Reserve members involves several topics.

Statistics tell us that more than half of veterans will elect to extend their service in the Guard or the Reserve.[19] Their motivations might range from completing their service obligation to qualifying for a pension to contributing to a cause greater than themselves. Table 8-3 shows the many benefits to continuing their service.

Educational	Financial	Quality of Life
◆ Tuition assistance ◆ College credit ◆ Montgomery GI Bill—Selected Reserve ◆ On-the-job training ◆ Post-9/11 GI Bill ◆ Student loan repayment ◆ Reserve Educational Assistance Program (REAP) ◆ VA Veteran Readiness and Employment (VR&E)	◆ Extra Income ◆ Grocery and department store privileges ◆ Low-cost insurance ◆ Healthcare—medical and dental ◆ Pension ◆ Potential bonus ◆ Disability compensation ◆ VA home loan guaranty ◆ VA burial and memorial services ◆ Military discounts ◆ Tax deductions for RC job-related expenses ◆ Differential pay (from some employers)	◆ Sense of self-worth ◆ Service to the nation ◆ Camaraderie ◆ Direct transfer from active duty ◆ Doing the extraordinary ◆ Keep their rank ◆ Networking ◆ No need to move ◆ Access to: 　◇ Fitness centers 　◇ Chaplain services 　◇ Childcare services 　◇ Financial counseling 　◇ Family centers 　◇ Legal assistance 　◇ Recreation facilities

Table 8-3: Summary of Reserve Component Benefits[20]

But now, they likely have a civilian boss in addition to a military one, which can lead to complications when called to active duty or to regular drills (and those activations and deployments may be more frequent; see "The Operational Reserve" on page 168). Those complications will depend on your policies and approaches to members of the Reserve Component. Those complications will be different from their active-duty peers, as the support systems available to members of the Reserve Component are not as robust. As a result, they tend to lead to more stress at home and within their families.

The Operational Reserve

The Reserve Component changed from a strategic to an operational reserve in 2008 by US Department of Defense Directive 1200.17.[21] How so? Twenty years ago, Guard or Reserve members could reliably assume that they would involuntarily mobilize only once throughout their Reserve service. Employers could expect their citizen-soldier employees to have relatively predictable schedules (one weekend of service per month and two weeks of active duty per year). That is no longer the case. That Department of Defense Directive effectively put Reserve Component (RC) forces on par with Active Component (AC) forces, at least related to their regularly scheduled participation in overseas contingency operations. In short, as it relates to the frequency and duration of deployments and the kinds of missions they could be activated to support, RC members may be busier than members of a generation ago.

Despite that increased frequency of deployment activity, recognize that you have your own set of rights and resources to manage members of the Reserve:

+ You may request that some of your workers be named "key employees" who cannot mobilize.[22]

   ◇ Given the disproportionate impact on smaller employers, you might consider such a designation as of their initial hire date.

+ The US Department of Defense (DoD) is supposed to proactively engage employers with relevant USERRA information based on the Civilian Employment Information (CEI) that RC members provide. Should that outreach not occur, you should reach out to the Employer Support of the Guard and Reserve organization (ESGR). ESGR is a DoD program established in 1972 to promote cooperation and understanding between RC members and their civilian employers, and help resolve conflicts arising from an employee's military commitment.

   ◇ ESGR offers several helpful employer programs.[23]

   ◇ ESGR administers an awards program for supportive employers.[24]

◇ ESGR also provides free mediation services to RC members and their employers.[25]

♦ According to DoD Instruction 1205.12, RC members must fulfill the following obligations to be eligible for reemployment rights under USERRA:[26]

◇ Provide notice to their employer of the pending military service, preferably in writing and at least thirty days before departure.

◇ Provide a return notification letter to their employer, samples of which you can find at the Employer Support of the Guard and Reserve (ESGR).[27]

◇ Provide documentation of service performed to their employer.[28]

◇ Limit cumulative absences to no more than five years per employer.

◇ Not be separated from the service under a disqualifying discharge.

♦ The burden of proof of discrimination under USERRA rests with the veteran.

♦ There is no obligation to continue full or differential/partial pay during an RC member's absence, although many leading companies have such policies.[29]

Different organizations have chosen various ways to manage these individuals. My general guidance is to take the opportunity to implement such policies that will further embellish your brand in the marketplace—yes, even smaller organizations. Larger organizations can do even more. To wit, Schlumberger has chosen to go above and beyond the requirements of USERRA. They will hold the job for a deployed veteran beyond five years. Also, while they provide differential pay for an entire year for deployed veterans, they are working to make it even longer. They believe this sends a positive message to aspiring veteran hires.[30]

. . . .

COMPANIES IN THE COCKPIT

"Walmart has a robust Military Leave of Absence (MLOA) policy. Since 2008, Walmart has offered differential pay to associates taking a leave of absence for specific military assignments. If an associate's military salary is less than what they make at their job at Walmart, the company will pay them the difference while they're on MLOA. Walmart has since announced enhancements to this policy to include any eligible military assignment, including basic training, allowing associates who are considering enlisting in the Armed Forces to do so without fear of losing wages."

Brynt Parmeter, Senior Director, Non-Traditional Talent
I Head of Walmart Military & Veterans Affairs

A critical role that your veteran affinity group might play when a member of the Guard or Reserve is activated or deployed is "rear detachment support." When active-duty units deploy, their commands assign a small contingent to stay behind and, in large part, provide support to family members impacted by the deployment. Why? As stated by Basil Liddell Hart: "Man has two supreme loyalties—to country and to family. . . . So long as their families are safe, they will defend their country, believing that by their sacrifice they are safeguarding their families also. But even the bonds of patriotism, discipline and comradeship are loosened when the family itself is threatened."[31] And so, as the theory goes, those same loyalties (and resultant impacts on retention) will accrue to you when you provide similar support.

According to the Army's handbook on the topic, such support may take the form of:

◆ Maintaining contact with families, including those returning to their home of record or otherwise leaving the area during the deployment.

◆ Furnishing important information to families regularly. Answer their questions and concerns.

◆ Attending and supporting any family group meetings or activities. Coordinate social or recreational activities to build and sustain morale and camaraderie.

◆ Providing families with administrative and logistical support. Resolve family issues by referring families to appropriate military or community agencies.

◆ Conducting counseling as required.

◆ Coordinating with American Red Cross regarding emergency information on the deployed personnel and family members.

◆ Maintaining a record of contacts, actions taken, and follow-ups with families.[32]

While the support your organization provides need not be as formal, any help that would complement that provided by their military unit would most certainly be appreciated and fondly recalled.

UTILIZE TACTICS TO INCREASE RETENTION RATES

As a rule, veterans are a reasonably loyal group as long as you give them a reason for being so. In theory, executing the previously described veteran hiring process in a way that results in a veteran-ready culture should have increased retention as a byproduct. The proposed approaches directly address the usual root causes of lower retention rates. Moreover, it always serves to study the leading practices of organizations that have had success in this area. Please note that organizations implement most of the tactics specified below at the outset of a veteran's employment.

Amazon feels that transparency is one of the keys to retention. This includes:

♦ Providing more frequent and detailed feedback, especially early on.

♦ Identifying career track options and requirements from the outset, to include time in grade and schooling requirements to reach various levels in each track.

♦ Providing more transparent guidance around what it takes to get promoted to successive levels in those career tracks.[33]

COMPANIES IN THE COCKPIT

"Retention is a challenge. Getting veterans over the initial hump of transition from the military to the corporate world is hard. Focusing on sponsorship programs, mentoring programs, local warrior community chapters, and developing more clear career paths are all efforts being utilized to improve retention for our veteran hires. Our track record shows that if we can get the veterans that join Amazon to the eighteen-month to two-year mark within the company, their future trajectory is better than their non veteran peers."

Beau Higgins, Senior Manager, Amazon Military Recruiting Center of Excellence | Worldwide Operations Talent Acquisition

Like many corporate entities, USAA has had difficulty retaining new veteran hires. Their experience has been that many veterans don't have a good sense of what they want to do. Transitioning veterans seemingly just don't want to be unemployed, so they tend to take the first job offer they come across regardless of personal fit. Thus, USAA has aggressively addressed this problem by developing a transitioning checklist that helps in these situations (and you don't have to be a veteran member to review it).[34] Even better, they implemented VetsLeaD, a twelve-month program focused on helping veterans make a successful transition at USAA. It involves monthly training that touches on various aspects of transition. The expectation is that, upon conclusion, the transitioning veteran is relatively equal to their civilian peers in adjusting to USAA culture. Program content is the same as their civilian peers. However, by spreading the curriculum over twelve monthly (one- to two-day) events, rather than delivering it all in five weeks, they can actively engage the new veteran employees for the duration of their first year. Facilitators of the training are veterans themselves, and those facilitators help the transitioning veterans mesh their military experiences with USAA behavioral norms and culture. Moreover, executive-level mentors and peer-level sponsors actively engage with VetsLeaD employees throughout the year. As a result, first-year retention of VetsLeaD employees is 98 percent, which is more than forty points higher than the nationwide average of veterans in their first post-military job (56 percent first-year retention).[35]

COMPANIES IN THE COCKPIT

"There is a much better chance of retaining veteran hires if:

- They feel engaged, supported, and empowered.

- They have an understanding of the company's mission.

- They are able to make a positive impact on their team and on the business.

- They have a clear vision of their future (pathway) within the organization."

Brynt Parmeter, Senior Director, Non-Traditional Talent
| Head of Walmart Military & Veterans Affairs

Some organizations with widely dispersed geographic entities or highly variable product lines might consider a segmented approach. For example, JPMorgan Chase's veteran retention efforts are focused and specific to each of the firm's multiple lines of business. Another example is how Tesla's veterans group facilitates a regular comfort care package event for its deployed Guard and Reserve members in each business line.[36]

Also worth considering are rotational programs for newly hired veterans. General Electric has experienced success with its Junior Officer Leadership Program (JOLP). JOLP is a two-year program in which members—both junior officers and non-commissioned officers—rotate through four roles, each for a six-month duration. The rotational nature of these roles exposes them to multiple areas of the organization, which allows them to better and more quickly understand the organization's culture and where and how their strengths might best fit within it. Other organizations replicate the nature of such rotational programs simply by their work routine. The work at Cajun Industries, for example, is project-based; and projects tend to have durations of no more than a few months. And so, veteran hires are routinely exposed to various roles and aspects of the organization, which has the same benefits as the more formal programs. The result of both approaches tends to be increased retention rates.

- -

COMPANIES IN THE COCKPIT

"What's key to retaining veteran hires is keeping them working, keeping them active in moving from job to job. Rolling stones gather no moss."

Chris Newton, Workforce Development Manager at Cajun Industries

Another tactic some organizations utilize is allowing veterans, who tend to have varied interests and passions outside of work, flexible work schedules to accommodate those personal passions. For example, given the physical activity they experience and the leadership skills they gain while serving, some veterans enjoy giving back through coaching or teaching opportunities, whose commitments often conflict with standard work hours. Allowing some flexibility to enable the achievement of both work and life goals will enhance their loyalty.

Regardless of the tactics used, the bottom line is this: early and consistent engagement with organizational leaders who understand veterans and demonstrate care about their ongoing advancement via tailored policies will reap the retention rewards.

As you approach the end of the process, it is worth taking stock for a moment to capture some secrets for success. What is required to enable a supportive environment for a transitioning veteran?

- Senior executives with good intentions and active sponsorship

- An educated base of employees who understand and appreciate the dynamics of a military culture

- Transparency regarding the hiring process, promotion timing and expectations, and career path upon arrival

- Willing and involved mentors within the employee base

- Regular and substantive feedback regarding the new hire's performance

- An active military or veteran affinity program

- Sufficiently robust and widely available training programs and tools

The last part of this journey involves monitoring progress, ensuring success, and sharing best practices with the broader community. That is the subject of the next and final chapter.

KEYS TO SUCCESS

- Acceptance of the offer should not end your veteran support efforts. Ensure a sequential assimilation approach that begins with peers and trained organizational leaders.

- Invest appropriately in onboarding and career development of veteran hires to support retention efforts.

  ◇ Ensure new veteran hires are assigned a mentor and a peer sponsor.

  ◇ Ensure new veteran hires receive regular and substantive feedback.

  ◇ Administer an in-house "one-stop" support center for veteran employees.

- Training civilians on veterans is just as important as the inverse.

- Transparency is the best policy in onboarding and professional development activities.

- Capitalize on the opportunity that military spouse hires represent.

- Fully support the ongoing service of Guard and Reserve employees, especially during times of activation and deployment.

- Take advantage of federal resources to supplement your onboarding and training activities.

- Consider rotational programs for the initial assignments of newly hired veterans.

- Track veteran performance and retention metrics to understand which tactics and investments provide the greatest return.

CHAPTER 9

VALIDATE ASSIMILATION, MEASURE SUCCESS, AND SHARE LESSONS LEARNED

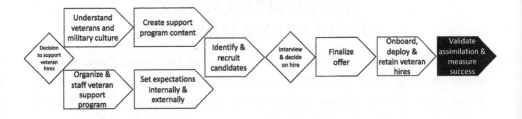

"You've been told that you're broken, that you're damaged goods and should be labeled victims. I don't buy it. The truth, instead, is that you are the only folks with the skills, determination, and values to ensure American dominance in this chaotic world."

—**James Mattis,** 2014 speech to veterans of the Iraq and Afghanistan wars (during the question-and-answer portion), Marine's Memorial Club, San Francisco, California[1]

While General Mattis spoke of the nation, the same sentiment applies to your organization. With all of the time, money, and effort you've put forth in your program thus far, you owe it to yourself to ensure that it achieves its goals and is sustainable. That is the intent of this final chapter. The topics we will cover include how to:

- Facilitate defined, periodic check-ins with new veteran hires.
- Monitor and report on progress against established metrics.
- Make programmatic adjustments as needed.
- Outplace veterans.
- Apply for military-friendly recognition programs.
- Share lessons learned with the broader veteran community.

Assuming you follow through on these topics, your veteran support program will be a competitive advantage in the marketplace—something your executive leaders can publicly tout and leverage in recruiting even more members of this valuable talent pool.

FACILITATE DEFINED, PERIODIC
CHECK-INS WITH NEW VETERAN HIRES

Retention rates improve if you can keep a veteran hire beyond two years. A key to enabling that is validating cultural assimilation. As I explained in my award-winning book *Mission Transition,* this can be the most tenuous time in a veteran's transition from the military. Providing them regular support, feedback, and mentoring will be critical in helping them make needed adjustments. Pull again on your veteran affinity group members to carry the weight here. The resulting tribal behavior will support success.

It's time to put the mentoring content covered in Chapters 3 and 4 to work. Here are a couple of approaches to consider:

1. For the first few months, have affinity group members conduct a semiformal check-in with new hires. Clear thirty minutes to discuss how things are going in their new roles. These "sounding board" sessions do not require formal documentation. They're an opportunity for affinity group members to encourage new hires to communicate any time they have questions or concerns. These simple acts can

represent a lifeline to new hires. The sessions are most important in the first six to twelve months of a new hire's tenure; their frequency can wane in the ensuing months.

2. Administer an organizational culture assessment to understand how new veteran hires fit into the culture of the specific workplace assigned to them. This assessment will enable workplace leaders and mentors to identify the gap between the type of organizational culture veterans prefer to work in and the current culture of their workplace. Working through any cultural disconnects will help the veteran and workplace leaders address issues developed after onboarding and hiring. This approach is a powerful way to improve collaboration, business performance, and personal effectiveness when coupled with mentoring. Consider these four assessments:

   ◆ The Organizational Culture Assessment Instrument (OCAI).[2] This cultural assessment is based on the Competing Values Framework, one of the most used frameworks in business. More than ten thousand companies have used it. It features six aspects that represent an organization's culture. The assessment involves distributing one hundred points among four "Competing Values," which correspond to four types of organizational culture. Every organization has its mix of these four types of organizational culture.

   ◆ The Hofstede Culture in the Workplace Questionnaire™ (Hofstede CWQ).[3] The Hofstede CWQ is perhaps the best-known measure of culture. This questionnaire is a profiler that measures a person's cultural preferences on six dimensions. It compares an individual's culture orientation to that which they interact with at work and enables respondents to improve their effectiveness by developing a greater understanding of personal attitudes and values toward work.

   ◆ The Organizational Culture Inventory (OCI).[4] The OCI is one of the most widely used and thoroughly researched tools for measuring organizational culture globally. The OCI measures twelve behavioral norms that describe the thinking and behavioral styles that might be implicitly or explicitly required for people to "fit in" and "meet expectations" in an organization or organizational subunit. These behavioral norms specify how all members of an organization—or at least those in similar positions or organizational locations—should approach their work and interact with one another.

- ◆ The Organizational Culture Assessment Questionnaire (OCAQ).[5] The OCAQ is a diagnostic aid designed to be a first step in building better-functioning organizations and strengthening and improving their cultures. The OCAQ asks thirty questions to measure how its members believe the organization is doing in five crucial culture functions. The OCAQ then provides members with information showing the discrepancies between the way things are and how they should be. Once the existing patterns of culture are unfrozen, managers and administrators can become leaders.

Even with that support, you may still experience some veteran hires who struggle. Assuming your organization has one, you might refer these veterans struggling with adjusting to the workplace to your organization's Employee Assistance Program (EAP). According to the Society for Human Resource Management,

---

an EAP is a work-based intervention program designed to assist employees in resolving personal problems that may be adversely affecting the employee's performance. Programs are delivered at no cost to employees by stand-alone EAP vendors or providers who are part of comprehensive health insurance plans. Services are often delivered via phone, video-based counseling, online chatting, e-mail interactions, or face-to-face.[6]

A study conducted by the Department of Veterans Affairs (VA) identified EAPs as a vital factor in veteran retention. It maintains a website that describes veteran-friendly EAP practices.[7] All federal agencies have EAPs. (See "Employee Assistance Programs in Federal Agencies. on page 181.").

Employee Assistance Programs in Federal Agencies

All federal agencies have access to Employee Assistance Programs (EAPs). According to the Office of Personnel Management, EAP services include assessments, counseling, and referrals for additional services to employees with personal and/or work-related concerns, such as stress, financial issues, legal issues, family problems, office conflicts, and alcohol and substance use disorders. EAPs also often work with management and supervisors providing advanced planning for situations, such as organizational changes, legal considerations, emergency planning, and response to unique traumatic events.[8]

Your organization's EAP should also use the services and programs of some of the more prominent national veteran service organizations that exist to support veterans in transition. Veterans Affairs maintains a lengthy list of these organizations online.[9] Among this group, you might consider:

- Iraq and Afghanistan Veterans of America (IAVA)
- National Association of American Veterans (NAAV)
- Wounded Warrior Project
- American Legion
- Veterans of Foreign Wars (VFW)
- American Veterans (AMVETS)
- United Service Organizations (USO)
- Disabled American Veterans (DAV)
- Paralyzed Veterans of America
- Vietnam Veterans of America
- The VA's own Center for Women Veterans (CWV)

Recall that one of the most important aspects of a successful transition from the military is to enable the veteran a sense of "tribe" with their peers. And so, your EAP might make use of another group of volunteering and civic engagement organizations. The following maintain a nationwide footprint and are worth considering:

- The Mission Continues
- Team Rubicon

- Team Red White and Blue (RWB)

- Travis Manion Foundation

MONITOR AND REPORT ON PROGRESS AGAINST ESTABLISHED METRICS

There's an adage from business guru Eliyahu Goldratt: "Tell me how you measure me, and I'll tell you how I behave."[10] And so, if you want to change the behavior of the organization when it comes to supporting veteran hires, you ideally measure and report on the veteran support program's established metrics (as defined in Chapter 3), and senior management ideally monitors and rewards progress against those measures (as noted in Chapter 1). The formality of the process for doing so must align with your corporate culture. Whatever the approach, the reporting ideally occurs regularly and allows for feedback and the opportunity for continuous improvement.

COMPANIES IN THE COCKPIT

"Prudential's Inclusive Solutions department receives a regular report on veteran hires—communicated as a percent of new hires—broken down by business unit and corporate function. In order to assist with military talent and diverse hiring, these numbers are shared with each business leader periodically—showcasing areas of strength, as well as any areas of improvement."

James Beamesderfer, former Vice President, Veterans Initiatives, Prudential

MAKE PROGRAMMATIC ADJUSTMENTS AS NEEDED

In Chapter 5, you identified internal and external stakeholder groups. Each reporting period brings the opportunity to solicit feedback from these stakeholders and make programmatic adjustments. You need not hit up the same groups every time; feel free to mix it up and garner different perspectives. However, whatever the input, make sure that it gets recognized and used to further your efforts. If stakeholders feel their feedback offers little value, they may stop offering it. Their inputs, combined with the feedback from organizational leadership and benchmarking of other veteran programs across industry, will enable a cutting-edge veteran support program. Simple surveys and interview techniques can suffice for soliciting these inputs.

COMPANIES IN THE COCKPIT

"The biggest thing to understand in hiring veterans is that you can't expect recruiting to go out and make it happen without some prior planning. You have to break down some barriers to entry first. You have to build your own house first. You need to look at minimum job requirements to know what skills you need to bring in and then go from there. Table stakes is having a veteran-friendly reputation and advertising that. You have to reach out in person and visit bases. If the perception of your organization is negative, you have to work hard to change that perception. Bottom line, you have to work hard to establish your name brand in a positive light in the veteran environment."

Nick B. Tran, Manager, Community and Veteran Affairs at Schlumberger

You might also consider critical reviews of your program implementation from reputable sources. For example, the Institute for Veterans and Military Families (IVMF) at Syracuse University authored an assessment of the implementation of Executive Order 13518—The Veterans Employment Initiative (VEI), which aimed to boost the employment of military veterans from Iraq and Afghanistan in twenty-four agencies of the federal government.[11] In its review, it made several recommendations for those responsible for implementing the policy:

- For the Council on Veterans Employment:

  ◇ Provide dedicated and sustained leadership to ensure agency representatives possess the necessary authority to remain engaged with the goals and objectives identified by the Council.

  ◇ Direct and oversee the development of a coordinated strategic planning process to address the findings and lessons learned from the implementation assessment.

  ◇ Establish a formal outreach process with veteran employment coalitions such as the Department of Defense's (DoD) Hiring Heroes Program, DoD Operation Warfighter, and the private sector's Hiring Our Heroes and the Veteran Jobs Mission initiatives.

- For Office of Personnel Management (OPM) and Human Resource Professionals:

  ◇ Consult with experts in industrial and organizational psychology, public management, and veteran-focused social science research to develop a strategic-planning framework to achieve desired agency outcomes through innovation, learning, and workforce intelligence.

◇ Develop a comprehensive plan to identify the most effective means to translate veterans' military-acquired skills, education, and competencies for civilian employment.

◇ Design a tailored, data-driven performance management system to guide goal setting, action steps, and resource allocation for the next phase of the VEI.

◇ Conduct a targeted assessment to determine how human resource professionals can address differing views related to civil-military culture within the workforce and how gaps in understanding and opinions may be impacting perceptions of fairness, diversity, and inclusion.

◆ For agency and department heads:

◇ Identify critical occupations, skills, licenses, and professional certifications that support agency-specific workforce needs and align them with established career skills programs and other established workforce readiness initiatives for transitioning military and veterans.

◇ Conduct assessments to identify human capital requirements supporting VEI strategic planning objectives.

◇ Ensure Veteran Employment Program Offices (VEPOs) are fully staffed and resourced. Continue to identify learning and resource-sharing opportunities with other VEPOs, particularly between well-resourced and under-resourced agencies.

◇ Ensure that agency heads and their deputies provide a dedicated and sustained commitment to VEI requirements, including full participation in council and steering committee meetings, training, and internal veteran-related employment activities.

◇ Conduct, in cooperation with OPM and the Council, an agency assessment of employee, managerial, and executive-level perceptions and knowledge gaps in current veteran employment policies and hiring preference rules.

Regardless of whether you lead a federal agency, I think you will find the opportunity for parallel application of their guidance in your organization.

OUTPLACE VETERANS

There are two scenarios in which hired veterans leave your organization: voluntarily and involuntarily.

Voluntary. Despite your best efforts, there will still be some portion of your veteran hires that decide to leave the organization. Rather than fret over this outcome, you might consider this an opportunity in hiding. How you treat those departing the organization will comprise their last memory of your organization. Veterans talk, and word gets around. So, make this final memory a good one. These good stories may well produce future veteran applicants.

- First, consider offering these departing veterans access to your organization's outplacement services even though they may be leaving voluntarily. If they have yet to read it, I recommend providing a copy of my award-winning book *Mission Transition: Navigating the Opportunities and Obstacles to Your Post-Military Career.*

- Second, consider incorporating a member of your veteran affinity group in the exit interview. Have among the interview's primary purposes understanding their reasons for departing and improving your organization's veteran support processes. Take the opportunity to plow these lessons back into your veteran support program.

- Third, upon understanding why the individual is leaving and the alternate opportunity they are considering, you might offer them employment alternatives inside or outside your organization that better meet their needs. They will fondly recall this kindness.

- Finally, you might consider providing the outgoing veteran an open door if they should decide to return. It may be their first employment outside the military, so they might find the "grass isn't always greener" at other organizations. Knowing that they could return prevents them from burning a bridge.

Involuntary. Call it a Reduction in Force (RIF), call it a layoff, a downsizing, call it what you will. There will inevitably be situations in which organizations must part with some personnel. Human resource managers must understand that veterans are one of several protected classes for equal opportunity purposes in the United States. That means several laws and regulations noted in Chapter 2 make it illegal to discriminate in the terms and conditions of employment based on an individual's status as a veteran. Thus, it's not illegal to fire a veteran, but you can't discriminate against one (or a group of them) in doing so.

The Society for Human Resource Management (SHRM) offers some guidance on how to minimize your risk in conducting such involuntary outplacements.[12] The US Department of Labor details requirements in a handy pamphlet if you are a federal contractor.[13] Despite the reasons for an involuntary action, organizations might consider taking approaches with veterans similar to those noted in the voluntary section above. Doing so may help retain a bridge for potential future employment opportunities. To that end, and considering the time, effort, and resources you applied in bringing them into your organization in the first place, you might consider placing these displaced personnel into openings elsewhere in your organization where they may be a fit.

Veterans' Preference in Reductions in Force (RIFs)

While this US Code is specific to federal hires, civilian organizations might consider using a similar approach. Per 5 United States Code (USC), federal hires who are veterans have advantages over non veterans in a reduction in force (RIF). Also, special provisions apply in determining whether retired military members receive preference in a RIF and whether their military service counts. Depending on their tenure, veteran's preference, length of service, and performance, veterans may bump others or retreat into positions with lower standing. Special conditions also apply if a veteran has a 30 percent or more compensable disability. Further, if impacted by a RIF, veterans have the right to appeal those decisions and will maintain re-employment priority in the same agency. However, affected veterans must first meet specific eligibility requirements detailed in 5 US Code 3501, 3502; 5 CFR 351.501.[14]

APPLY FOR MILITARY-FRIENDLY RECOGNITION PROGRAMS

After putting in all the work to build a successful veteran support program, you and your organization should consider the advantages of being recognized for your efforts. There are several programs available to enable such recognition. This recognition will help build your organization's brand, which will, in turn, improve your standing in the eyes of prospective veteran hires. Once again, good goes around.

On a national level, there are several opportunities for being recognized. First, the Department of Labor established the *HIRE Vets Medallion Program* under the Honoring Investments in Recruiting and Employing American Military Veterans Act (HIRE Vets Act). The HIRE Vets Medallion Program recognizes employers "for their investments in recruiting, employing, and retaining our nation's heroes."[15] This program is the only federal-level veterans' employment award that recognizes an organization's commitment to veteran hiring, retention, and professional development.

There are two levels of award (Gold and Platinum) for three tiers of employers: Large employers (500-plus employees), Medium employers (51–499 employees), and Small employers (50 or fewer employees). For each award, the employer must satisfy criteria that include the percentage of employees hired who are veterans and the percentage of veterans retained. Verification of these criteria consists of a self-attestation by the applicant and a check for violations of veteran-related labor laws by the US Department of Labor. For details on the program and to apply, please see their website.

Secondly, Employer Support of the Guard and Reserve (ESGR) offers several progressive awards,[16] including:

- **Patriot Award.** Patriot Awards are given to individual supervisors of veterans, not organizations. Individual employees serving in the National Guard or Reserve (collectively, the Reserve Component), or the spouse of a Guard or Reserve member, may nominate individual supervisors for support provided to the service member and their family. "Support" includes flexible schedules, time off before and after deployment, caring for families, and granting leaves of absence.

- **Spouse Patriot Award.** Much like Patriot Awards, Spouse Patriot Awards are given to individual supervisors of spouses of Reserve Component members, not organizations. The nomination process and criteria used are similar, although the focus is on spousal support.

- **Seven Seals Award.** The most inclusive ESGR award, it is presented in recognition of a significant individual or organizational achievement, initiative, or support that promotes and supports the ESGR mission. Service members may nominate their organization or individuals within it.

- **Above and Beyond Award.** This award intends to recognize employers who have gone "above and beyond" the legal requirements of the Uniformed Services Employment and Reemployment Rights Act (USERRA) by providing their Reserve Component employees additional, non-mandated benefits such as differential or full pay to offset lost wages, extended health benefits, and other similar benefits. Service members may nominate their organization for the award.

- **Pro Patria Award.** The highest award bestowed at the state level, the Pro Patria Award is presented annually to one small, one large, and one public sector employer. Awardees must demonstrate significant support to Guard and Reserve employees through their leadership and practices, including adopting personnel policies that make it easier for employees to participate in the National Guard and Reserve. Only those organizations that 1) have signed a Statement of Support, 2) have received the Above and Beyond Award, and 3) have at least one supervisor that earned a Patriot Award are eligible.

- **Extraordinary Employer Support Award.** This award recognizes sustained employer support of employees' Reserve Component service. Only prior recipients of the Secretary of Defense Employer Support Freedom Award or the Pro Patria Award, who have demonstrated sustained support for three years after receiving one of those awards, are eligible for consideration. Organizations may earn subsequent awards in three-year increments following the initial award.

- **Secretary of Defense Employer Support Freedom Award.** This is the highest recognition the US government provides employers for supporting their employees who serve in the Guard and Reserve. Reserve Component employees or their family members may nominate the employer. There are three categories for the award: small employer, large employer, and public sector. A national selection board comprised of senior Department of Defense officials, business leaders, and prior awardees selects up to fifteen employers annually to receive this prestigious award.

Third, in concert with the Thayer Leader Development Group at West Point, *Chief Executive* magazine sponsors the annual **Patriots in Business Award** to recognize the best companies with military and veteran programs. As its website notes:

[the] award recognizes outstanding businesses that lead our nation in supporting active-duty military members, veterans, and their families and exemplify the values of Duty, Honor, and Country through their business practices and throughout their community and industry. Through their initiatives on hiring, training, supporting, and honoring active duty, veterans, and military families, these outstanding companies are the gold standard for other companies who seek to support those who serve.[17]

All for-profit organizations are eligible to apply, and there are three categories of awards:

♦ Large (>$1B in annual revenue) companies

♦ Medium-sized (between $10M and $1B in annual revenue) companies

♦ Small (less than $10M in annual revenue) companies

Criteria categories include:

♦ Hire veterans and military spouses

♦ Train, retain, and support veterans, National Guard, Reserve, and spouses

♦ Honor veterans and their families within the company and community

Please see the magazine's website for additional details and procedures for applying.

Fourth, VETS Indexes sponsors a free annual employer awards program for organizations—companies large and small, government agencies and departments, nonprofit groups, colleges, and universities—that prove to be the best veteran employers based on the following criteria:[18]

♦ Veteran employee development and retention, including:

  ◊ Employee retention rates for all employees, veterans, and military-connected personnel

  ◊ Seniority levels of veteran employees within an organization

  ◊ Proportion of internal promotions going to veteran employees

♦ Veteran-inclusive policies and culture, including:

  ◊ Veteran employee resource groups: activity levels and sizes

- ◇ Proportion of vendor/supplier budget spent at veteran-owned businesses
- ◇ Contributions to veteran employment efforts beyond your own organization
- ◆ Veteran recruiting and hiring, including:
    - ◇ Proportion of new hire and overall employee populations who are veterans
    - ◇ Proportion of recruiting budget earmarked for veterans
    - ◇ Relative size of veteran-focused recruiting staff
- ◆ Guard and Reserve support, including:
    - ◇ Compliance with employment rules for Guard/Reserve employees
    - ◇ Pay policies for serving Guard and Reserve employees
    - ◇ Employer Support of the Guard and Reserve (ESGR) award received
- ◆ Military spouse and family support, including:
    - ◇ Proportion of new hire and overall employee populations who are military spouses
    - ◇ Flexible work locations, scheduling for military spouse employees
    - ◇ Military spouse recruiting and job application policies

Fifth, some national nonprofits sponsor award programs to recognize organizations that hire veterans.

- ◆ **Disabled American Veterans (DAV)** sponsors an annual National Commander Employer Awards Program for small, midsize, and large businesses.[19]

- ◆ The **American Legion** sponsors National Veterans Employment & Education Awards every year. There are more than a half dozen categories of awards.[20]

Sixth, Viqtory offers an annual survey, upon whose completion companies and schools that meet their discerning criteria might be considered **Military Friendly** in one of several categories.[21]

Lastly, there likely exist additional programs at the state and local levels for which you might be eligible. As noted in Chapter 2, please see the Resources section of my website (*www.matthewjlouis.com*) for opportunities at the state level as of this writing.

Consider applying for all recognition programs for which you are eligible, as being recognized by any of these programs will portray your organization in a positive light in the minds of veteran talent seeking careers post-service. Your veteran support program lead should be responsible for these applications.

SHARE LESSONS LEARNED WITH THE BROADER VETERAN COMMUNITY

There are two dimensions to lessons learned: those aimed at other organizations interested in hiring veterans and those aimed at veterans themselves. Throughout this book, you find examples of the former in the "Companies in the Cockpit" excerpts. For the latter and adding your own to both lists, please see the Resources section of my website (*www.matthewjlouis.com*).

COMPANIES IN THE COCKPIT

"You should be willing to help other companies with their veteran support programs. At the end of the day, it's about getting the veteran situated and helping the industry, not just our company. We've been at it six years, and we are proof positive that focusing on veteran talent has been a strategic differentiator for us."

David Theriot, Military Workforce Development at Performance Contractors

Here are some examples of efforts that leading organizations are taking:

- Procter & Gamble's veterans affinity group conducts an annual cultural survey across the entire company to understand what impact their approach is having.[22]

- Nick Tran at Schlumberger regularly visits the Pentagon and the White House to share what the company does for its veterans.[23]

- Many organizations participate in the annual National Veteran Workforce Development Conference (NVWDC), a national conference highlighting best practices in veteran workforce development and employment.[24]

- ◆ Federal hiring managers might consider:

  - ◇ Following the regular postings on the Chief Human Capital Officers Council webpage for updates on veterans' employment issues.[25]

  - ◇ Leveraging best practices captured in the US Office of Personnel Management's Reintegration Framework for Guard and Reserve members.[26]

COMPANIES IN THE COCKPIT

"In general, we would suggest that any labor market program such as this begin with the end in mind. Start with what the business requires, the demand side of the labor market. Then identify the various means of supply to successfully meet those demands and strategize on how to best engage those populations. Specifically, I would encourage organizations to:

1. Do your homework. Understand the nature of the human capital asset you are bringing on board and how to best recruit/onboard/train/deploy/retain them.

2. Know the actors in the veteran talent arena. Understand government requirements as well as organizational opportunities (recognition programs, tax incentives, etc.).

3. Get started. Take the basic tenets portrayed in this book, begin hiring non-traditional talent, and adjust your program as outcomes dictate."

Brynt Parmeter, Senior Director, Non-Traditional Talent
I Head of Walmart Military & Veterans Affairs

For a final example of the evolution of—and motivations for—a leading organization supporting veteran efforts, see "Spotlight on Prudential" below.

Spotlight on Prudential

Prudential decided to focus on veterans as a high-quality talent pipeline in 2010 when there was high unemployment among this population. They thought they could lean in and make a difference, as they always look for talent as a differentiator for their business. At the time, Prudential felt that, of their talent options, veterans were one where they could make a difference. And so, they created an Office of Veteran Initiatives (OVI), which subsequently spawned a Business Resource Group called VetNet. The overall intent of their effort was to support veteran- and military-serving organizations while recruiting high-quality talent to Prudential. It was not a ploy to grandstand; there were no big, bold pronouncements and media plays. Prudential wanted to provide veterans careers (not jobs)—at Prudential or elsewhere—by helping them transition successfully. While their leaders would like graduates of their veteran programs to work for Prudential, that doesn't necessarily need to be so. They have two primary goals:

- First is to provide and support best-in-class veteran programs that have an impact on a local basis which could be recognized nationally once those efforts are aggregated.

- Prudential also aims to be a nationally recognized thought leader on veteran employment and financial wellness. While they don't hire 100K veterans a year like some others, they excel in having great retention rates among their hires. They believe they should share programs enabling this success with other companies.[27]

If your veteran support program can mimic the intent of that at Prudential, you will be well on your way to success.

Amid World War II, Winston Churchill noted, "Never in the field of human conflict was so much owed by so many to so few."[28] It is this sentiment with which I'd like to leave you. The idea is not that we owe our veterans jobs. Far from it. They will need to earn those roles the same as they ever earned anything in the military. I posit that what we owe our veterans is the opportunity and support to compete on a level playing field for those roles. We must recognize the vast divide they need to cross, and the current, well-intentioned support systems provided to them upon leaving the military cannot do this job successfully. If your organization can accomplish that, as many others in this book have demonstrated across many industry segments, you will be richly rewarded. As I've said several times, good goes around. You are now effectively trained to do just that and help other organizations do the same.

Congratulations on deciding to hire and retain veterans. As with any employee group, there will be challenges along the way, but you will not be disappointed in the return on your investment. I wish you the best with your efforts, and I stand ready to support them. Godspeed and all good wishes!

- Validate the cultural assimilation of new veteran hires to get them beyond the second anniversary of their hire date. Use leading cultural assessments to augment your mentoring approach in doing so.

- Track and report on progress to ensure executive-level engagement.

- Solicit and incorporate feedback from internal and external stakeholder groups to continuously improve your program.

- Use outplacement as an opportunity to build a bridge and further improve your program.

- Apply to all available military initiative recognition programs.

- Apply for all tax incentives for which you are eligible.

- Be active in the community of organizations sharing lessons learned regarding their veteran support programs. Communal support benefits everyone.

- Provide veterans a hand up, not a handout.

- Consider incorporating an experienced external advisor to enable your program's success.

USERRA EMPLOYER SUPPORT CHECKLISTS

These pre- and demobilization checklists contain guidance the military provides to mobilized members of the Guard and Reserve on how to inform and continually update their employers throughout a military contingency.[1] Actions suggested set expectations that enable mutual understanding and coordination during the employee's mobilization. As such, they are useful references for both employers and the managers of mobilized members of the Guard and Reserve. A good practice is to share these with Guard and Reserve members upon being hired, along with Employer Support of the Guard and Reserve (ESGR)'s demobilization briefing.[2]

PRE-MOBILIZATION EMPLOYER SUPPORT CHECKLIST

◆ BEFORE YOU LEAVE: Communicate with your employer. Maintaining an open dialogue with your employer will help ensure you both have reasonable expectations for what will happen before, during, and after your absence. Most problems result from miscommunication between employers and employees, so work with your employer to ensure that you both understand your mutual rights and responsibilities.

◆ You have rights and responsibilities under USERRA. To be eligible for reinstatement following your service:

☐ You must provide prior notice to your employer that you will be absent from your employment due to military service. You should provide notice as early as you have information concerning your departure.

☐ You must leave your place of employment for the purpose of performing military service.

- [ ] You must serve under honorable conditions for USERRA to apply.

- [ ] You must not be absent for more than five cumulative years from any one employer performing military service (with some exceptions).

- [ ] You must report back to work following your service in a timely fashion.

- Following is a checklist of suggested items to verify or execute before your departure:

  - [ ] Review USERRA.

  - [ ] Notify your employer, in person if possible, of your activation. ESGR has sample letters you may use as a template to notify your employer of your service obligation.

  - [ ] Department of Defense policy strongly suggests you provide your employer with at least thirty days of advance notice whenever possible.

  - [ ] If orders become available, you may present a copy to the appropriate supervisor and human resource (HR) representative.

  - [ ] Review military and company policy with supervisor and HR personnel.

  - [ ] Determine whether you would like to use leave before or during your mobilization. Share this plan with your employer.

  - [ ] Update beneficiaries and family information.

  - [ ] Resolve pay and compensation issues.

  - [ ] Determine if you will continue or suspend any employer-sponsored healthcare plans, including health, dental, and vision plans. Notify your employer of your intentions.

  - [ ] Provide forwarding address, telephone numbers, and email address.

  - [ ] Clear all employer-owned supplies and equipment in compliance with the employer's policy for extended leaves of absence.

☐ Share with your employer your projected return-to-work date.

☐ Keep a record of names, dates, and a summary of your conversations with your employer.

☐ Thank your employer and supervisor for their support and cooperation. Nominate them for a Patriot Award by completing the form at ESGR's online nomination page.

This checklist contains suggested actions to consider before active service. All actions are not required to gain or maintain USERRA protections.

DEMOBILIZATION EMPLOYER SUPPORT CHECKLIST

♦ WHEN YOU RETURN: To ensure a smooth transition back to work, you need to communicate with your employer. You have rights and responsibilities under USERRA. To be eligible for reinstatement following your service:

☐ You must provide prior notice to your employer that you will be absent from your employment due to military service. You should provide notice as early as you have information concerning your departure.

☐ You must leave your place of employment for the purpose of performing military service.

☐ You must serve under honorable conditions for USERRA to apply.

☐ You must not be absent for more than five cumulative years from any one employer performing military service (with some exceptions).

☐ You must report back to work following your service in a timely fashion.

☐ You must apply for reemployment or report back to work within the following guidelines:

1–30 days of service	Report to work the next scheduled workday
31–180 days of service	Apply within 14 days after completion of service
181+ days of service	Apply within 90 days after completion of service

- It is recommended that you present the appropriate supervisor and human resource (HR) representative with a copy of your discharge/separation order. If you were gone for more than 30 days and your employer requests proof of your service, you must provide it once it is available.

- Following is a checklist of suggested items to verify or execute upon your return:

  - ☐ Accumulation of seniority.

  - ☐ Reinstatement of health insurance, dental, and vision plans without waiting periods for you and any dependents.

  - ☐ Update beneficiaries and family information.

  - ☐ Resolve pay and compensation issues.

  - ☐ Review 401K or other pension plans and determine if and how make-up contributions will be made. Share your plans with your employer.

  - ☐ Review retirement and life insurance benefits.

  - ☐ Determine if training or retraining of job skills is necessary and share this with your employer.

  - ☐ Update personal data: address, telephone numbers, and email address.

  - ☐ Keep a record of names, dates, and a summary of your conversations with your employer.

  - ☐ Expect protection against discrimination and harassment.

  - ☐ Thank your employer and supervisor for their support and cooperation. Nominate them for a Patriot Award by completing the form at ESGR's online nomination page.

This checklist contains suggested actions to consider after completing your service. All actions are not required to gain or maintain USERRA protections.

SAMPLE VETERAN SUPPORT PROGRAM JOB DESCRIPTIONS

Ideally, both roles get filled from within your organization's ranks. But if you must post for them externally, following are draft descriptions for each.

PROGRAM LEAD

<u>Title:</u> [Organization] Veteran Support Program Lead

<u>Job Summary:</u> Our organization is looking for a Veteran Support Program Lead who will help us build and maintain various programs for our recruited and hired veterans. The Program Lead will be responsible for achieving all program goals, ensuring all staff members are appropriately certified, and meeting all government guidelines. If you are a veteran and have previous experience in a leadership position at a commercial organization with a veteran support program, a compassionate nature, and a dedication to improving veteran employees' lives, we encourage you to apply today.

<u>Responsibilities and Duties:</u>

- Accountable for all veteran support program activities in the organization

- Actively promote the program internally and externally while developing and maintaining relationships with key stakeholders

- Personally facilitate critical aspects of the program

- Maintain the professional credentials of each program staff member

- Stay updated on all laws and regulations and ensure that all program operations are within their scope; advise organizational executives on veteran-related matters

- Establish and maintain an annual program budget

- Develop and submit comprehensive progress reports on program activity to the executive staff each quarter

- Maintain and deliver all documentation required to ensure the organization's certifications remain intact and in good standing

Qualifications and Skills:

- Military veteran or retiree with active security clearance

- Bachelor's degree required; MBA or similar advanced degree preferred

- 5+ years of experience in a commercial entity, preferably within the same industry

- Experience as a veteran support program lead desired

- Ability to maintain workflow efficiently in a fast-paced environment

- Strong communication and leadership skills

- Proficiency in MS Office

- Compassionate and understanding nature

PROGRAM TALENT TRANSLATOR

Title: [Organization] Veteran Support Program Talent Translator

Job Summary: We are a global leader in the [industry name] industry, and we are growing quickly. We are currently in need of an experienced and professional Veteran Support Program Talent Translator to join our team. The Program Talent Translator will be responsible for producing materials and facilitating programs that enable our civilian employees to better understand our employees with military backgrounds and vice versa. The ideal candidate is a veteran, has previous experience in talent development in commercial entities, and is enthusiastic about being part of a team at the top of its game. If this sounds like you, please apply!

Responsibilities and Duties:

- Responsible for helping to close the civil-military gap in our organization
- Work with learning professionals to develop and manage the curricula associated with veteran-related programs
- Review all materials provided to veteran recruits and new hires to ensure mutual understanding, including interview questions
- Provide tools and training to veteran recruits on résumé preparation and terminology translation
- Facilitate the training of employees that interact with veteran recruits and new hires, including all recruiters, interviewers, onboarding personnel, and first-line managers
- Train additional facilitators as the program scales; coordinate their participation in veteran-related programs
- Conduct all new veteran hire onboarding sessions
- Participate in strategic planning concerning program development
- Monitor the execution of veteran-related programs and incorporate continuous improvement feedback from each
- Act as a resource for career counselors and all civilian managers of veterans
- Identify software and technology applications that stand to improve program effectiveness and efficiency

Qualifications and Skills:

- Bachelor's degree
- 3+ years' experience in talent development in a commercial organization
- Knowledge of [name of industry] industry
- Strong attention to detail
- Able to work well on a team
- Willingness to travel
- Strong Microsoft Excel and PowerPoint skills

SAMPLE VETERAN SUPPORT PROGRAM DASHBOARD

Overall Summary:

Lifecycle Component	Year to Date	Year-over-Year Trend	Status	Summary Highlights
Identify	# Identified			• A • B • C
Recruit	% Screened			• A • B • C
Interview	% Interviewed			• A • B • C
Hire	% Accepted			• A • B • C
Onboard / Train	% Mentor Assigned			• A • B • C
Deploy / Develop	% Reviews Completed			• A • B • C
Retain / Separate	% First-Year Retention			• A • B • C

Measure	Year to Date	Year-over-Year Trend
Productivity		
Revenue		
Margin		
Etc.		

As of: [DATE]

Legend: ○ On Track   ◐ Behind Plan   ● Off Track

Identify and Recruit Status

Source / Location	Annual # Identified	Year-over-Year Trend	% Interviewed	Year-over-Year Trend	% Hired	Year-over-Year Trend	Status	Summary Highlights	Upcoming Activity	Risks / Issues to Be Addressed
1								A B C • • •		
2								A B C • • •		
3								A B C • • •		
4								A B C • • •		
5								A B C • • •		
Etc.								A B C • • •		
TOTAL								A B C • • •		

Legend: ◯ On Track   ◯ Behind Plan   ● Off Track

Interview and Hire Status

Measure	KPI	Y-O-Y Trend	Status	Summary Highlights	Upcoming Activity	Risks / Issues to Be Addressed
# to Be Trained and Interviewed				• A • B • C		
% Pass Screening Interview				• A • B • C		
% Pass Formal Interview				• A • B • C		
% Pass Informal Interview				• A • B • C		
# Offers Made				• A • B • C		
# Offers Accepted				• A • B • C		
% Accept				• A • B • C		
Feedback: Why Accept or Decline	• A • B • C					

Legend: ◯ On Track   ◔ Behind Plan   ● Off Track   *As of: [DATE]*

Onboard and Train Status

Measure	KPI	Y-O-Y Trend	Status	Summary Highlights	Upcoming Activity	Risks / Issues to Be Addressed
% Assigned Vet Buddy				• A • B • C		
% Assigned Mentor				• A • B • C		
% Members of Affinity Group				• A • B • C		
% Complete Training 1, 2, 3, etc. within first month				• A • B • C		
% Civilian Managers Trained						
Etc.				• A • B • C		

Feedback:
• A
• B
• C

How Improve Training

Legend: ○ On Track ◐ Behind Plan ● Off Track

As of: [DATE]

Deploy/Develop Status

Measure	KPI	Y-O-Y Trend	Status	Summary Highlights	Upcoming Activity	Risks / Issues to Be Addressed
% Annual Goals Completed				• A • B • C		
% Quarterly Feedback Completed				• A • B • C		
% Biannual Reviews Completed				• A • B • C		
% Annual Reviews Completed				• A • B • C		
Etc.				• A • B • C		
Feedback: Performance Trends	• A • B • C					

Legend: ○ On Track ◐ Behind Plan ● Off Track   *As of: [DATE]*

Retain / Separate Status

Measure	KPI	Y-O-Y Trend	Status	Summary Highlights	Upcoming Activity	Risks / Issues to Be Addressed
% in Guard or Reserve			N/A	• A • B • C		
# Deployed			N/A	• A • B • C		
% Retained First Year				• A • B • C		
% Retained Second Year				• A • B • C		
% Exit Interviews Completed				• A • B • C		
Etc.				• A • B • C		
Feedback: Why Leave Organization	• A • B • C					

Legend: ○ On Track ◐ Behind Plan ● Off Track

As of: [DATE]

APPENDIX D

CONSIDERATIONS FOR DISABLED VETERANS

America's employers have an essential role in ensuring the success of disabled veterans in the workplace. Often, a few simple workplace adaptations are all that is necessary for an employer to benefit from a dedicated, skilled employee who has sacrificed in service to our nation. Strangely enough, the US government doesn't define disabled veterans. They use "Wounded, Ill, and/or Injured." According to the US Department of Veterans Affairs:

- Wounded generally means any injury inflicted by an external force during combat. Combat wounded are a subset of all injured individuals.

- Ill means any disease process that changes an individual from healthy to not healthy.

- Injury means any skin, tissue, or organ damage inflicted by an external force.[1]

However, Carnegie Mellon University has produced some workable definitions for application in the workplace:

- Individual with a Disability

  ◇ A person who has a physical or mental impairment which substantially limits one or more of such person's major life activities;

  ◇ A person who has a record of such an impairment; or

  ◇ A person who is regarded as having such an impairment.

- Disabled Veteran

  - A veteran of the US military, ground, naval, or air service who is entitled to compensation (or who but for the receipt of military retired pay would be entitled to compensation) under laws administered by the Secretary of Veterans Affairs, or

  - A person who was discharged or released from active duty because of a service-connected disability.

- Special Disabled Veteran

  - A veteran entitled to compensation (or who but for the receipt of military retired pay would be entitled to compensation) under the laws administered by the Department of Veterans Affairs for disability who is rated at 30 percent or more or who is rated at 10 or 20 percent in the case of a veteran who has been determined under Section 3106 of Title 38, US Code to have a serious employment handicap, or

  - A person who was discharged or released from active duty because of a service-connected disability."[2]

Pejoratively, you might call members of this group "wounded warriors," "disabled veterans," or "recovering warriors." Whatever the definition, there are more of these individuals in our talent pools today. With Iraq and Afghanistan, the longest war efforts on record and during a time when advancements in medical treatment have saved many more combatants who would have perished in past conflicts, we thankfully have many more of these talented individuals returning home. There are more than you may think. According to the Bureau of Labor Statistics, 25 percent of veterans have a service-connected disability.[3] Moreover, few of their injuries are visible. Some of the most common physical impairments for which veterans receive disability benefits include:

Arthritis	Head injury	Radiculopathy
Asthma	Heart disease	Rheumatoid arthritis
Back arthritis	Hypertension	Sleep apnea
Back pain	Joint disorder	Sleep disorder
Bronchitis	Knee pain/injuries	Spinal fusion
Cancer	Migraine headaches	Spine disorder
Chronic fatigue syndrome	Military sexual trauma	Thyroid disorder
COPD	Neck arthritis	Tinnitus/hearing loss
Diabetes	Neck pain	Traumatic brain injury
Fibromyalgia	Prostate cancer	Varicose veins

Some of the most common mental impairments for which veterans receive disability benefits include:

◆ Anxiety	◆ Panic Disorder
◆ Bipolar disorder	◆ PTSD
◆ Depression	◆ Schizoaffective disorder
◆ Major depressive disorder	◆ Schizophrenia[4]

So, how many of those would you be able to recognize by simply viewing someone's physical presence? Hardly any is the likely answer. Visible or not, the unemployment rate of disabled veterans is almost 50 percent higher than those without a disability.[5]

To turn this tide and to further optimize the productivity that you can extract from the veteran talent pool, consider the following in hiring these heroes:

◆ Educate yourself and your fellow employees on who disabled veterans are and how you can help them.

  ◇ Read the portions of Chapter 2 that refer to the Uniformed Services Employment and Reemployment Rights Act (USERRA) and the Americans with Disabilities Act (ADA). A few points of note:

    ◆ Under the ADA, a person has a disability if they have a physical or mental impairment that substantially limits one or more major life activities, a record of such an impairment, or is regarded as having such an impairment. And so . . .

    ◆ The ADA does not automatically protect veterans with service-connected disabilities. The veteran must meet ADA's above definition.

    ◆ The earlier lists of physical and mental impairments may or may not qualify as disabilities under the ADA.

  ◇ Understand reporting requirements. As noted in Chapter 2, federal contractors must regularly report on hiring benchmarks to comply with the Vietnam Era Veterans' Readjustment Assistance Act (VEVRAA).[6]

◇ Understand the nature of—and myths surrounding—PTS and TBI.

 ◆ According to DAV:

Post-traumatic stress disorder, or PTSD, is an anxiety disorder that can develop after exposure to a traumatic event or ordeal in which a person thinks that his or her life or others' lives are in danger. PTSD can be diagnosed in anyone who has trouble coping with or recovering from a trauma. Some traumatic events that may trigger PTSD include violent personal assaults (physical, sexual, child abuse), witnessing death or injury, natural or human-caused disasters, accidents, and military combat. In fact, 60 percent of all men and half of all women will likely experience at least one trauma during their lives. Not every traumatized person develops ongoing or even short-term PTSD—and not everyone with PTSD has been through a dangerous event.[7]

 ◆ Also, from DAV:

Traumatic brain injury, or TBI, occurs in both civilian and military populations. In fact, TBI in the civilian population is eight times as frequent as breast cancer, AIDS, spinal cord injury, and multiple sclerosis combined. According to the Center for Deployment Psychology, an estimated 10 to 20 percent of all service members who served in Iraq and Afghanistan sustained a TBI, with most being mild (sometimes referred to as concussions).[8]

 ◆ Both conditions are treatable. Symptoms will wane with treatment and time, regardless of the source of the condition.

 ◆ Unfortunately, many media outlets have covered this topic in a way that leaves many with a stereotype that most Iraq- and Afghanistan-era veterans suffer from PTSD or TBI. As noted in Appendix H, veterans comprise a tiny percentage of your employee population that suffer from this impairment. And those who do can make very effective employees with minimal accommodations.

◇ The Employer Assistance and Resources Network for Disability Inclusion (EARN) offers answers to a thorough list of frequently asked questions.[9] For example, hiring members of this group does not increase your insurance rates and may improve your safety rating. Furthermore, the same tax incentives described in Chapter 2 apply here.

♦ Seek out disabled veterans. Chapter 6 lists many avenues for identifying qualified candidates in this talent pool. Consider emphasizing these during October to support National Disability Employment Awareness Month.

♦ Apprenticeship opportunities. If you are hesitant to hire disabled veterans full-time, you might consider internship or apprenticeship opportunities. Doing so could represent your "try before you buy" option. As noted in Chapter 6, there are many options for this approach in the federal and civilian marketplaces. And as mentioned in Chapter 2, several federal programs exist to incentivize and support your efforts:

◇ VA Veteran Readiness and Employment (VR&E) program

◇ Special Employer Incentives (SEI) program

◇ The Department of Labor's CareerOneStop Business Center

♦ When hiring, try to get disabled veterans to self-identify as such for affirmative action purposes. The US Equal Employment Opportunity Commission provides enforcement guidance of the Americans with Disabilities Act for disability-related inquiries.[10] And the Code of Federal Regulations provides a Sample Invitation to Self-Identify for federal contractors who are considered covered entities under VEVRAA.[11]

♦ Understand accommodation requirements and their impact.

◇ Title I of ADA requires employers to provide reasonable accommodation to qualified individuals with disabilities who are employees or applicants for employment unless to do so would cause undue hardship. There are three categories of "reasonable accommodations":

- Modifications or adjustments to a job application process that enable a qualified applicant with a disability to be considered for the position such qualified applicant desires; or

- Modifications or adjustments to the work environment, or to the manner or circumstances under which the position held or desired is customarily performed, that enable a qualified individual with a disability to perform the essential functions of that position; or

- Modifications or adjustments that enable a covered entity's employee with a disability to enjoy benefits and privileges of employment equal to those enjoyed by its other similarly situated employees without disabilities.[12]

◇ However, accommodations need not be expensive or burdensome to have a high impact. The Job Accommodation Network (JAN) documents that

---

the benefits employers receive from making workplace accommodations far outweigh the associated costs. Employers reported providing accommodations that resulted in such benefits as retaining valuable employees, improving productivity and morale, reducing workers' compensation and training costs, and improving company diversity. The employers . . . reported a high percentage (58%) of accommodations cost absolutely nothing to make ($0), while the rest of the accommodations made had a typical cost of only $500.[13]

See below for some examples.

Sample Accommodations

- Flexible work schedules
- Uninterrupted work time
- Written job instructions with clear expectations

- ◆ Increased natural lighting
- ◆ Desk organizers
- ◆ Schedulers
- ◆ White noise machines
- ◆ Screen readers
- ◆ Voice recognition systems

- ◆ As part of onboarding disabled veterans:

  - ◇ Include information and resources that are specific to their needs.

  - ◇ Assign veteran mentors, initially others with disabilities for orientation purposes, but quickly normalize them into the rest of the employee population.

  - ◇ Alert HR and EAP of best practices in employing and retaining disabled veterans.

  - ◇ Consider how you configure workstations. Some considerations may be necessary. Check to see how a veteran's new surroundings work for them within their first week.[14]

- ◆ Once you have onboarded disabled veterans, be prepared to support them. Understand what resources are available. There are many:

  - ◇ The DAV provides a guide to hiring and retaining veterans with disabilities called *The Veteran Advantage*.[15]

  - ◇ The Department of Defense offers a handy compensation and benefits handbook for this talent pool.[16]

  - ◇ The Job Accommodation Network (JAN) is a free source for guidance on workplace accommodations and disability employment issues provided by the US Department of Labor's Office of Disability Employment Policy (ODEP).[17] They offer consultants to help with individual cases and offer two programs you should investigate: the Employer Assistance and Resource Network on Disability Inclusion (EARN) and the Partnership on Employment & Accessible Technology (PEAT). Among JAN's many offerings, there are two guides of note:

- The Employers' Practical Guide to Reasonable Accommodation Under the Americans with Disabilities Act.

- The Employees' Practical Guide to Negotiating and Requesting Reasonable Accommodations under the Americans with Disabilities Act (ADA).

◇ The Web Accessibility Initiative offers evaluation tools, resources for inclusive designs, principles of website accessibility, and other resources to enable website content to meet accessibility guidelines and standards.[18]

◇ Another good resource is the National Resource Directory, a searchable database of resources vetted for the use of service members, veterans, family members, and caregivers.[19]

◇ The US Equal Employment Opportunity Commission offers "Veterans and the Americans with Disabilities Act (ADA): A Guide for Employers."[20]

◇ The Wounded Warrior Project provides a series of fact sheets that employers will find helpful.[21]

◇ For federal agencies, the Office of Personnel Management offers guidance on disability employment and reasonable accommodations.[22]

◇ For those suffering from PTSD or TBI, consider Make the Connection and the Veterans Crisis Line.[23] The VA's National Center for PTSD is another good resource for further education.

- Periodically solicit feedback from disabled veteran hires and their managers and act on it.

REGISTERED APPRENTICESHIP PROGRAMS, VETERANS, AND THE GI BILL

An apprenticeship program enables planned, day-to-day training on the job and experience under proper supervision, combined with related technical instruction. Participants are workforce members working a regular workweek and sign an agreement that stipulates the skills they are to learn and the hours and wages for each training period. Upon its conclusion, they receive certificates representing their qualification to work within the field.[1]

Apprenticeships are proven vehicles for helping veterans transition into a new industry or profession. They vary from organization to organization and from industry to industry. However, for a program to be considered a Registered Apprenticeship Program (RAP), it must meet specific federally approved standards mandated by the US Department of Labor's (DoL) Employment and Training Administration (ETA).[2] The registration takes place through regional and state Offices of Apprenticeship (OA) or State Apprenticeship Agencies (SAA) approved by OA.[3] Advantages of registering a program include:

- ◆ State-based tax credits related to apprenticeship programs.[4]

- ◆ Resources from federal programs to help reduce costs and support your apprentices.[5]

- ◆ Access to a nationwide network of expertise and support at no cost.

If you have a registered apprenticeship program, you may be able to qualify the program as "Approved for GI Bill," which means that eligible veterans in your program can receive Post-9/11 GI Bill education benefits in addition to their apprenticeship wages.[6,7] Specifically, they would receive:

- A monthly housing allowance (MHA) at an E-5 rate with dependents (and based on the geographic location of the employer) prorated as follows:

  ◇ 100% of the applicable MHA in the first six months of training.

  ◇ 80% of the applicable MHA in the second six months of training.

  ◇ 60% of the applicable MHA in the third six months of training.

  ◇ 40% of the applicable MHA in the fourth six months of training.

  ◇ 20% of the applicable MHA in the remainder of the training.[8]

- A monthly stipend for books and supplies, prorated by the veteran's eligibility percentage.

- A one-time rural benefit payment, as applicable.

To ensure the veterans in your registered apprenticeship program receive these benefits, you will need to complete and send the following information to your SAA (the SAA can typically authorize programs within thirty days):

- Employer's Application to Provide Job Training (VA Form 22-8865)[9]

- Designation of a Certifying Official(s) (VA Form 22-8794)[10]

- Proof of having met the Registered Apprenticeship Program (RAP) Standards[11]

Upon SAA approval, participating veterans will then need to secure individual approval from the VA to receive their GI Bill benefits. While participation is entirely voluntary for your organization, while there is no charge for the service, and while it is ultimately the veteran's decision on whether and how to use their GI Bill benefits, additional advantages accrue to your organization for doing so:

- Earning the reputation as a veteran-friendly organization

- Helping your veteran program participants earn the benefits to which they are entitled

- Reinforcing and further enabling the marketing materials of your organization's veteran hiring program in meeting its recruitment goals

- Having the ability to advertise your program's eligibility in your internal and external veteran apprentice recruitment efforts

Veterans with a service-connected disability may also be eligible for custom apprenticeship programs approved by a VA Veteran Readiness and Employment (VR&E) counselor. The US Department of Veterans Affairs, through its Veteran Readiness and Employment (VR&E) program, incentivizes the hiring of these veterans in several ways:[12]

- **Salary subsidies.** Through its on-the-job training program, VR&E subsidizes veterans' salaries so that employers pay an apprentice-level wage while training veterans. As the veteran progresses, the employer pays a larger portion of the veteran's salary until they complete the training program, after which the employer pays the full salary.

- **Assistive technology.** VR&E may provide specialized tools, equipment, and workplace modifications to eligible veterans, allowing them to perform their duties without cost to the employer.

- **Salary reimbursement.** Through the Special Employer Incentive program, employers may receive an incentive to hire veterans facing extraordinary obstacles to employment, which includes reimbursement of as much as 50 percent of the veteran's salary for up to six months.

- **Federal tax credit.** Please see Chapter 2 for details on the Work Opportunity Tax Credit.

- **Nonpaid work experience training.** This program allows local, state, and federal government offices to temporarily employ a veteran without having the position count against the agency's full-time equivalent allocation. VR&E pays the veteran a monthly subsistence allowance while they learn valuable work-related skills and experience.

For more information on this topic, please see:

- Apprenticeship.gov, which allows you to post apprenticeship job openings.[13]

- American Job Centers, which can help identify available qualified veterans looking for job opportunities.[14]

- Regional veteran collaboratives (see Chapter 6), which can also help identify available qualified veterans.

- Other organizations with Registered Apprenticeship Programs by state.[15]

PERSONA MATRIX: PERTINENT FACTS AND SUMMARY RESPONSIBILITIES

Chapter	Persona / Role					
	CXO Sponsor	Human Resources	Hiring Manager / Recruiting	Veteran Program Manager	Veteran Talent Translator	Veteran Affinity Group
Introduction: Opportunity by Another Name	• Inclusive organizations realize 22% *increase in productivity* • Veteran presence among corporate leaders is at an all-time low (2.6%) and shrinking	• 90% of HR managers say vets promoted *faster* • 75% say vets *easier* to manage • 68% say vets perform *better* than peers	• 98% of vets have HS education level or higher • Vets are 160% more likely to have graduate or other advanced degree • Vets are 30% more likely to be *underemployed*	• 80% of organizations do *not* have veteran-specific recruiting programs • 71% do *not* provide training to hiring managers • 52% do *not* provide onboarding support		
1: Understand the Veteran and Military Culture	• Top-down support is critical • Talk the talk—and walk the talk • Provide needed resources	• Cultural fit correlates with higher job performance levels • 50-90% of job satisfaction correlates to culture fit • Understand cultural differences and make those known to veteran applicants • Train employees on those same cultural differences				
2: Understand Governing Regulations	Encourage: • Compliance with all regulatory obligations • Participation in incentive and reward programs	• Understand all pertinent regulatory obligations • Take advantage of all applicable incentive programs • Ensure best intentions in utilizing veterans in program participation		Support: • Compliance with all regulatory obligations • Participation in all applicable incentive and reward programs		
		Where appropriate, maintain a security clearance				

Chapter	CXO Sponsor	Human Resources	Hiring Manager / Recruiting	Veteran Program Manager	Veteran Talent Translator	Veteran Affinity Group
			Persona / Role			
3: Organize and Staff a Veteran Support Program	• Robust DEI efforts include a veteran component • Ensure enabling infrastructure is in place • Link program's purpose to organizational values	• Ensure program linked to organization's DEI efforts • Select a veteran to lead the program • Ensure program tracks and reports progress to CXO sponsor	• Support selection of appropriate talent to lead and support the program	• Track & report on program metrics • Identify needed program staffing and support • Hire & train support program staff • Define program scope	• Act as a talent development resource for veterans and those that work with them, especially career counselors and all supervisors of veterans	Support: • Staffing of veteran support program • Tracking and reporting on program metrics • Identification of needed program staffing & support
			More than 80% of companies lack training to help civilian employees relate to veterans			
4: Create Support Program Content	• Advocate for the involvement of veteran affinity group in program creation and administration • Oversee selection of potential supporting third parties	• First, organize a veteran affinity group • Leverage that group to create and administer program content • Encourage training of civilian employees on that same content	• Support the creation of a veteran affinity group and selection of its leaders • Help vet potential supporting third parties	• Create & administer program content with support from affinity group • Train civilian employees on that same content • Establish program community-building and recruiting goals • Identify needed third party entities	• Develop & manage program curricula • Maintain a library of veteran-related educational materials • Produce translated job descriptions for veteran candidates • Train program personnel	Support: • Creation and administration of program content • Program community-building and recruiting goals • Collaboration with supporting third party entities
5: Set Expectations – Internally & Externally	• Advocate for military-friendly goals • Champion program with internal and external stakeholders	• Define specific military-friendly goals • Identify program stakeholders • Establish communication plan to influence relevant stakeholders • Establish selection criteria for veteran applicants; transparently share the same with them		• Engage with stakeholders to solicit program support • Maintain ESGR statement of support	• Train veteran candidates on résumé prep and terminology translation • Translate veteran résumés for internal consumption	Support: • Military-friendly goals • Stakeholder analysis • Communication plan execution • Sharing selection criteria with veteran applicants

Chapter	Persona / Role					
	CXO Sponsor	Human Resources	Hiring Manager / Recruiting	Veteran Program Manager	Veteran Talent Translator	Veteran Affinity Group
6: Identify and Recruit Candidates	• Help prioritize applicable sources of veteran talent • Provide guidance for updating outreach platforms	Monitor veteran program manager efforts to: • Prioritize applicable sources of veteran talent • Allocate recruiting resources to most productive sources • Update outreach platforms	• Translate role descriptions with help from veteran affinity group • Ensure recruiting processes resonate with veteran applicants • Encourage self-identification; update application forms to enable	• Prioritize applicable sources of veteran talent • Allocate recruiting resources to most productive sources • Update outreach platforms	• Maintain a database of potential veteran hires • Support the update of outreach platforms	Support program recruiting efforts: • Help identify priority sources of veteran talent • Help translate role descriptions • Participate in outreach activities • Help gain access to military installations
7: Interview Candidates and Initiate Offers	Champion: • Transparency • A competency-based behavioral interviewing (CBBI) approach • Support throughout the entire hiring lifecycle	• Ensure a CBBI approach with veterans • Consider pre-employment assessment to ensure cultural fit • Monitor veteran program manager efforts	• Train on how to interview veterans • Use standard interviewing forms that leverage a CBBI approach • Use ice-breakers and be transparent • Provide tools that enable compensation package comparison and take emotion out of the job offer decision	• Train hiring managers on CBBI approach • Ensure standard CBBI interview forms • Ensure job offers detail components of compensation package on a comparative basis • Develop tools that help veterans take emotion out of job offer decisions	• Facilitate training of hiring managers on CBBI approach • Produce standard CBBI interview forms • Help prepare veterans for interviews • Participate in interviews of veteran candidates • Maintain materials that support veteran decision-making process	• Participate in interviews with veterans • Support training of hiring managers • Support creation of CBBI interview questions • Help enable compensation package comparisons • Support veteran applicants in their decision-making process

Chapter	Persona / Role				
	CXO Sponsor	Human Resources	Veteran Program Manager	Veteran Talent Translator	Veteran Affinity Group
8: Onboard, Train and Retain Veteran Hires	• 52% of organizations do not provide onboarding support to veteran employees • More than 50% of new veteran hires leave their jobs within the first year. Why? ○ Lack of career development, lack of meaningful work, inadequate professional development				
	• Ensure appropriate investments in onboarding and career development of veteran hires • Monitor program performance metrics and act on feedback to continuously improve the program • Champion transparency in policies and culture	• Provide effective support for members of the Guard and Reserve • Support the hiring of military spouses • Administer an in-house "one-stop" support center for veteran hires • Monitor veteran program manager efforts	• Ensure a sequential assimilation approach, first leveraging peers and trained organizational leaders • Ensure new hires have an assigned mentor, a peer sponsor, and receive regular and substantive feedback • Administer onboarding training for new veteran hires and the training of supervisors of newly hired veterans • Leverage outside resources to supplement onboarding and training activities • Encourage rotational assignments for newly hired veterans • Structure effective support for Guard and Reserve employees • Champion hiring of military spouses	• Facilitate onboarding sessions for new veteran hires • Facilitate training of supervisors of new veteran hires • Train additional facilitators as the program scales • Improve means by which veterans may self-identify • Orchestrate mentor and peers sponsor programs • Oversee any rotational assignment programs	• Participate in onboarding training • Participate in training of supervisors of new veteran hires • Support Guard and Reserve members and their families – especially during deployments • Encourage hiring of military spouses
9: Validate Assimilation, Measure Success, and Share Lessons Learned	• Engage with the community of organizations sharing lessons learned on their veteran support programs • Incorporating an experienced external advisor can help enable program success	• Monitor veteran program manager effort • Use outplacement as an opportunity to build a bridge with veteran talent	• Track and report on program progress • Validate cultural assimilation of veteran hires; aim for two-year retention • Apply for all available military initiative recognition programs and tax incentives • Solicit and incorporate feedback from all stakeholder groups to continuously improve the veteran support program	• Monitor program execution • Incorporate continuous improvement feedback • Vet any software programs or apps that improve program effectiveness or efficiency	• Support efforts to document and share lessons learned from program formation and execution • Test and help implement any technologies that stand to improve program effectiveness or efficiency

SUCCESS CHECKLIST

Introduction: Opportunity by Another Name

Do you accept that:

- ☐ Your ability to effectively engage and attract veterans and military spouses as a talent pool represents an organizational productivity opportunity and potential competitive advantage?

- ☐ To successfully hire veterans and military spouses, your organization must enhance some of its existing processes and educate its employee base?

- ☐ When you design hiring programs for inclusion, you design your organization for the betterment of all?

- ☐ Veterans are not a "broken" talent pool; they are a misunderstood and underutilized talent pool?

- ☐ Veterans will need more support than a typical new hire—throughout their transition as they acclimate and develop with mentorship?

Chapter 1: Understand the Veteran and Military Culture

- ☐ Why have you decided to support the hiring of veterans and military spouses?

- ☐ Are the senior leaders in your organization directly supporting your efforts?

☐ Are you prepared to provide the support that transitioning service members need throughout the hiring process to ensure their success?

☐ Have you defined the cultural differences between the military and your organization?

☐ Are those differences addressed throughout the entirety of your veteran support program?

Chapter 2: Understand Governing Regulations

☐ Do you understand the regulatory obligations of your organization, given the expected scope of your veteran support program?

☐ Have you identified all veteran and military spouse hiring support and incentive programs available at the federal, state, and local levels?

    ☐ Have you decided which of those you will leverage?

Chapter 3: Organize and Staff a Veteran Support Program

☐ What is the scope of your veteran support program?

    ☐ Is it directly linked to your organization's values?

☐ Is your program a component of the broader organization's diversity and inclusion efforts?

☐ Is your veteran support program leader a tenured member of your organization who previously served in the military?

☐ Is that leader accountable to an executive-level individual in your organization?

☐ Did you establish metrics for the program and create a dashboard to document program outcomes?

    ☐ How frequently will the program leader report on those metrics?

    ☐ Are performance trends documented and addressed?

☐ Is the program's enabling infrastructure in place (to include all needed support staff)?

- [ ] If applicable, have you applied for support from your organization's philanthropic foundation?

Chapter 4: Create Support Program Content

- [ ] Did you first enable a veteran affinity group? Did you use them to create your program content?

- [ ] Have you created onboarding materials unique to incoming veteran and military spouse hires?

- [ ] How have you decided to integrate incoming veterans with the balance of the employee population upon their hire?

- [ ] Have you considered utilizing third parties in composing and executing program content?

- [ ] Have all managers of incoming veterans been trained on their nature and that of the military?

  - [ ] What resources have you provided them to enable this new responsibility?

Chapter 5: Set Expectations—Internally and Externally

- [ ] Have you identified all internal and external stakeholders of your program?

- [ ] Have you defined how your organization can be veteran-friendly?

  - [ ] What is your plan for making it so?

- [ ] How will you influence internal and external stakeholders to support your program?

  - [ ] Did you conduct a stakeholder analysis before updating your recruiting and marketing materials?

  - [ ] How will you update your recruiting and marketing materials?

  - [ ] What is your communications plan for engaging with all of these audiences?

- ☐ Given the scope of your program, what are the criteria for admitting veteran and veteran-related applicants?
- ☐ Where and how have you shared this with them?

Chapter 6: Identify and Recruit Candidates

- ☐ Have you taken advantage of all relevant veteran and military spouse talent sources?
- ☐ Have you allocated recruiting resources to the most productive sources of veteran talent?
- ☐ Have you translated role descriptions into language that veterans understand?
  - ☐ Did you use your in-house veteran talent in doing so?
- ☐ Have you used all of the above to update the venues and processes to connect with potential veteran applicants?
- ☐ Are you prepared to educate applicants on overcoming the typical challenges associated with Applicant Tracking Systems (ATS)?

Chapter 7: Interview Candidates and Initiate Offers

- ☐ Do members of your veteran program participate in interviews of all veteran applicants?
- ☐ Are all interviewers trained in conducting interviews with veterans and military spouses?
  - ☐ Do they understand what questions to—and not to—ask?
  - ☐ Do they utilize a competency-based behavioral interviewing approach?
  - ☐ Do they use standard interview forms that reflect that approach?
  - ☐ What do interviewers do to make the veteran feel comfortable?
- ☐ Do veteran applicants understand the components of your compensation package vis-à-vis their military compensation package (or perhaps those of a competing offer)?

- [ ] Do prospective veteran hires have a clear understanding of your organization's culture?

  - [ ] Have you considered psychometric testing to ensure compatibility?

- [ ] What support have you provided veterans and military spouses to help them decide on your offer?

Chapter 8: Onboard, Train, and Retain New Veteran Hires

- [ ] What onboarding and career development resources exist to support veteran and military spouse hires?

  - [ ] Have a mentor and peer sponsor been assigned?

  - [ ] Have all veteran hires been asked to join the veteran affinity group?

  - [ ] Is there an in-house "one-stop" support center available?

  - [ ] Are veteran hires deployed in accordance with their skill sets and career aspirations?

  - [ ] Have you emplaced a regular schedule for substantive feedback?

- [ ] Have you trained your non veteran employees on the nature of veterans and military culture?

  - [ ] Have you taken advantage of all available federal resources and nonprofit programs?

- [ ] Have you considered rotational programs as a means to assimilate new veteran hires?

- [ ] Are you tracking veteran performance and retention and acting on those report outcomes?

- [ ] Have you capitalized on the employment opportunity that military spouses represent?

- [ ] Are you fully supporting the ongoing service of Guard and Reserve employees?

Chapter 9: Validate Assimilation, Measure Success, and Share Lessons Learned

- ☐ Have you validated the cultural assimilation of new veteran hires over at least two years?

- ☐ Are you using cultural assessments to augment your mentoring approach with veterans and military spouses?

- ☐ Are you tracking and regularly reporting on program progress to ensure executive-level engagement?

- ☐ Have you solicited feedback from internal and external stakeholders to continuously improve your program?

- ☐ Have you defined an outplacement approach that builds a bridge with a departing or displaced veteran or military spouse?

- ☐ Have you applied to all applicable military initiative recognition programs?

- ☐ Have you applied for all tax incentives for which you are eligible?

- ☐ Have you shared your program's lessons learned with other veteran support program leaders?

- ☐ Have you considered incorporating an experienced, external advisor to support and enable the success of your program?

Overall

- ☐ Have you taken advantage of my website (*www.matthewjlouis.com*) and all its available materials and additional resources?

DISPELLING VETERAN MYTHS

Many myths surround today's veterans, perpetuated by stereotypes presented in news stories, movies, and television. These unchecked portrayals make it difficult to separate fact from fiction. So, let's get some things straight.

Myth: Veterans are disproportionately affected by post-traumatic stress disorder (PTSD).

Fact: You likely have many more civilians in your organization who have PTSD than veterans. Let's first define what PTSD is. The National Center for PTSD defines it as "a mental health problem that some people develop after experiencing or witnessing a life-threatening event, like combat, a natural disaster, a car accident, or sexual assault."[1] Those triggers apply to most people. The Department of Veterans Affairs tells us that between 11 and 20 percent of post-9/11 veterans experience PTSD.[2] The VA also tells us that between 7 and 8 percent of the adult US population will experience PTSD at some point in their lives.[3] Now, let's apply those percentages to your workforce. Let's assume your workforce consists of one thousand people. Let's further assume that your workforce reflects the national average of 6 percent of veterans in the labor pool. That would mean you have sixty (6% of 1,000) veterans in your organization and about twelve (20% of 60) with PTSD. That would also mean that of the remaining 940 (1,000 minus 60) civilians, about sixty-six (7% of 940) have PTSD. Think about that. Even after applying conservative ends of the applicable percentage ranges, you would have *more than five times the number of civilians with PTSD as veterans.*

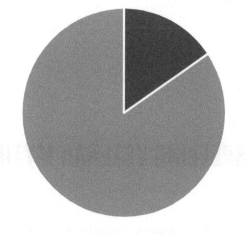

■ Veterans with PTSD in Workforce   ■ Civilians with PTSD in Workforce

Figure H-1. PTSD Population in a Notional 1000 Employee Organization

Myth: Most veterans have served in combat roles and may have killed people.

Fact: An overwhelming majority of transitioning veterans have not served in combat roles and have served in roles whose skill sets directly translate to the civilian world. As demonstrated in Chapter 1, the Bureau of Labor Statistics tells us that 15 percent of military specialties are combat-related.[4] Thus, even though *all* transitioning veterans have immediately accretive soft skills (as detailed in the Introduction), 85 percent work in active-duty roles whose skill sets directly translate to positions in your organization. Moreover, killing someone does not indicate that a veteran is maladjusted or dangerous. It is a reality of war and should not be a factor when hiring a veteran.

Myth: Most veterans that have served in combat roles suffer from traumatic brain injuries (TBI) and are permanently damaged.

Fact: As with PTSD, the incidence of TBI is much higher in the civilian population than in the military. However, what is different is that the severity of TBI related to combat injury tends to be higher and takes longer to remedy. As before, let's start with a definition. The National Center for PTSD says that TBI "occurs from a sudden blow or jolt to the head. Brain injury often occurs during some type of trauma, such as an accident, blast, or a fall."[5] When you think about it, things like concussions apply to a large portion of the population.

The Centers for Disease Control and Prevention says that a typical year sees 2.8 million TBI-related emergency department visits, hospitalizations, or deaths in the United States.[6] Eighty percent of those instances involve mild TBI, and "most people who have [mild TBI] will be back to normal by three months without any special treatment."[7] In the military, the Theater Medical Data Store of the Defense Medical Surveillance System indicates that more than 83 percent of all Department of Defense TBI instances in a typical year are mild.[8] Moreover, the Department of Defense and the Defense and Veteran's Brain Injury Center estimate that *only 22 percent of all combat wounds suffered in Iraq and Afghanistan were brain injuries*.[9] The Congressional Research Service found that over a fifteen-year period from 2000 to 2015, there was an annual average of 21,820 TBI-related injuries in the military.[10] That's *less than 1 percent of the occurrence in the civilian population*, and during the most intense fighting in Iraq and Afghanistan—so again, a conservative estimate. The VA reports the main causes of combat-related TBI are blasts, motor vehicle accidents, and gunshot wounds; because of that, symptoms may last eighteen to twenty-four months. "TBI symptoms are likely to last only a limited time. With proper treatment and healthy behaviors, they are likely to improve."[11]

Myth: Most veterans require disability accommodations, most of which are costly.

Fact: Most veterans do not require disability accommodations, 58 percent of which cost nothing. As the Department of Labor's Job Accommodation Network (JAN) details, of the 2,744 employers surveyed:

Most employers report no cost or low cost for accommodating employees with disabilities. Of the 776 employers [only 28% of the total surveyed] who could provide cost information related to accommodations they had provided, 453 (58%) said the accommodations needed by their employees cost absolutely nothing. Another 289 (37%) experienced a one-time cost. Only 25 (3%) said the accommodation resulted in an ongoing, annual cost to the company, and 9 (1%) said the accommodation required a combination of one-time and annual costs. Of those accommodations that did have a one-time cost, the median one-time expenditure as reported by the employer was $500. When asked how much they paid for an accommodation beyond what they would have paid for an employee without a disability in the same position, the median answer given by employers was $100.[12]

Myth: Veteran behavioral health challenges are specific to post–9/11 veterans.

Fact: Today's veterans are no more vulnerable to behavioral health challenges than previous generations and have access to better diagnostic and treatment resources.

Behavioral Health Challenge	Veteran Era		
	Vietnam	Gulf War I	Gulf War II (Post–9/11)
PTSD	15%	12%	11–20%
TBI	22% of combat wounds	20% of combat wounds[13]	12% of combat wounds

Table H-1: Occurrence of Behavioral Health Challenges by Veteran Era[14]

Myth: The military is not diverse, or racial and ethnic minority groups are misrepresented.

Fact: The diversity of our military is a strength and continues to change. Women now make up 16 percent of our active-duty military (up from 11 percent in 1990), and racial and ethnic minority groups make up more than 31 percent of the active-duty military. See tables H-2 and H-3 for details.

Service Branch	% of Total Active Force	% of Total Enlisted	% of Senior Enlisted (E-7, E-8, E-9)	% of Total Officers (Excludes Warrant Officers)	% of General / Flag Officers
Army	15.0%	14.4%	12.0%	18.7%	6.8%
Navy	19.7%	19.7%	12.0%	19.3%	8.6%
Marine Corps	8.6%	8.7%	5.7%	7.9%	2.1%
Air Force	20.2%	19.9%	20.4%	21.1%	9.2%
All DoD	**16.5%**	**16.2%**	**13.5%**	**18.6%**	**7.6%**

Notes: Total officer calculations exclude warrant officers for purposes of comparison as they are ineligible for General/Flag rank and the Air Force does not have warrant officers. Warrant officers are included in total active duty force calculation. Total active duty force does not include cadets and midshipmen. General/Flag officers include O-7s and above.

Table H-2: Female Representation in the Active-Duty Armed Forces[15]

Rank and Grade	White	Black	Asian	American Indian/ Alaskan Native	Native Hawaiian/ Pacific Islander	Multi/ Unknown	Hispanic*
General/Flag Officer (O-7 and above)	87.5%	8.1%	1.8%	None	0.3%	2.4%	2.1%
Officer (all)	77.3%	8.1%	5.2%	10.1%	0.5%	8.2%	7.6%
Warrant Officer	69.0%	16.0%	3.1%	0.8%	0.6%	10.4%	11.6%
Senior Enlisted (E-7 and above)	63.1%	19.1%	3.8%	1.3%	1.2%	11.5%	14.3%
Enlisted (all)	67.4%	18.5%	4.3%	1.3%	1.3%	7.3%	17.5%
Total Active Duty	**69.1%**	**16.8%**	**4.4%**	**1.2%**	**1.1%**	**7.5%**	**15.8%**
US Resident Population (age 18–64)	**76.2%**	**13.7%**	**6.3%**	**1.2%**	**0.3%**	**2.2%**	**17.9%**

Notes: *Race and Hispanic origin are self-identified.*

*The concept of race is separate from the concept of Hispanic origin. Hispanic may be more than one race (e.g., Hispanic and White or Hispanic and Black). Percentages for race should not be combined with percent Hispanic.

Table H-3: Race and Ethnic Representation in the Active Component and US Population[16]

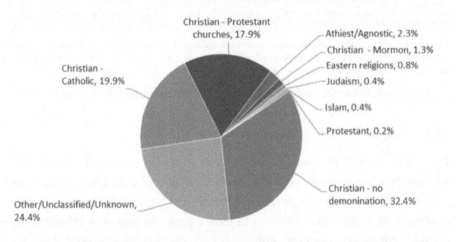

Figure H-2. Religious Diversity in the Active-Duty Force as of January 2019[17]

Myth: People who are poor or uneducated are over-represented in the military.

Fact: US soldiers are more likely to come from middle- to upper-middle-class backgrounds, as shown in Figure H-3. They may have fewer academic degrees than their college-age civilian counterparts, yet that's because people enlist in the military before going to college to take advantage of the educational opportunities provided by the GI Bill. People serve in the military for various reasons, including education, the opportunity to travel, patriotism, the opportunity to be a member of a strong team, meaningful work, and a chance to play a role in history. Service members don't appreciate being stereotyped as poor, uneducated, or desperate. These perceptions color the public's views of what veterans can do when they return home.[18]

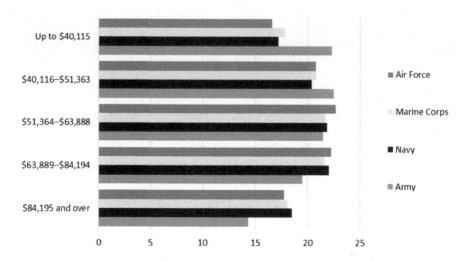

Notes: *Information applies to the census tract reported by individual accessions who report a home of record in the fifty states or the District of Columbia and who were matched to a census tract. The median census tract income ranges used in this table represent the income quintiles for all US households in the census.*

Figure H-3. Active Component Enlisted Accessions by Median Household Income[19]

Myth: Veterans are not sufficiently educated.

Fact: This stereotype couldn't be further from the truth. As noted in the Introduction, on average, veterans are more educated than their civilian peers, with 97 percent having a high school education or higher.[20] Veterans are 160 percent more likely than non veterans to have a graduate degree or other advanced degree.[21] Moreover, veterans with bachelor's degrees have almost three times more work experience than non veterans.[22]

Myth: Military families are no different from other families.

Fact: Military families have incredibly challenging jobs. Not only do they go through long separations from their loved ones, but on average, they move six to eight times during a military career. That means six to eight new homes, schools, jobs, friends, routines, and neighborhoods. Military families endure an enormous change, with moves often every two to four years.[23] The average child in a military family will move three times more frequently than in nonmilitary families.[24]

Myth: Female veterans don't have equivalent experiences to their male counterparts.

Fact: Women have been on the battlefield for as long as America has been a country. During the Revolutionary War, American Civil War, and Spanish–American War, women served as nurses, cooks, and support staff. They were officially allowed to serve in the military during the last two years of WWI, primarily as nurses, spies, and support staff. They gradually took on more duties through WWII, the Korean War, and the Vietnam War. Women began entering the nation's service academies in 1976, and during the 1990s they flew on combat missions, served on combat ships, and were deployed to the Persian Gulf. In the last two decades, women have served in more and more positions and can now serve in any combat role. Today, about two million women veterans make up 10 percent of the overall veteran population.[25] This lack of awareness is especially problematic because women veterans are two to four times as likely as their civilian counterparts to experience homelessness and make up the fastest-growing share of homeless vets.[26]

Myth: Veterans don't have the appropriate certifications, licenses, degrees, or other credentials or technical experience.

Fact: As with education, veterans bring more training and experience than you may realize. While much of the training veterans receive would qualify them for civilian-equivalent certifications in their fields, the military may not issue them. In recognition of this shortcoming, the military has recently initiated Credentialing Opportunities On-Line (COOL), a program to help veterans credentialize their military experience.[27] Furthermore, and as noted in the Introduction, transitioning veterans, regardless of rank or service, bring hands-on experience, technical training, and licenses and certifications that prepare them for the corresponding civilian certification.[28] Veterans also demonstrate many "soft skills" such as professionalism, teamwork, interpersonal and emotional intelligence, critical thinking, and the ability to solve problems, many of which were developed as a result of military service.[29] In sum, veterans have the skills that US employers need for success in the workplace.

Myth: Skills gained in the military are not transferrable to the civilian workplace.

Fact: As noted in the Introduction, veterans bring a combination of hard and soft skills gained via their experience in the military that US employers need for success in the workplace, as illustrated in Figure H-4.

Most Important Skills Cited by Employers for Workplace Success	Skills Strengthened or Enhanced by Military Service
• Professionalism / work ethic • Teamwork / collaboration • Oral and written communication • Critical thinking / problem-solving • Ethics / social responsibility	• Professionalism • Work ethic / discipline • Leadership & management skills • Mental toughness • Adaptation to different challenges

Figure H-4. Demand and Supply of Workplace Skills[30,31]

Veterans inject a significant amount of "human capital value" into any workplace. Let's define *Human Capital Value* as the combination of four factors: ability, behavior exhibited, effort applied, and time invested. (See Figure H-5.) When employees deliver a robust complement of these factors in their organizations, it generally results in a positive workplace contribution. Let's define *contribution* as the attainment of individual, team, and organizational goals. Human capital value is important to organizations because it generates high-performance results and creates a competitive advantage when aligned with corresponding employment opportunities. In today's world, human capital value is critical in enabling organizational transformation, which involves building new employee capabilities to meet the needs of constant work redesign with endless complexity. Veterans possess the human capital value to meet this talent challenge and ensure maximum contribution and high-performance results.

ABILITY

Skills
- Interpersonal
- Conceptual
- Technical

Knowledge
- Command of facts to do a job evidenced by credentials
  - Certificate
  - Badge
  - Certification
  - License
  - Diploma
  - Degree

Experience
- Learning & proficiency gained based on the length of time in a job or position.

+

BEHAVIOR EXHIBITED

Observable ways of acting that contribute to the accomplishment of a task (e.g., the way individuals behave & manifest their values, beliefs, & reactions to the world they live in).

×

EFFORT APPLIED

Conscious application of mental and physical resources toward a particular end. Applied effort goes to the heart of the work ethic. Applied effort activates skill, knowledge, & experience & harnesses behavior.

×

TIME INVESTED

The time one invests in a job and more importantly how an individual allocates that time and uses it wisely. Skill, knowledge, experience and dedication are meaningless without the investment of time in the job.

=

HUMAN CAPITAL VALUE

Contribution as measured by attainment of Individual, Team & Organization goals in the areas of :
- Productivity
- Quality
- Service
- Cost

& by attainment of Individual behavioral expectations in the areas of :
- Accountability
- Integrity
- Passion
- Collaboration
- Innovation
- Customer & Team Member Support & Care

Skills, Knowledge, Experience & Behavior as determined by Purepost's proprietary Cross-Industry Translational Framework & Skills Taxonomy Strataplex

- Level of Leadership
- Level of Education
- Nature of the Position
- Years of Experience
- Other Factors

Contribution Elements that Purepost examines & analyzes to capture and portray a person's Human Capital Value

Figure H-5. Factors and Formula for Measuring Human Capital Value[32]

Myth: Veterans only know how to follow orders. They don't know how to lead or think for themselves.

Fact: The idea that veterans can't think for themselves and don't know how to lead is untrue and offensive. Veterans are put into incredibly complex situations and have to think on their feet. In such cases, creative thinking isn't just good; it's essential. PsychArmor offers a course entitled "The Myths and Facts of Military Leaders" that speaks directly to this topic.[33] I highly recommend you review it.

Additionally, veterans consistently demonstrate the ability to engage in higher levels of organizational learning that go beyond Single Loop learning. These higher levels of learning, demonstrated in Figure H-6, are called Double Loop and Triple Loop learning, which are more critical to the success of organizations—especially during times of rapid change. Both Double Loop and Triple Loop learning involve "thinking outside of the box" (e.g., creativity, analytical thinking, the ability to deal with ambiguity and solve ill-defined, complex problems).

Double Loop learning focuses on "solving the right problem" and helps employees understand why some solutions work better than others in addressing a challenge or achieving a goal. Employees who engage in Double Loop learning can reflect on whether the "governing rules" (e.g., policy, process, or practice) should be changed rather than simply changing their actions and behaviors to correct errors based on governing rules. The focus of Triple Loop learning is on "identifying the right problem." Triple Loop learning is a deeper form of learning that considers the "governing rules," not only whether the rules should be changed. It involves "learning how to learn" by considering how we learn in the first place. Employees who engage in Triple Loop learning consider whether it is necessary to change the overall "organizational context" (e.g., values, purpose, and vision). Said differently, Triple Loop learning is Double Loop learning about Double Loop learning.

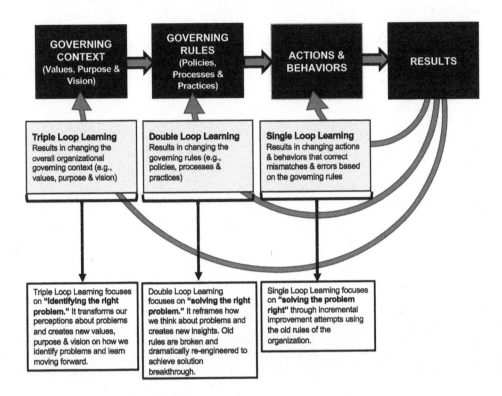

Figure H-6. Organizational Learning Loops[34]

Myth: I must assume that any veteran I hire might be in the Guard or Reserve and will not be available for large swaths of time.

Fact: More than half of veterans will elect to extend their service in the Guard or the Reserve.[35] A ten-year study by the Institute of Medicine documented that Guard and Reserve members experienced between one and two deployments within those ten years. The average length of those deployments was about eight months.[36] Please refer to the detail in Chapter 8 for guidance on optimizing your approach to this talent pool.

Myth: Fewer young people are serving in the military.

Fact: As of 2020, about 76 percent of active-duty military members were thirty-five and younger. Millennials make up about 36 percent of the total military, and the newest generation—the Network Generation (age twenty-five and younger)—makes up more than 40 percent of the entire active-duty population.[37]

GOVERNMENT-WIDE REINTEGRATION FRAMEWORK FOR GUARD AND RESERVE MEMBERS CALLED TO ACTIVE DUTY

On July 19, 2012, a presidential memorandum was issued to strengthen compliance with the Uniformed Services Employment and Reemployment Rights Act (USERRA) to protect veterans in the federal government from any discrimination due to their uniformed service, in accordance with 38 US Code 4301-4335. The memorandum discusses the need for service members "to be reintegrated as quickly and efficiently as possible when they return to civilian life" and calls upon federal agencies to support this effort through outreach, education, and oversight. And so, a White House working group and Council on Veterans Employment created a government-wide veteran Reintegration Framework to assist agencies and their Guard and Reserve members that may be called to active duty. Nongovernment organizations may also benefit from utilizing the framework.

Purpose. The Reintegration Framework outlines a systematic approach to reintegrating Guard and Reserve members by employing strategies to create a culture of support as they deploy and return to the federal workplace. This framework intends to help federal agencies develop effective workforce planning methods to improve reintegration while reducing substantiated USERRA violations and claims.

Workforce Planning and Mission Impact. Agencies should be able to identify their Guard and Reserve members using Department of Defense data. Once identified, agencies should conduct succession planning as part of their regular workforce planning meetings. Doing so will support the continued effective performance of the agency by identifying the work to be transitioned to other members in the event of the deployment of an employee.

Deployment Life Cycle. The deployment life cycle creates a reliable environment for a Guard or Reserve member who faces the possibility of deployment. Successful reintegration of Guard and Reserve members occurs in a three-stage process: pre-deployment, deployment, and post-deployment.

Pre-Deployment. The pre-deployment stage begins when the employee receives notification or orders to perform military service and ends when they depart the agency for the deployment assignment. Agencies should:

- Discuss USERRA protections.

- Understand deployment durations.

- Outline agency and employee responsibilities.

- Provide USERRA refresher training to Guard and Reserve members, immediate supervisors, and HR specialists.

- Draft an agreement between the Guard or Reserve member and supervisors/management on roles related to:

  ◊ An engagement plan.

  ◊ Communication methods.

  ◊ Storage of personal items.

Deployment. During the deployment stage, the deployed employee's primary focus is on their military mission and duties. However, exercising an engagement plan permits the employee to stay connected to the agency. Agency news, activities, and information will help promote a seamless return to the agency. Agencies should:

- Implement the engagement plan by:

  ◊ Contacting the Guard or Reserve member as agreed.

  ◊ Providing the employee information about the activities of the agency, job opportunities, and applicable training programs.

  ◊ Providing points of contact (e.g., supervisors, family members, HR).

- Provide opportunities for training or promotion by:

- ◇ Providing access to e-learning opportunities via the agency's learning management system.

- ◇ Notifying the employee of promotion opportunities and methods of consideration.

Post-Deployment. The post-deployment stage begins when the Guard or Reserve member notifies the agency of their pending return. The post-deployment stage can be a time of great stress for the returning employee and the agency. Successful navigation of this stage is essential to making the returning employee feel welcomed, honored, and smoothly transitioned back into the workforce. It is also an opportunity for agency supervisors and the employee to identify new skills developed while deployed and outline an approach to potentially utilize those new skills within the organization. Agencies should:

- ◆ Create a formal reboarding process to facilitate the employee's successful return to the agency by:

  - ◇ Reestablishing access to the building, personal items, and other resources (e.g., badge, computer, office).

  - ◇ Reacquainting the employee with the work environment and technology.

- ◆ Offer a "Welcome Back" celebration and written acknowledgment as appropriate, supported by agency leadership and fellow employees.

- ◆ Support returning Guard and Reserve member's resumption of assigned duties by:

  - ◇ Reviewing the alignment of their work with the mission and strategic priorities of the organization.

  - ◇ Identifying any assistance or training necessary to perform assigned duties.

  - ◇ Discussing new skills developed while the employee was away and how they may use them.

  - ◇ Communicating performance expectations.

  - ◇ Following agency procedures for performance feedback.

◇   Conducting follow-up conversations within six months of reintegration, including reintegration or exit interviews.[1]

Summary. By successfully employing a reintegration process for deployable Guard and Reserve members, an agency will demonstrate its commitment to enforcing USERRA while valuing veterans' service. The agency's actions should positively impact and enhance compliance with USERRA.

The US Office of Personnel Management created a toolkit to help agencies implement the Reintegration Framework. It consists of six components: references, guides, facts, frequently asked questions, training, and templates. The toolkit is for Guard and Reserve members who are also federal employees and their supervisors. It is well worth reviewing, if not incorporating, into your agency's program.[2]

ACKNOWLEDGMENTS

For those who haven't attempted it, writing a book can be one of the more daunting projects you'll ever undertake. It involves many trying days for all involved in its development, especially those closest to you. It can also be a thankless task, save for knowing that the eventual product may someday help your intended audience. I've been particularly blessed by a cast of supporting characters that have sustained me throughout this process.

Any foundation for taking on such an effort must start with family. I'll start with my mom (Anita) and dad (Patrick). Dad never lived to see the outcome of these efforts—or even their genesis. But I know he would be proud. Both instilled values in me and my siblings that stick with us today: the usefulness of discipline and hard work, the importance of persistence and continuous improvement, the significance of sacrifice and service, and the priorities of faith, family, and friends. Their sense of true north never wavered, and I can only hope to pass on the same to my own family.

My family has endured many days with an absentee husband and father. It is a sacrifice they have accepted to enable this work to be in your hands today. To them, I will be forever grateful. My wife, Michelle, and my boys, Jack, Nick, and Will, have been most patient and kind in ceding my time and efforts to this project and the good they know it will do for you and those veterans most in need of it.

Next, I must thank those individuals who have volunteered their time and organizations to act as case studies for this book. Their participation and input have brought many illustrations to life. And so, thanks to Jim Beamesderfer, Mark Elliott, Paul Fellinger, Brad Fittes, Maura Hart, Beau Higgins, Rhett Jeppson, Sean Lenahan, Harris Morris, John Myers, Chris Newton, Marcus "Ohley" Ohlenforst, Brynt Parmeter, Sean Passmore, Gary Profit, David Theriot, Nick Tran, and Dustin Whidden.

Several veteran friends also weighed in with input and support. And so, I must thank John Cook, Chris Galy, Anthony Garcia, Chris Gill, Major General David Hodne, Colonel (USA retired) Norm Litterini, and Stephanie Markich.

Thanks to friends for acting as a sounding board, providing feedback, and injecting perspective. Thanks to Kurt Babe, John Boerstler, Mark Cotteleer, the late Anthony DeToto, Doug Gish, Doug McCormick, Brian Melton, Brian Niswander, Nate Pelletier, Ted Russ, and Heather Yee.

Having achieved a "D" in plebe (freshman) English at West Point, I need all the help I can get from editors and reviewers. For that I have the following individuals to thank: Bill Bagley, Kate Bailey, Ron Henlein, and Robert Louderback.

Thanks to my website team: Kevin LeMasters at PixelParade and Kim Post at Kim Post Design.

Many thanks to my agent, Rita Rosenkranz, who again astutely guided an impatient author to a successful outcome. Thanks as well to Michael Pye and my publishing team at Career Press.

Finally, I'd like to thank all organizations willing to take a calculated risk on veteran talent and those service organizations that stand ready to support them in this task. If you follow the guidance provided herein, you will not be disappointed. You may even be pleasantly surprised.

ENDNOTES

PREFACE

1. Ash Carter, *Inside the Five-Sided Box: Lessons from a Lifetime of Leadership in the Pentagon* (New York: Random House, 2019), p. xi.

2. US Department of Defense, Office of the Deputy Assistant Secretary of Defense for Military Community and Family Policy (ODASD MC&FP), "2019 Demographics: Profile of the Military Community," accessed August 26, 2022, *militaryonesource.mil.*

3. US Department of Labor, US Bureau of Labor Statistics, "Labor Force Statistics from the Current Population Survey," Table A-40. Employment Status of Persons 18 Years and Over by Veteran Status, Age, and Sex, last updated September 3, 2021, accessed August 26, 2022, *bls.gov.*

INTRODUCTION

1. "A Quote from a Speech by Teddy Roosevelt to Veterans on July 4, 1903," Invictus Foundation, accessed August 26, 2022, *invictusfoundation.org.*

2. Tony Coray, "Marketing to the Military Explained," SheerID, August 9, 2022, accessed November 30, 2022, *sheerid.com.*

3. "Challenges on the Home Front: Underemployment Hits Veterans Hard," Call of Duty Endowment and ZipRecruiter, accessed August 26, 2022, *callofdutyendowment.org.*

4. Nathan D. Ainspan and Kristin N. Saboe, *Military Veteran Employment: A Guide for the Data-Driven Leader* (New York: Oxford University Press, 2021), p. 2.

5. See the US Country/Economy report from each of the World Economic Forum's Global Competitiveness Reports from the past decade. The most recent is featured here: World Economic Forum, The Global Competitiveness Report 2017-2018, United States Economy Profile, "Most Problematic Factors for Doing Business," p. 302, accessed August 26, 2022, *weforum.org.*

6. Mark Kaplan and Mason Donovan, *The Inclusion Dividend: Why Investing in Diversity & Inclusion Pays Off* (Brookline, MA: Bibliomotion, 2013), p. 37.

7. J. M. Haynie, *Revisiting the Business Case for Hiring a Veteran: A Strategy for Cultivating Competitive Advantage* (Workforce Readiness Briefs, Paper No. 2) (Syracuse, NY: Institute for Veterans and Military Families, Syracuse University, April 2016).

8. "The Business Case for Hiring a Veteran: Beyond the Clichés," Institute for Veterans and Military Families, March 5, 2012, accessed August 26, 2022, *ivmf.syracuse.edu*. See also: Chad Storlie, "10 Amazing Reasons You Don't Know to Hire a Military Veteran," Material Handling Network, July 22, 2019, accessed August 26, 2022, *mhnetwork.com*.

9. Amy Schafer, Andrew Swick, Katherine Kuzminski, and Phillip Carter, *Onward and Upward: Understanding Veteran Retention and Performance in the Workforce* (Washington, DC: Center for a New American Security, November 2016).

10. US Department of Labor, Bureau of Labor Statistics, Economic News Release, "Table 3: Employment Status of Persons 25 Years and Over by Veteran Status, Period of Service, and Educational Attainment, 2021 Annual Averages," accessed August 26, 2022, *bls.gov*.

11. Melissa Boatwright and Sarah Roberts, "Veteran Opportunity Report: Understanding an Untapped Talent Pool," LinkedIn, accessed August 26, 2022, *socialimpact.linkedin.com*.

12. D. A. Bradbard, N. J. Armstrong, and R. Maury, *Work after Service: Developing Workforce Readiness and Veteran Talent for the Future* (Workforce Readiness Briefs, Paper No. 1). (Syracuse, NY: Institute for Veterans and Military Families, Syracuse University, February 2016).

13. Security Executive Agent Directive 4: National Security Adjudicative Guidelines, Office of the Director of National Intelligence, December 10, 2016, accessed August 26, 2022, *odni.gov*.

14. The Conference Board Inc., the Partnership for 21st Century Skills, Corporate Voices for Working Families, and the Society for Human Resource Management, "Are They Really Ready to Work? Employers' Perspectives on the Basic Knowledge and Applied Skills of New Entrants to the 21st Century U.S. Workforce," 2006, last accessed May 18, 2023, *eric.ed.gov/*.

15. Ibid.

16. C. Zoli, R. Maury, and D. Fay, "Missing Perspectives: Servicemembers' Transition from Service to Civilian Life: Data-Driven Research to Enact the Promise of the Post-9/11 GI Bill" (Syracuse, NY: Institute for Veterans & Military Families, Syracuse University, November 2015).

17. Vanessa Fuhrmans, "Generals Bring Battlefield Expertise to the Business World: Employers Are Tapping Military Leaders to Develop Leadership Talent, Provide Corporate Governance and Oversee Cybersecurity Strategy," *Wall Street Journal*, August 29, 2017, accessed January 29, 2023, *wsj.com*.

18. Ibid.

19. Aaron Kay, "Research Shows Military Service Can Hurt Some Job Seekers' Prospects," Duke Fuqua School of Business, September 23, 2019, accessed August 26, 2022, *fuqua.duke.edu*. See also: Steven Shepherd, Aaron C. Kay, Kurt Gray, "Military Veterans Are Morally Typecast as Agentic but Unfeeling: Implications for Veteran Employment," *ScienceDirect, Volume 153*, July 2019, pp. 75–88.

20. Melissa Boatwright and Sarah Roberts, "Veteran Opportunity Report: Understanding an Untapped Talent Pool," LinkedIn, accessed August 26, 2022, *social impact.linkedin.com*.

21. US Government Publishing Office, "United States Code 2011, Title 38 Section 101," accessed August 26, 2022, *gpo.gov*.

22. "The Business Case for Hiring Veterans," CEB Corporate Leadership Council, 2013, accessed August 26, 2022, *img.en25.com*.

23. Roy Maurer, "8 in 10 Employers Lack Recruitment Programs for Veterans," Medium.com, May 25, 2015, accessed August 26, 2022, *medium.com*.

24. "Small Business Index: The Voice of Small Business Owners," *Metlife & US Chamber of Commerce*, Q3 2019, accessed August 26, 2022, *uschamber.com/ sbindex/uploads/SBI_2021_Q1.pdf*.

CHAPTER 1

1. *The Public Papers and Addresses of Franklin D. Roosevelt*, 1943 volume, The Tide Turns: Compiled with Special Material and Explanatory Notes by Samuel I. Rosenman, "Message to Congress," November 23, 1943, pp. 523–528, accessed August 26, 2022, *archive.org*.

2. A recent study by LinkedIn that found veterans remain with their initial company more than 8 percent longer than non veterans. See: Melissa Boatwright and Sarah Roberts, "Veteran Opportunity Report: Understanding an Untapped Talent Pool," LinkedIn, accessed August 26, 2022, *socialimpact.linkedin.com*.

3. J. M. Haynie, *Guide to Leading Policies, Practices & Resources: Supporting the Employment of Veterans and Military Families* (Syracuse, NY: Institute for Veterans and Military Families, Syracuse University, August 2021), p. 42.

4. Victoria A. Hoevemeyer, *High-Impact Interview Questions, Second Edition* (New York: AMACOM, 2018), p. 40.

5. Mark Murphy, "Why New Hires Fail (Emotional Intelligence vs. Skills)," Leadership IQ, June 22, 2015, accessed August 26, 2022, *leadershipiq.com*.

6. Dr. Kerry Schofield, "Culture Fit in the Workplace: What It Is and Why It's Important," *Good & Co*, June 14, 2016, accessed August 26, 2022, *linkedin.com*. See also: Amy L. Kristof-Brown, Ryan D. Zimmerman, and Erin C. Johnson, "Consequences of Individuals' Fit at Work: A Meta-Analysis of Person-Job, Person-Organization, Person-Group, and Person-Supervisor Fit," *Personnel Psychology 58*, 2, Summer 2005, ABI/INFORM Global, p. 281, accessed August 26, 2022, *nreilly.asp.radford.edu*.

7. "The Army Values," US Army, accessed August 26, 2022, *army.mil*.

8. "Marine Corps Values," Marines, accessed August 26, 2022, *marines.com*.

9. "About," America's Navy, accessed August 26, 2022, *navy.mil*.

10. "Our Principles: Core Values," US Air Force, accessed August 26, 2022, *airforce.com*.

11. "CSO Unveils Guardian Ideal, Space Force Values at AFA," *Space Force News*, September 21, 2021, accessed April 17, 2022, *spaceforce.mil*.

12. "Training Center Cape May," US Coast Guard, accessed August 26, 2022, *forcecom .uscg.mil*.

13. USAA also funds the US Chamber of Commerce Foundation's Hiring Our Heroes initiative, which includes an Employer Roadmap for hiring veterans. See: "Employer Roadmap," Hiring Our Heroes, US Chamber of Commerce, accessed January 29, 2023, *vetemployerroadmap.org*.

14. For additional educational resources for understanding military culture, please see: "Courses for Military Culture," Psycharmor.org, accessed August 26, 2022, *learn. psycharmor.org*. See also: "Information & Resources for Providers Who Serve Veterans," Community Provider Toolkit, US Department of Veterans Affairs, accessed August 26, 2022, *mentalhealth.va.gov*. See also: "Military Cultural Competence," Uniformed Services University, Center for Deployment Psychology, accessed August 26, 2022, *deploymentpsych.org/*.

15. Michael Abrams, "Mission Critical: Unlocking the Value of Veterans in the Workplace," Center for Talent Innovation, 2015, p. 5, accessed August 26, 2022, *talentinnovation.org*.

16. Dan Witters, "Active Duty Military Leads US in Well-Being; Veterans Lag," Gallup, June 30, 2010, accessed August 26, 2022, *gallup.com*.

17. Ibid.

18. John R. P. French Jr. and Bertram Raven, "Bases of Social Power," ValueBased Management.net, 1959, accessed August 26, 2022, *valuebasedmanagement.net*.

19. Phillip Carter, Amy Schafer, Katherine Kidder, and Moira Fagan, "Lost in Translation: The Civil-Military Divide and Veteran Employment," Center for a New American Security, June 15, 2017, p. 16, accessed August 26, 2022, *cnas.org*.

20. "US Military Rank Insignia," US Department of Defense, accessed August 26, 2022, *defense.gov*.

21. Ibid.

22. Ryan Blackburn, "Military Culture," Ohio Department of Veterans Services Employer Training, pp. 5–16.

23. Bureau of Labor Statistics, US Department of Labor, *Occupational Outlook Handbook*, Military Careers, accessed September 20, 2022, *bls.gov*.

24 "The Age Discrimination in Employment Act of 1967," US Equal Opportunity Employment Commission, accessed August 26, 2022, *eeoc.gov*.

25. See: *Handbook No. 15-6: Military Decision-Making Process (MDMP): Lessons and Best Practices,* Center for Army Lessons Learned, March 2015, accessed August 26, 2022, *usacac.army.mil/sites/default/files/publications/15-06_0.pdf*.

26. "How to Improve Your Personal Wellness: Guidelines and Resources," Free Management Library, accessed August 26, 2022, *managementhelp.org*.

27. See also: Stephen R. Covey, A. Roger Merrill, and Rebecca R. Merrill, *First Things First* (New York: Simon & Schuster Inc., 1994), pp. 36–42.

28. Mary Burtzloff, archivist, Eisenhower Presidential Library and Museum, August 4, 2017. See also Stephen R. Covey, A. Roger Merrill, and Rebecca R. Merrill, *First Things First* (New York: Simon & Schuster, 1994), p. 37.

29. Maxwell Wessel, "Why Big Companies Can't Innovate," *Harvard Business Review*, September 27, 2012, accessed August 26, 2022, *hbr.org*.

30. George K. Pitchford, Esq., "An Examination of the At-Will Employment Doctrine," ALA Allied Professional Association, August, 2005, accessed August 26, 2022, *ala-apa.org*. Also see: Charles J. Muhl, "The Employment-at-Will Doctrine: Three Major Exceptions," *Monthly Labor Review,* January 2001, accessed August 26, 2022, *bls.gov*.

31. See: Capt. Bill Wicks Trial Counsel, 13th ESC, "Leaving on Good Terms: Types of Discharges, Their Consequences," *Fort Hood Sentinel*, December 22, 2015, accessed August 26, 2022, *forthoodsentinel.com*. See also: Army Regulation 635-200: Personnel Separations—Active Duty Enlisted Administrative Separations, Headquarters, Department of the Army, Washington, DC, June 28, 2021, accessed August 26, 2022, *armypubs.army.mil*.

CHAPTER 2

1. "Abraham Lincoln—Quotes—Quotable Quote," Goodreads.com, accessed August 26, 2022, *goodreads.com.*

2. "USERRA Statute," The US Department of Justice, accessed August 26, 2022, *justice.gov.* See also: "Elaws: Employment Laws Assistance for Workers & Small Businesses—USERRA Advisor," US Department of Labor, accessed August 26, 2022, *webapps.dol.gov.*

3. "Vietnam Era Veterans' Readjustment Assistance Act of 1974, as Amended," US Department of Labor Office of Federal Contract Compliance Programs, accessed August 26, 2022, *dol.gov.*

4. "Information and Technical Assistance on the Americans with Disabilities Act," US Department of Justice Civil Rights Division, accessed August 26, 2022, *ada.gov.*

5. "Family and Medical Leave Act," US Department of Labor Wage and Hour Division, accessed August 26, 2022, *dol.gov.*

6. "Veterans' Preference," US Office of Personnel Management FedsHireVets Job Seekers, accessed August 26, 2022, *fedshirevets.gov.*

7. "§ 668.18 Readmission Requirements for Servicemembers," Code of Federal Regulations Title 34—Education, Volume 3, Part 668 Student Assistance General Provisions, Subpart B—Standards for Participation in Title IV, HEA Programs, July 1, 2017, accessed August 26, 2022, *govinfo.gov.*

8. "Rehabilitation Act of 1973," US Government Printing Office, August 13, 2019, accessed August 26, 2022, *govinfo.gov.*

9. Haynie, *Guide,* pp. 24–27.

10. "Frequently Asked Questions: Institutional Readmission Requirements for Servicemembers," US Department of Education, September 25, 2017, accessed August 26, 2022, *ed.gov.*

11. "Compliance Assistance," US Department of Labor Veterans' Employment & Training Service, accessed August 26, 2022, *dol.gov.*

12. "Compliance Assistance Guides," US Department of Labor Office of Federal Contract Compliance Programs, accessed August 26, 2022, *dol.gov.*

13. "VETS-4212 Federal Contractor Reporting," US Department of Labor Veterans' Employment & Training Service, accessed August 26, 2022, *dol.gov.*

14. "5 Ways Not Complying with OFCCP Regulation Can Cost You," BirdDog HR, an ARCORO Company, October 21, 2019, accessed August 26, 2022, *blog.birddoghr.com.*

15. "Special Hiring Authorities for Veterans," FedsHireVets, US Office of Personnel Management, accessed August 26, 2022, *fedshirevets.gov*. See also: "Veterans and the Americans with Disabilities Act (ADA): A Guide for Employers," US Equal Opportunity Employment Commission, accessed August 26, 2022, *eeoc.gov*.

16. For training and detailed documentation, see: "Disability Employment, Hiring: Schedule a Hiring Authority," US Office of Personnel Management, accessed August 26, 2022, *opm.gov*.

17. "Non-Competitive Special Hiring Authorities for Veterans: A Quick Reference for Veterans," US Department of Veteran Affairs, accessed August 26, 2022, *vaforvets.va.gov*.

18. "3 CFR 13518—Executive Order 13518 of November 9, 2009. Employment of Veterans in the Federal Government," US Government Publishing Office, accessed August 26, 2022, *govinfo.gov*. See also: "Governmentwide Veterans Recruitment and Employment Strategic Plan FY 2014—FY 2017," FedsHireVets, US Office of Personnel Management, accessed August 26, 2022, *fedshirevets.gov*.

19. "Military Spouse Hiring Authority," FedsHireVets, US Office of Personnel Management, accessed August 26, 2022, *fedshirevets.gov*.

20. "Enhancing Noncompetitive Civil Service Appointments of Military Spouses," National Archives Federal Register, accessed August 26, 2022, *federalregister.gov*.

21. "5 US Code § 3330d. Appointment of Military Spouses," Legal Information Institute, Cornell University, accessed August 26, 2022, *law.cornell.edu*.

22. "Work Opportunity Tax Credit," US Department of Labor Employment & Training Administration (ETA), accessed August 28, 2022, *doleta.gov*.

23. "Tax Benefits for Businesses Who Have Employees with Disabilities," Internal Revenue Service, accessed August 28, 2022, *irs.gov*.

24. See: "State Veterans Affairs Offices," US Department of Veterans Affairs, accessed August 28, 2022, *va.gov*.

25. "Veteran Readiness and Employment (VR&E)," US Department of Veterans Affairs, accessed August 29, 2022, *benefits.va.gov*.

26. J. Marc Burgess, *The Veteran Advantage: DAV Guide to Hiring & Retaining Veterans with Disabilities* (Cold Spring, KY: DAV, 2018) pp. 4–5, accessed August 28, 2022. See also: "Veterans Employment Toolkit," US Department of Veterans Affairs, accessed August 28, 2022, *va.gov*.

27. "Special Employer Incentive (SEI) Program," US Department of Veterans Affairs Veterans Benefits Administration, accessed August 28, 2022, *benefits.va.gov*.

28. Burgess, *The Veteran Advantage*.

29. "Toolkit," US Department of Labor CareerOneStop Business Center, accessed August 28, 2022, *careeronestop.org.*

CHAPTER 3

1. "Quotes about Veterans," Inspirational Quotes, accessed August 28, 2022, *inspirationalquotes4u.com.*

2. "Veteran Employment Program Offices (VEPO) Directory," FedsHireVets, US Office of Personnel Management, accessed August 28, 2022, *fedshirevets.gov.*

3. Harris Morris, ADP, interview by Matthew Louis, October 12, 2018.

4. Rhett Jeppson, JPMorgan Chase, interview by Matthew Louis, October 18, 2021.

5. John Myers, Procter & Gamble Veterans Affinity Group (Cincinnati, OH), interview by Matthew Louis, March 1, 2018.

6. James Beamesderfer, telephone interview by Matthew Louis, October 4, 2018. Updated via email May 10, 2022.

7. Nick Tran, telephone interview by Matthew Louis, March 14, 2018. Updated May 16, 2022.

8. Dustin Whidden, telephone interview by Matthew Louis, January 19, 2018. Updated May 5, 2022.

9. Brynt Parmeter, interview by Matthew Louis, May 12, 2022.

10. Sean Lenahan, telephone and email interview by Matthew Louis, July 9, 2019, and July 31, 2019.

11. Brad Fittes, email interview by Matthew Louis, June 10, 2019. Subsequent updates provided by Paul Fellinger via email, May 4, 2022.

12. John Myers, Procter & Gamble Veterans Affinity Group (Cincinnati, OH), interview by Matthew Louis, March 1, 2018.

13. Rhett Jeppson, JPMorgan Chase, interview by Matthew Louis, October 18, 2021.

14. Dustin Whidden, telephone interview by Matthew Louis, January 19, 2018. Updated May 5, 2022.

15. Brynt Parmeter, interview by Matthew Louis, May 12, 2022.

16. Sean Passmore, telephone and email interview by Matthew Louis, April 26, 2018. Subsequent updates provided by Marcus "Ohley" Ohlenforst via email exchange, February 4, 2021.

17. James Beamesderfer, telephone interview by Matthew Louis, October 4, 2018. Updated via email May 10, 2022.

18. Nick Tran, telephone interview by Matthew Louis, March 14, 2018. Updated May 16, 2022.

19. Chris Newton, telephone interview by Matthew Louis, January 30, 2018. Updated May 13, 2022.

20. Brad Fittes, email interview by Matthew Louis, June 10, 2019. Subsequent updates provided by Paul Fellinger via email, May 4, 2022.

21. Brynt Parmeter, interview by Matthew Louis, May 12, 2022.

22. "VEVRAA Hiring Benchmark," US Department of Labor Office of Federal Contract Compliance Programs, accessed February 1, 2023, *dol.gov*.

23. Nick Tran, telephone interview by Matthew Louis, March 14, 2018. Updated May 16, 2022.

24. Rhett Jeppson, JPMorgan Chase, interview by Matthew Louis, October 18, 2021.

25. Dustin Whidden, telephone interview by Matthew Louis, January 19, 2018. Updated May 5, 2022.

26. Sean Passmore, telephone and email interview by Matthew Louis, April 26, 2018. Subsequent updates provided by Marcus "Ohley" Ohlenforst via email, February 4, 2021.

27. Brad Fittes, email interview by Matthew Louis, June 10, 2019. Subsequent updates provided by Paul Fellinger via email, May 4, 2022.

28. Sean Lenahan, telephone and email interview by Matthew Louis, July 9, 2019, and July 31, 2019.

29. "Workforce Recruitment Program," US Department of Labor's Office of Disability Employment Policy and the US Department of Defense, accessed August 28, 2022, *wrp.gov*.

30. Sean Passmore, telephone and email interview by Matthew Louis, April 26, 2018. Subsequent updates provided by Marcus "Ohley" Ohlenforst via email, February 4, 2021.

31. Brynt Parmeter, interview by Matthew Louis, May 12, 2022.

CHAPTER 4

1. James Charlton, *The Military Quotation Book* (New York: St. Martin's Press, 1990), p. 68.

2. Sebastian Junger, *Tribe: On Homecoming and Belonging* (New York: Twelve Books, 2016), pp. 101–103.

3. Eric Milzarski, "This Is How 'RED Friday' Became a Thing and Why It Still Matters Today," Military.com, accessed August 28, 2022, *military.com.*

4. "DoD SkillBridge," US Department of Defense, accessed August 28, 2022, *skillbridge .osd.mil.*

5. "ACP," American Corporate Partners, accessed August 28, 2022, *acp-usa.org.*

6. "Creating a Nationwide Hiring Effort," US Chamber of Commerce Foundation, accessed August 28, 2022, *hiringourheroes.org.*

7. "The JPMorgan Chase Pathfinder Playbook: A Veteran Acclimation Program Development Roadmap," JPMorgan Chase & Co., June 2018, accessed August 29, 2022, *veteranjobsmission.com.*

8. See this example: "Mentoring Handbook," American Corporate Partners, January 2018, accessed August 28, 2022, *acp-usa.org.*

9. "ACP."

10. "America's Mentoring Network for the Military," Veterati, accessed August 28, 2022, *veterati.com.*

11. See: Ainspan and Saboe, *Military Veteran,* pp. 205–215.

12. CORE Success Faculty Guide, Deloitte Services LP, 2017, pp 3–4.

13. Harris Morris, telephone interview by Matthew Louis, October 12, 2018.

14. "Workforce Opportunity Services," Workforce Opportunity Services, accessed August 28, 2022, *wforce.org.*

15. James Beamesderfer, telephone interview by Matthew Louis, October 4, 2018. Updated via email May 10, 2022.

16. See: "15 Things Veterans Want You to Know," PsychArmor Institute, accessed August 28, 2022, *psycharmor.org.* See also: "Committed to Empowering HR Professionals to Attract, Hire and Retain Veterans," Society for Human Resource Management Foundation, accessed August 28, 2022, *veteransatwork .org.* See also: "Reinventing Michael Banks," Will Interactive, accessed August 28, 2022, *willinteractive.com.* See also: "HR Professionals and Supervisors," VA for Vets, accessed August 29, 2022, *vaforvets.va.gov.* See also: "Employers," US Chamber of Commerce Hiring Our Heroes, accessed May 18, 2023, *hiringourheroes.org.* See also: "Veteran Supportive Supervisor Training," Study for Employment Retention of Veterans (SERVe), accessed August 28, 2022, *servestudy.org.* See also: "Community Resources," WorkforceGPS, US Department of Labor Employment and Training Administration, accessed August 28, 2022, *veteranspriority.workforcegps.org.*

17. "Veterans Employment Training," FedsHireVets, US Office of Personnel Management, accessed August 28, 2022, *opm.gov*.

18. John Myers, Procter & Gamble Veterans Affinity Group (Cincinnati, OH), interview by Matthew Louis, March 1, 2018.

CHAPTER 5

1. Charlton, *The Military*, p. 31.

2. John Myers, Procter & Gamble Veterans Affinity Group (Cincinnati, OH), interview by Matthew Louis, March 1, 2018.

3. See: Marc Holliday, "Employee Retention vs. Turnover: Key Differences & Why It Matters," *Oracle Netsuite*, February 9, 2021, accessed August 28, 2022, *netsuite.com*.

4. See: "What Does It Mean to Be a Military Friendly Company?" Military Friendly, accessed August 28, 2022, *militaryfriendly.com*.

5. See: "Become Veteran Ready," Psycharmor Institute, accessed August 28, 2022, *psycharmor.org*.

6. See: "Accredited Representatives: VSOs at Regional Benefit Offices," US Department of Veterans Affairs, accessed August 29, 2022, *benefits.va.gov*.

7. See: "Why Military Friendly?" Military Friendly, accessed August 28, 2022, *militaryfriendly.com*.

8. Dustin Whidden, telephone interview by Matthew Louis, January 19, 2018. Updated May 5, 2022.

CHAPTER 6

1. Charlton, *The Military*, p. 57.

2. See: "Résumé Formats: Which Type of Résumé Is Best for You?" Jobscan, accessed April 14, 2022, *jobscan.co*.

3. See: "What Happens to Résumé Tables and Columns in an ATS? See for Yourself," Jobscan, accessed April 14, 2022, *jobscan.co*.

4. See: "The Best Fonts for Your Résumé in 2022 + Best Résumé Formatting Tips," Jobscan, accessed April 14, 2022, *jobscan.co*.

5. See: "5 Sections You Should Never Leave Off Your Résumé" Jobscan, accessed May 18, 2023, *jobscan.co*.

6. National Center for Veterans Analysis and Statistics, "Profile of Veterans: 2017," US Department of Veterans Affairs, March 2019, accessed August 28, 2022, *va.gov*.

7. Office of the Deputy Assistant Secretary of Defense for Military Community and Family Policy (ODASD (MC&FP)), "2020 Demographics Profile of the Military Community," US Department of Defense, p. 32, accessed August 28, 2022, *militaryonesource.mil.*

8. Beau Higgins, telephone interview by Matthew Louis, December 18, 2017. Update via email May 6, 2022.

9. "Transition Survey Results, 2017 Veteran Survey," p. 9," Military-Transition.org, accessed August 28, 2022, *military-transition.org.*

10. "Best Colleges for Veterans," *US News & World Report*, accessed August 28, 2022, *usnews.com.*

11. Student Veterans of America, accessed August 28, 2022, *studentveterans.org.*

12. Sarah E. Minnis, PhD, "What Does It Mean to Be 'Veteran Friendly'?" LinkedIn, June 10, 2014, accessed August 28, 2022, *www.linkedin.com.* See also: J. Keef, Z. Huitink, and P. Donegan, *Advancing Veteran Success in Higher Education: Case Studies of Student Veteran Support Programs at San Diego State University, the University of Texas-Arlington, the University of South Florida, and Florida State College Jacksonville* (Leading Practice Briefs, Paper No. 2), (Syracuse, NY: Institute for Veterans and Military Families, Syracuse University (September 2016), accessed August 28, 2022, *veterans.syr.edu.* See also: Brian Borsari, et al., "Student Service Members/Veterans on Campus: Challenges for Reintegration," *The American Journal of Orthopsychiatry*, vol. 87,2 (2017): 166–175, accessed August 28, 2022, *ncbi.nlm.nih.gov.*

13. "NASPA Symposium on Military-Connected Students," NASPA Student Affairs Administrators in Higher Education, accessed August 29, 2022, *naspa.org.*

14. "Military Evaluations," American Council on Education, accessed August 28, 2022, *acenet.edu.* See also: "College Credit by Examination," DoD VolEd Programs, accessed August 28, 2022, *dantes.doded.mil.*

15. "Transition from Active Service to College and the Workforce," edX, accessed August 28, 2022, *edx.org.* See also: Center for Veteran Transition and Integration, Columbia University in the City of New York, accessed August 28, 2022, *veterans.columbia.edu.*

16. "Student Financial Services, Veterans & Service Members," Columbia University in the City of New York, accessed August 28, 2022, *sfs.columbia.edu.*

17. See also: "Resources for Schools," US Department of Veterans Affairs, accessed August 30, 2022, *va.gov/school-administrators/.* See also: "School Certifying Official Handbook," US Department of Veterans Affairs, accessed August 30, 2022, *va.gov/school-administrators/.*

18. See: "Yellow Ribbon Program," US Department of Veterans Affairs, accessed August 30, 2022, *benefits.va.gov*. See also: "Yellow Ribbon Program Agreement," US Department of Veterans Affairs, accessed August 30, 2022, *va.gov*.

19. "8 Keys to Veterans' Success Sites," US Department of Education, accessed August 30, 2022, *ed.gov*.

20. See: "Principles of Excellence Program," US Department of Veterans Affairs, accessed August 30, 2022, *va.gov*. See also: David Bergeron, "Establishing Principles of Excellence for Educational Institutions Serving Service Members, Veterans, Spouses, and other Family Members," *Federal Register, Vol. 77, No. 85*, May 2, 2012, accessed August 30, 2022, *fsapartners.ed.gov*.

21. "The College Financing Plan," US Department of Education, accessed August 31, 2022, *ed.gov*.

22. To become accredited, see: "Accreditation in the United States," US Department of Education, accessed August 31, 2022, *ed.gov*. See also: "How to Use the Military Tuition Assistance Program," Military Onesource, accessed August 31, 2022, *militaryonesource.mil*.

23. "DoD Voluntary Education Partnership Memorandum of Understanding (MOU)," Military Onesource, accessed August 31, 2022, *https://download.militaryonesource.mil/12038/Project%20Documents/Voluntary%20Education%20Portal/mou_dod_voled.pdf*.

24. See: "School Program Approval" US Department of Veterans Affairs, accessed August 31, 2022, *benefits.va.gov*. See also: "VetSuccess on Campus," US Department of Veterans Affairs, accessed August 31, 2022, *benefits.va.gov* and *va.gov*.

25. "VA Campus Toolkit," PsychArmor, accessed August 31, 2022, *learn.psycharmor.org*.

26. "Toolkit for Veteran Friendly Institutions," American Council on Education, accessed August 31, 2022, *acenet.edu*.

27. "Workforce Recruitment Program," US Department of Labor's Office of Disability Employment Policy and the US Department of Defense, accessed August 31, 2022, *wrp.gov*.

28. "Building the Next Generation of Leaders," Pat Tillman Foundation, accessed August 31, 2022, *pattillmanfoundation.org*.

29. "Bass Military Scholars Program," Vanderbilt University, accessed August 31, 2022, *vanderbilt.edu*.

30. Veterans in Global Leadership, accessed August 31, 2022, *vetsgl.org*.

31. "Veteran Leadership Accelerator," The Mission Continues, accessed August 31, 2022, *missioncontinues.org*.

32. "ServiceCorps Fellowship," ServiceCorps, accessed August 31, 2022, *servicecorps .org.*

33. "AMVETS Scholarships," American Veterans, accessed August 31, 2022, *amvets .org.*

34. "Scholarships," Armed Forces Communications and Electronics Association, accessed August 31, 2022, *afcea.org.*

35. "Scholarship Program," Army Women's Foundation, accessed August 31, 2022, *awfdn.org.*

36. "Scholarships," Divine Mercy University, accessed August 31, 2022, *divinemercy .edu.*

37. "Heroes Fund Scholarship," Liberty University, accessed August 31, 2022, *liberty .edu.*

38. "Lunacap Foundation Scholarships," Lunacap Foundation, accessed August 31, 2022, *lunacapfoundation.org.*

39. "Scholarship Program," Military Order of the Purple Heart, accessed August 31, 2022, *purpleheart.org.*

40. "Education Support," Air Force Aid Society, accessed August 31, 2022, *afas.org.*

41. "Scholarships," Army Emergency Relief, accessed August 31, 2022, *armyemergency relief.org.*

42. "Army Scholarship Foundation," Army Scholarship Foundation, accessed August 31, 2022, *armyscholarshipfoundation.org.*

43. "Our Scholarship," Chief Petty Officer Scholarship Fund, accessed August 31, 2022, *cposf.org.*

44. "Scholarships," Coast Guard Foundation, accessed August 31, 2022, *coastguard foundation.org.*

45. "Scholarships," Folds of Honor, accessed August 31, 2022, *foldsofhonor.org.*

46. "Military Spouse Scholarships & Caregiver Scholarships," Hope for the Warriors, accessed August 31, 2022, *hopeforthewarriors.org.*

47. "Programs," Marine Corps League, accessed August 31, 2022, *mclnational.org.*

48. "Spouse Scholarships" and "Careers," National Military Family Association, accessed August 31, 2022, *militaryfamily.org.*

49. "Education Assistance," Navy-Marine Corps Relief Society, accessed August 31, 2022, *nmcrs.org.*

50. "ThanksUSA Scholarship Program," ThanksUSA, accessed August 31, 2022, *thanksusa.org.*

51. "Administered Scholarships," Wings over America Scholarship Foundation, accessed August 31, 2022, *wingsoveramerica.us.*

52. "Scholarship," National Ranger Foundation, accessed August 31, 2022, *national rangerfoundation.com.*

53. "National Veterans Leadership Foundation," National Veterans Leadership Foundation, accessed August 31, 2022, *nvlfoundation.org.*

54. "Scholarship Program," Paralyzed Veterans of America, accessed August 31, 2022, *pva.org/find-support.*

55. "The Posse Veterans Program," Posse Foundation, accessed August 31, 2022, *possefoundation.org.*

56. "Student Veteran Support," Veterans of Foreign Wars, accessed August 31, 2022, *vfw.org.*

57. "Empowering Veterans in the Classroom," Warrior-Scholar Project, accessed August 31, 2022, *warrior-scholar.org.*

58. "Search Career Events," National Labor Exchange, accessed August 31, 2022, *jobs.usnlx.com.*

59. "Upcoming Hiring Events," VA For Vets, accessed August 31, 2022, *vaforvets.va.gov.*

60. "DOD Civilian Employment," Department of Defense Civilian Careers, accessed August 31, 2022, *dodciviliancareers.com.*

61. Service Academy Career Conference, accessed August 31, 2022, *sacc-jobfair.com.*

62. "Job Fairs Calendar," Soldier for Life-Transition Assistance Program, accessed August 31, 2022, *armytap.army.mil.*

63. "Veterans Career Fairs," The American Legion, accessed August 31, 2022, *legion.org.*

64. "Choice Career Fairs," Choice Career Fairs , accessed August 31, 2022, *choicecareerfairs.com.*

65. "Hire Veterans through RecruitMilitary Hiring Programs and Events," RecruitMilitary, accessed August 31, 2022, *recruitmilitary.com.*

66. "Corporate Gray Job Fairs," Corporate Gray, accessed August 31, 2022, *corporategray.com.*

67. ClearedJobs.net, accessed August 31, 2022, *clearedjobs.net.*

68. "Job Fair Schedule," Job Zone, accessed August 31, 2022, *jobzoneonline.com.*

69. "Upcoming Job Fairs," Military.com, accessed August 31, 2022, *military.com.*

70. "Veteran Recruiting Center," VeteranRecruiting.com, accessed August 31, 2022, *veteranrecruiting.com*.

71. Elite Meet, accessed August 31, 2022, *elitemeetus.org*.

72. "Women Veterans Alliance Unconference," Women Veterans Alliance, accessed August 31, 2022, *womenveteransalliance.com*.

73. "National Conference," Student Veterans of America, accessed August 31, 2022, *studentveterans.org*.

74. "MBA Veterans Conference," MBA Veterans Network, accessed August 31, 2022, *mbaveterans.com*.

75. See the National Association of State Workforce Agencies website for their upcoming Veterans Conference: *naswa.org*.

76. "American Veterans Center Annual Conference," American Veterans Center, accessed August 31, 2022, *americanveteranscenter.org*.

77. "Officer Women Leadership Symposium (OWLS)," Academy Women, accessed August 31, 2022, *militaryowls.org*.

78. "Hire Veterans," Hire Heroes USA, accessed August 31, 2022, *hireheroesusa.org*.

79. "American Job Centers," CareerOneStop, accessed August 31, 2022, *careeronestop.org*.

80. "CareerOneStop Business Center," CareerOneStop, accessed August 31, 2022, *careeronestop.org*.

81. "Service Members and Veterans," US Department of Labor ApprenticeshipUSA, accessed August 31, 2022, *apprenticeship.gov*. See also: "Hire Veterans," US Department of Labor ApprenticeshipUSA, accessed August 31, 2022, *apprenticeship.gov*.

82. "Fellowships—Growing Meaningful Careers," US Chamber of Commerce Hiring Our Heroes, accessed August 31, 2022, *hiringourheroes.org*.

83. "DOD SkillBridge," US Department of Defense, accessed August 25, 2022, *skillbridge.osd.mil*.

84. "Career Skills Program," US Army Installation Management Command, accessed August 31, 2022, *home.army.mil*. See also: "Hire Military," HireMilitary LLC, accessed August 31, 2022, *hiremilitary.us*.

85. "Veterans Innovation Partnership Fellowship," US Department of State, accessed August 31, 2022, *careers.state.gov*.

86. "Explore Veteran Programs," US Department of Energy, accessed August 31, 2022, *energy.gov*.

87. "OSD Fellows Program," Office of the Assistant Secretary of Defense for Sustainment, accessed August 25, 2022, *acq.osd.mil.*

88. "United Services Military Apprenticeship Program (USMAP)," US Department of Defense, accessed August 25, 2022, *usmap.osd.mil.*

89. "On-the-Job Training and Apprenticeships," US Department of Veterans Affairs, accessed August 31, 2022, *vets.gov.*

90. "Accelerating Business, Launching Careers," US Department of Labor and Fastport, accessed August 31, 2022, *nationalapprenticeship.org.*

91. "ForgeNow," accessed May 18, 2023, *forgenow.com.*

92. "Helmets to Hardhats," *Helmuts to Hardhats,* accessed June 1, 2023, *helmetstohardhats.org.*

93. Operation Socrates, accessed August 5, 2022, *operationsocrates.org.*

94. "The Painters and Allied Trades Veterans Program," Finishing Trades Institute, accessed August 31, 2022, *ifti.edu.*

95. "Purdue Cyber Apprenticeship Program," Purdue University, accessed August 31, 2022, *polytechnic.purdue.edu.*

96. "Hire Vetted Military Talent in the Right Roles," Shift.org, accessed August 31, 2022, *shift.org.*

97. "Developing Coaches Who Inspire," Soldiers to Sidelines, accessed August 5, 2022, *soldierstosidelines.org.*

98. "Serve Your Community in the Skilled Trades," Explore the Trades, accessed August 31, 2022, *explorethetrades.org/military/.*

99. "VIP Program Trades," United Association Veterans in Piping Program, accessed August 31, 2022, *uavip.org.*

100. "Education Programs—Weams Institution Search," US Department of Veterans Affairs, accessed August 31, 2022, *inquiry.vba.va.gov.*

101. "Get Trained and Certified in Four Months," Workshops for Warriors, accessed August 31, 2022, *wfw.org.*

102. "Find the Right Trade or Vocational School for You," Real Work Matters, accessed August 31, 2022, *rwm.org.*

103. VetsInTech, accessed August 31, 2022, *vetsintech.co.*

104. "Veterans' Employment and Training Service: Hire a Veteran," US Department of Labor, accessed August 31, 2022, *dol.gov.*

105. "Partnerships," US Department of Labor Veterans' Employment and Training Service, accessed February 2, 2023, *dol.gov.*

106. To find DVOPs near you, see the various state employment services located here: "Veterans Employment Services," US Department of Labor Veterans' Employment and Training Service, accessed August 31, 2022, *dol.gov*. See also: "American Job Center Finder," US Department of Labor CareerOneStop Veteran and Military Transition Center, accessed August 31, 2022, *careeronestop.org*.

107. "Veteran Readiness & Employment (VR&E)," US Department of Veterans Affairs, accessed August 31, 2022, *benefits.va.gov*.

108. To find LVERs near you, see the various state employment services located here: "Veterans Employment Services," US Department of Labor Veterans' Employment and Training Service, accessed August 31, 2022, *dol.gov*. See also: "American Job Center Finder," US Department of Labor CareerOneStop Veteran and Military Transition Center, accessed August 31, 2022, *careeronestop.org*.

109. "Military Spouse Employment Partnership," US Department of Defense Military OneSource, accessed February 5, 2023, *msepjobs.militaryonesource.mil*.

110. "Operation Warfighter," US Department of Defense Warrior Care, accessed August 31, 2022, *warriorcare.dodlive.mil*.

111. "Hiring Information," US Office of Personnel Management, accessed August 31, 2022, *opm.gov*.

112. "Veteran Initiatives," FedsHireVets US Office of Personnel Management, accessed August 31, 2022, *fedshirevets.gov*.

113. Ibid.

114. "Employment of Women Veterans in the Federal Government," FedsHireVets US Office of Personnel Management Council on Veterans Employment, accessed August 31, 2022, *fedshirevets.gov*.

115. Frances M. Murphy, MD, MPH, and Dr. Sherrie Hans, PhD, "Women Veterans: The Long Journey Home," Disabled American Veterans (DAV), accessed August 31, 2022, *dav.org*.

116. "Care Coordination: Education and Employment Initiative," US Department of Defense Warrior Care, accessed August 31, 2022, *warriorcare.dodlive.mil*.

117. See also: "Training Partners," Hire Heroes USA, accessed August 31, 2022, *hireheroesusa.org*.

118. "Find Your Next Career," American Corporate Partners, accessed August 31, 2022, *acp-usa.org*.

119. "Preparing Top Performers for Careers in Tech," BreakLine, accessed August 31, 2022, *breakline.org*.

120. "CORE Leadership Program," Deloitte, accessed August 31, 2022, *deloitte.com*.

121. "Employers," FourBlock, accessed August 31, 2022, *fourblock.org*.

122. "Transition to Tech with MSSA," Microsoft Military Affairs, accessed February 5, 2023, *military.microsoft.com/mssa*.

123. "Onward to Opportunity," Institute for Veterans and Military Families, Syracuse University, accessed August 31, 2022, *ivmf.syracuse.edu*.

124. "Hire the Most Qualified Veterans," SHRM HireVets, accessed August 31, 2022, *hirevets.shrm.org*.

125. "USO Pathfinder—Transition Program," USO.org, accessed August 31, 2022, *uso.org*.

126. "A Leader in Employment for Military & Veteran Communities," VetJobs Powered by Corporate America Supports You (CASY), accessed August 31, 2022, *vetjobs .com*.

127. "Warriors to Work: A Resource for Employers," Wounded Warrior Project, accessed August 31, 2022, *woundedwarriorproject.org*. See also: "Employer Resources," Wounded Warrior Project, accessed August 31, 2022, *woundedwarriorproject.org*.

128. "Jobs for Veterans," National Veterans Foundation, accessed August 31, 2022, *jobs .nvf.org*.

129. "Military Spouse Jobs," MilitarySpouseJobs.org, accessed August 31, 2022, *militaryspousejobs.org*.

130. "Team Room to Boardroom," Green Beret Foundation, accessed August 31, 2022, *greenberetfoundation.org/transition-support/*.

131. "Your Next Adventure," The Honor Foundation, accessed August 31, 2022, *honor.org*.

132. "Vets2Industry," Vets2Industry Foundation Inc., accessed August 31, 2022, *vets2industry.com*.

133. "Directory of Centers for Independent Living (CILs) and Associations," Independent Living Research Utilization (ILRU) program of TIRR Memorial Hermann, accessed August 31, 2022, *ilru.org*.

134. "Ticket to Work," Social Security Administration, accessed August 31, 2022, *choosework.ssa.gov*.

135. "The Net," Council of State Administrators of Vocational Rehabilitation, accessed August 31, 2022, *csavr.org*.

136. "State Vocational Rehabilitation Agencies," Employer Assistance and Resource Network on Disability Inclusion (EARN), accessed August 31, 2022, *askearn.org*.

137. "Employment Referral Resource Directory," US Department of Labor Office of Federal Contract Compliance Programs (OFCCP), accessed August 31, 2022, *dol.gov.*

138. "AAPD Career Center," American Association of People with Disabilities, accessed August 31, 2022, *jobs.aapd.com.*

139. "Employment," Association of University Centers on Disability (AUCD), accessed August 31, 2022, *aucd.org.*

140. "About Us" Workforce Recruitment Program, accessed August 31, 2022, *wrp.gov.*

141. "Largest Job Site for People with Disabilities," abilityJOBS, accessed August 31, 2022, *abilityjobs.com.*

142. AbilityLinks, accessed August 31, 2022, *abilitylinks.org.*

143. "How ESGR Can Help," Employer Support of the Guard and Reserve, accessed August 31, 2022, *esgr.mil.* See also: "State / Local Contacts," Employer Support of the Guard and Reserve, accessed August 31, 2022, *esgr.mil.*

144. "CVSO State Directory," National Association of County Veterans Service Officers, accessed August 31, 2022, *nacvso.org.*

145. "Chambers of Commerce," Association of Chamber of Commerce Executives, accessed August 31, 2022, *secure.acce.org.*

146. For a directory of local chambers of commerce, see: "Chamber of Commerce Directory," US Chamber of Commerce, accessed August 31, 2022, *uschamber.com/co/chambers.*

147. "Military Spouse Chamber of Commerce," Military Spouse Chamber of Commerce, accessed August 31, 2022, *milspousechamber.org.*

148. "Military Times Job Board," *Military Times,* accessed August 31, 2022, *jobboard.militarytimes.com.*

149. "Veteran Job Center," *Stars and Stripes,* accessed August 31, 2022, *veteranjobs.stripes.com.*

150. "View the Competencies That Are Essential for Workplace Success," Competency Model Clearinghouse, CareerOneStop, accessed August 31, 2022, *careeronestop.org.*

151. "Building Blocks Model Download," Competency Model Clearinghouse, CareerOneStop, US Department of Labor, accessed February 2, 2023, *careeronestop.org.*

152. "Building Blocks Model," Competency Model Clearinghouse, CareerOneStop, US Department of Labor, accessed February 2, 2023, *careeronestop.org.*

153. "Civilian to Military Occupation Translator," CareerOneStop Business Center, accessed August 31, 2022, *careeronestop.org.*

154. "Military Crosswalk Search," O*Net OnLine, accessed August 31, 2022, *onetonline .org.*

155. "Military Skills Translator," Military.com, accessed August 31, 2022, *military.com.*

156. "Where Skills Meet Opportunities," Purepost, accessed May 18, 2023, *purepost.co.*

157. See: "Google Resources for Veterans and Families," Accelerate with Google, accessed August 31, 2022, *accelerate.withgoogle.com.*

158. "Marketing to the Military Explained," SheerID, August 9, 2022, accessed August 31, 2022, *sheerid.com/business/blog/marketing-to-the-military/.*

159. "Statement of Support Program," Employer Support of the Guard and Reserve, accessed August 31, 2022, *esgr.mil.*

160. "Marketing to the Military Explained," SheerID, August 9, 2022, accessed August 31, 2022, *sheerid.com/business/blog/marketing-to-the-military/.*

161. Ibid.

CHAPTER 7

1. Charlton, *The Military,* p. 8.

2. Victoria A. Hoevemeyer, *High-Impact Interview Questions, Second Edition* (New York: AMACOM, 2018), p. 15.

3. Ibid, p. 17.

4. Ibid, p. 33.

5. Ibid, pp. 22–28.

6. Charlton, *The Military,* p. 125.

7. Based on Hoevemeyer, *High-Impact,* p. 58.

8. For a thorough list of sample questions for a voluminous list of competencies, please see Hoevemeyer, *High-Impact,* pp. 63–136.

9. For additional detail and examples, please see: Hoevemeyer, *High-Impact.* See also: Paul Falcone, *96 Great Interview Questions to Ask before You Hire* (New York: AMACOM, 2018).

10. For additional detail and examples, please see: Hoevemeyer, *High-Impact.* See also: "Interview Guide," Society of Human Resource Management, accessed August 31, 2022, *shrm.org.*

11. Dustin Whidden, telephone interview by Matthew Louis, January 19, 2018. Updated May 6, 2022.

CHAPTER 8

1. Roy Maurer, "8 in 10 Employers Lack Recruitment Programs for Veterans," *Medium*, May 25, 2015, accessed August 31, 2022, *medium.com*.

2. "Veterans in the Workplace: Understanding the Challenges and Creating Long-Term Opportunities for Veteran Employees," Hiring Our Heroes, US Chamber of Commerce Foundation, November 2, 2016, p. 8, accessed August 31, 2022, *uschamberfoundation.org*.

3. Rosalinda Maury, MS, Brice Stone, PhD, and Jennifer Roseman, MA, *Veteran Job Retention Survey Summary* (Syracuse, NY: Institute for Veterans and Military Families at Syracuse University and VetAdvisor, October 1, 2014), p. 6.

4. "Military Spouse Employment Partnership," Department of Defense, accessed August 31, 2022, *msepjobs.militaryonesource.mil*.

5. D. A. Bradbard, R. Maury, and N. J. Armstrong, *The Force behind the Force: A Business Case for Leveraging Military Spouse Talent* (Employing Military Spouses, Paper No. 1). (Syracuse, NY: Institute for Veterans and Military Families, Syracuse University, July 2016) accessed August 31, 2022, *ivmf.syracuse.edu*. See also: *Employing Military Spouses—The Force behind the Force Series* (Syracuse, NY: Institute for Veterans and Military Families, Syracuse University), accessed August 31, 2022, *ivmf.syracuse.edu*.

6. "2008 Survey of Active Duty Spouses," US Department of Defense, Defense Manpower Data Center, accessed August 31, 2022, *opa.mil*. Similar percentages have been found with federal data such as the American Community Survey: 78% obtained some college education or higher, 25% obtained a bachelor's degree, and 7% obtained a master's degree.

7. "2015 Annual Military Family Lifestyle Survey Comprehensive Report," Blue Star Families, accessed August 31, 2022, *bluestarfam.org*.

8. Molly Clever, and David R. Segal, "The Demographics of Military Children and Families," *The Future of Children 23*, no. 2 (2013): 13–39, accessed August 31, 2022, *jstor.org*.

9. "2015 Annual."

10. "Volunteering in the United States, 2015," US Department of Labor Bureau of Labor Statistics, February 25, 2016, accessed August 31, 2022, *bls.gov*.

11. See: "Affirmative Action: Post-Offer Invitation to Self-Identify as a Veteran VETS-4212," Society for Human Resource Management, accessed August 31, 2022,

shrm.org. See also: "Sample VEVRAA Self-Identification Form," US Department of Labor Office of Federal Contract Compliance Programs, accessed August 31, 2022, *dol.gov.*

12. John Myers, Procter & Gamble Veterans Affinity Group (Cincinnati, OH), interview by Matthew Louis, March 1, 2018.

13. *Occupational Outlook Handbook,* Military Careers, Bureau of Labor Statistics, US Department of Labor, accessed August 31, 2022, *bls.gov.*

14. See: Ainspan and Saboe, *Military Veteran,* p. 173.

15. See: Haynie, "Revisiting."

16. "Career Map Links," Competency Model Clearinghouse, US Department of Labor, Employment & Training Administration (ETA), accessed August 31, 2022, *careeronestop.org.* For additional guidance on developing career paths and ladders, see: "Developing Employee Career Paths and Ladders," Society of Human Resource Management, accessed August 31, 2022, *shrm.org.*

17. See: "Education and Training: Forever GI Bill—Harry W. Colmery Veterans Educational Assistance Act," US Department of Veterans Affairs, accessed August 31, 2022, *benefits.va.gov.*

18. "Transition Resources," Military-Transition.org, accessed August 31, 2022, *military-transition.org.*

19. Gwendolyn Jaffe, "Reserve Forces: DOD Actions Needed to Better Manage Relations between Reservists and Their Employers," US General Accounting Office, June 13, 2002, accessed February 19, 2018, *gao.gov.*

20. See "Summary of VA Benefits for National Guard and Reserve Members and Veterans," US Department of Veterans Affairs, September 2012, accessed August 31, 2022, *benefits.va.gov.* See also "Air Force Reserve Benefits," Air Force Reserve, 2018, accessed August 31, 2022, *afreserve.com.*

21. "Managing the Reserve Components as an Operational Force," US Department of Defense Directive 1200.17, October 29, 2008, accessed August 31, 2022, *esd.whs.mil.*

22. "Guidance to Screening the Ready Reserve," Appendix A to 32 CFR 44, July 1, 2017, accessed August 31, 2022, *govinfo.gov.* See also "Department of Defense Instruction 1205.12," US Department of Defense, February 24, 2016, accessed August 31, 2022, *esd.whs.mil.* See also: "HR Professionals and Supervisors," VA for Vets, accessed August 31, 2022, *vaforvets.va.gov.*

23. "Employer Programs," Employer Support of the Guard and Reserve, accessed August 31, 2022, *esgr.mil.*

24. "Employer Awards," Employer Support of the Guard and Reserve, accessed August 31, 2022, *esgr.mil.*

25. Inquiries are handled through contacts here: "USERRA Contact," Employer Support of the Guard and Reserve, accessed August 31, 2022, *esgr.mil.*

26. "Department of Defense Instruction 1205.12."

27. "USERRA for Employers," Employer Support of the Guard and Reserve, accessed August 31, 2022, *esgr.mil.*

28. For types of documentation satisfying this requirement, see "Application for Reemployment," 20 CFR § 1002.123, April 1, 2017, accessed August 31, 2022, *govinfo.gov.*

29. "2013 Status of Forces Survey of Reserve Component Members," Defense Manpower Data Center, March 2014, pp. 252–260, 350–354.

30. Nick Tran, telephone interview by Matthew Louis, March 14, 2018. Updated May 16, 2022.

31. "US Army Rear Detachment Commander's Handbook (Edition 3; Revised 2006)," Army Community Service, March 26, 2007, p. 3, accessed April 21, 2021, *asktop.net.*

32. Ibid.

33. Beau Higgins, telephone interview by Matthew Louis, December 18, 2017. Update via email May 6, 2022.

34. See: "Military Separation: Create a Step-by-Step Checklist," USAA, accessed August 31, 2022, *usaa.com.*

35. Sean Passmore, telephone and email interview by Matthew Louis, April 26, 2018. Subsequent updates provided via email by Marcus "Ohley" Ohlenforst, February 4, 2021.

36. Dustin Whidden, telephone interview by Matthew Louis, January 19, 2018. Updated May 6, 2022.

CHAPTER 9

1. Quotefancy, "TOP 20 James Mattis Quotes," YouTube video, January 16, 2018, 2:20, accessed August 31, 2022, *youtube.com.*

2. "About the Organizational Culture Assessment Instrument (OCAI)," OCAI, accessed April 27, 2022, *ocai-online.com.*

3. "The Hofstede Culture in the Workplace Questionnaire™ Is an Online Cross-Culture Tool That Is Based on the Extensive Research of and Endorsed by Prof. Geert Hofstede," *Culture in the Workplace*, accessed April 27, 2022, *cultureinworkplace.com*.

4. Robert A. Cooke, PhD, and Janet L. Szumal, PhD, "Using the *Organizational Culture Inventory* to Understand the Operating Cultures of Organizations" (Human Synergistics International, 2013), accessed April 27, 2022, *google.com*.

5. Marshall Sashkin, PhD, and William E. Rosenbach, PhD (2013), "Organizational Culture Assessment Questionnaire," accessed April 27, 2022, Marshall Sashkin, *leadingandfollowing.com*.

6. "General: What Is an Employee Assistance Program (EAP)?" Society for Human Resource Management, accessed August 31, 2022, *shrm.org*.

7. "Veterans Employment Toolkit: Veteran-Friendly EAP Practice," US Department of Veterans Affairs, accessed August 31, 2022, *va.gov*.

8. "Work Life: Employee Assistance Programs," Office of Personnel Management, accessed August 31, 2022, *opm.gov*. To find your agency's work-life coordinator, see: "Work-Life Agency Coordinators," Office of Personnel Management, accessed August 31, 2022, *opm.gov*.

9. "VSOs at Regional Benefit Offices," US Department of Veterans Affairs, accessed August 31, 2022, *benefits.va.gov*. See also: "Accreditation Search," US Department of Veterans Affairs, accessed August 31, 2022, *va.gov*.

10. Eliyahu M. Goldratt, *What Is This Thing Called Theory of Constraints and How Should It Be Implemented?* (Great Barrington, MA: North River Press, 1990), p. 161.

11. N. J. Armstrong, Z. S. Huitink, M. Hidek, R. V. Maury, R. L. Uveges., N. Birnbaum, and F. Hyseni, *Implementation Assessment of Executive Order 13518—The Veterans Employment Initiative (Final Technical Report)* (Syracuse, NY.: Institute for Veterans and Military Families, Syracuse University, 2017), accessed August 31, 2022, *ivmf.syracuse.edu*.

12. "How to Conduct a Layoff or Reduction in Force," Society for Human Resource Management, accessed August 31, 2022, *shrm.org*.

13. "Protected Veterans' Rights," US Department of Labor Office of Federal Contract Compliance Programs, accessed August 31, 2022, *dol.gov*.

14. See: "Veterans Services," US Office of Personnel Management, accessed August 31, 2022, *opm.gov*.

15. "HIREVets Medallion Program," US Department of Labor HIREVets.gov, accessed August 31, 2022, *hirevets.gov*. See also: Veterans' Employment Outreach Team,

"Employer Guide to Hiring Veterans," US Department of Labor Veterans' Employment & Training Service (DOL VETS), May 11, 2021, accessed August 31, 2022, p. 14, *dol.gov.*

16. "Employer Awards," Employer Support of the Guard and Reserve, accessed August 31, 2022, *esgr.mil.*

17. "Patriots in Business Award: Best Companies with Veteran & Military Initiatives," *Chief Executive*, accessed August 31, 2022, *chiefexecutive.net.*

18. "VETS Indexes Employer Awards," VETS Indexes, accessed October 13, 2022, *vetsindexes.com.*

19. "National Commander's Award Nomination Form," Disabled American Veterans, accessed August 31, 2022, *dav.org.* See also: "DAV Patriot Employer Program," Disabled American Veterans, accessed August 31, 2022, *dav.org.*

20. "National Veterans Employment & Education Awards," The American Legion, accessed August 31, 2022, *legion.org.*

21. "Military Friendly Companies Overview," Military Friendly, Viqtory, accessed January 30, 2023, *militaryfriendly.com.*

22. John Myers, Procter & Gamble Veterans Affinity Group (Cincinnati, OH), interview by Matthew Louis, March 1, 2018.

23. Nick Tran, telephone interview by Matthew Louis, March 14, 2018. Updated May 16, 2022.

24. "National Veteran Workforce Development Conference," National Veteran Workforce Development Conference, accessed August 31, 2022, *nvwdc.com.*

25. "Transmittals," Chief Human Capital Officers Council, accessed August 31, 2022, *chcoc.gov.*

26. "Reintegration Framework," FedsHireVets, US Office of Personnel Management, accessed August 31, 2022, *fedshirevets.gov.*

27. James Beamesderfer, telephone interview by Matthew Louis, October 4, 2018. Updated via email May 10, 2022.

28. Charlton, *The Military,* p. 95.

APPENDIX A

1. "Deployment Tips and Checklist," Employer Support of the Guard and Reserve (ESGR), accessed August 31, 2022, *esgr.mil.*

2. "Demobilization Briefing," Employer Support of the Guard and Reserve (ESGR), accessed August 31, 2022, *esgr.mil.*

APPENDIX D

1. US Department of Veterans Affairs, "VA Handbook 0802: Federal Recovery Coordination Program" (Washington, DC: Department of Veterans Affairs, March 23, 2011), accessed August 31, 2022, *va.gov.*

2. "Definitions of Disability/Veteran's Status," Carnegie Mellon University Human Resources, accessed August 31, 2022, *cmu.edu.*

3. "Employment Situation of Veterans—2021," US Department of Labor Bureau of Labor Statistics, accessed August 31, 2022, *bls.gov.*

4. "Physical Conditions for VA Disability Benefits," Woods and Woods, LLC, accessed August 31, 2022, *woodslawyers.com.*

5. "Employment Situation of Veterans—2021."

6. "Vietnam Era Veterans' Readjustment Assistance Act of 1974," Employer Assistance and Resource Network on Disability Inclusion (EARN), accessed August 31, 2022, *askearn.org.*

7. Burgess, *The Veteran Advantage.*

8. Ibid.

9. "Disabled Veterans," Employer Assistance and Resource Network on Disability Inclusion (EARN), accessed August 31, 2022, *askearn.org.*

10. "Enforcement Guidance on Disability-Related Inquiries and Medical Examinations of Employees under the Americans with Disabilities Act (ADA)," US Equal Employment Opportunity Commission, accessed August 31, 2022, *eeoc.gov.*

11. "Title 41—Public Contracts and Property Management," US Code of Federal Regulations, accessed August 31, 2022, *govinfo.gov.* See also: "Affirmative Action: Post-Offer Invitation to Self-Identify as a Veteran (VEVRAA)," Society for Human Resource Management (SHRM), February 2, 2021, accessed August 31, 2022, *shrm.org.*

12. 29 C.F.R. § 1630.2(o)(1)(i-iii) (1997), US Government Printing Office, accessed August 31, 2022, *govinfo.gov.*

13. "Costs and Benefits of Accommodation," Job Accommodation Network, accessed August 31, 2022, *askjan.org.*

14. Kathy Crenshaw and Linda Maddy, "Building and Sustaining a Veteran-Informed Culture: A Guide for HR Professionals," Society for Human Resource Management, June 1, 2017, accessed August 31, 2022, *shrm.org.*

15. Burgess, *The Veteran Advantage.*

16. "Wounded, Ill, and/or Injured Compensation and Benefits Handbook," US Department of Defense, accessed August 31, 2022, *warriorcare.dodlive.mil.*

17. "Job Accommodation Network," US Department of Labor Office of Disability Employment Policy, accessed August 31, 2022, *askjan.org.*

18. "W3C Website Accessibility Initiative," World Wide Web Consortium, accessed May 18, 2023, *w3.org.*

19. "National Resource Directory, accessed May 18, 2023, *nrd.gov.*

20. "Veterans and the Americans with Disabilities Act (ADA): A Guide for Employers," US Equal Employment Opportunity Commission, accessed September 1, 2022, *eeoc.gov.*

21. "Employer Resources," Wounded Warrior Project, accessed September 1, 2022, *woundedwarriorproject.org.*

22. "Disability Employment," US Office of Personnel Management, accessed September 1, 2022, *opm.gov.*

23. See: "Make the Connection," US Department of Veterans Affairs, accessed September 1, 2022, *maketheconnection.net.* See also: "Veterans Crisis Line," US Department of Veterans Affairs, accessed September 1, 2022, *veteranscrisisline.net.*

APPENDIX E

1. Elizabeth H. Oakes, *Career Resource Guide to Apprenticeship Programs, Third Edition, Volume 1* (New York: Ferguson, 2006), p. ix.

2. See: "Apprenticeship," US Department of Labor, accessed September 1, 2022, *dol.gov.* To register your program, please visit: "Employers: Explore Apprenticeship," US Department of Labor ApprenticeshipUSA, accessed September 1, 2022, *apprenticeship.gov.*

3. See: "NASAA State Contacts," National Association of State Approving Agencies, accessed September 1, 2022, *nasaa-vetseducation.com.*

4. "State Tax Credits and Tuition Support," US Department of Labor ApprenticeshipUSA, accessed September 1, 2022, *apprenticeship.gov.*

5. "The Federal Resources Playbook for Registered Apprenticeship," US Department of Labor ApprenticeshipUSA, accessed September 1, 2022, *apprenticeship.gov.*

6. See: "Post-9/11 GI Bill (Chapter 33)," US Department of Veterans Affairs Education and Training, accessed September 1, 2022, *va.gov.*

7. Veterans already participating in an apprenticeship program at the time of your application may be eligible to receive up to twelve months of retroactive MHA and books and supplies stipend.

8. For all other GI Bill programs (e.g., Montgomery GI Bill), the payment rates are as follows: 75% of the full-time GI Bill rate for the first six months of training; 55% of the full-time GI Bill rate for the second six months of training; 35% of the full-time GI Bill rate for the remainder of the training program. See: "On-the-Job Training and Apprenticeships," US Department of Veterans Affairs Education and Training, accessed September 1, 2022, *va.gov.*

9. "About VA Form 22-8865—Employer's Application to Provide Job Training," US Department of Veterans Affairs VA Forms, accessed September 1, 2022, *va.gov.*

10. This form is not available online. It is available only to school officials, who must contact their VA representative for receipt.

11. "Legislation, Regulations, and Guidance: Registered Apprenticeship Programs (Title 29, CFR Part 29, Subpart A)," US Department of Labor ApprenticeshipUSA, accessed September 1, 2022, *apprenticeship.gov.*

12. "Veteran Readiness and Employment (VR&E)," US Department of Veterans Affairs, accessed September 1, 2022, *benefits.va.gov.* See also: "Veterans Employment Toolkit," US Department of Veterans Affairs, accessed September 1, 2022, *va.gov.* See also: "Veteran Readiness and Employment (Chapter 31)," US Department of Veterans Affairs, accessed September 1, 2022, *va.gov.*

13. "Employers," US Department of Labor ApprenticeshipUSA, accessed September 1, 2022, *apprenticeship.gov.*

14. "America's Service Locator: Find an American Job Center," US Department of Labor CareerOneStop, accessed September 1, 2022, *careeronestop.org.*

15. "Education Programs—Weams Institution Search," US Department of Veterans Affairs, accessed September 1, 2022, *inquiry.vba.va.gov.*

APPENDIX H

1. "PTSD Basics," US Department of Veterans Affairs, PTSD: National Center for PTSD, accessed September 1, 2022, *ptsd.va.gov.*

2. "How Common Is PTSD in Veterans?" US Department of Veterans Affairs, PTSD: National Center for PTSD, accessed September 1, 2022, *ptsd.va.gov.*

3. "How Common Is PTSD in Adults?" US Department of Veterans Affairs, PTSD: National Center for PTSD, accessed September 1, 2022, *ptsd.va.gov.*

4. Bureau of Labor Statistics, US Department of Labor, *Occupational Outlook Handbook*, Military Careers, accessed September 1, 2022, *bls.gov.*

5. "Traumatic Brain Injury and PTSD," US Department of Veterans Affairs, PTSD: National Center for PTSD, accessed September 1, 2022, *ptsd.va.gov.*

6. "Get the Facts about TBI," Centers for Disease Control and Prevention, accessed September 1, 2022, *cdc.gov*.

7. "Traumatic Brain Injury and PTSD."

8. "DoD Worldwide Numbers for Traumatic Brain Injury," Theater Medical Data Store of the Defense Medical Surveillance System, 2013, accessed September 1, 2022, *biami.org*.

9. "Traumatic Brain Injury and PTSD."

10. Hannah Fischer, "A Guide to US Military Casualty Statistics: Operation Freedom's Sentinel, Operation Inherent Resolve, Operation New Dawn, Operation Iraqi Freedom, and Operation Enduring Freedom," Congressional Research Service, August 7, 2015, accessed September 1, 2022, *fas.org*.

11. "Traumatic Brain Injury and PTSD."

12. "Costs and Benefits of Accommodation," Job Accommodation Network, accessed September 1, 2022, *askjan.org*.

13. Michael McCrea (Chair), Neil Pliskin (Chair, Division 40 Practice Affairs Committee), Jeffrey Barth, David Cox, Joseph Fink, Louis French, Thomas Hammeke, David Hess, Alan Hopewell, Daniel Orme, Matthew Powell, Ron Ruff, Barbara Schrock, Lori Terryberry-Spohr, Rodney Vanderploeg, and Ruth Yoash-Gantz, "Official Position of the Military TBI Task Force on the Role of Neuropsychology and Rehabilitation Psychology in the Evaluation, Management, and Research of Military Veterans with Traumatic Brain Injury," *The Clinical Neuropsychologist*, *22:1* (2008): 10–26, DOI: *10.1080/13854040701760981*.

14. "How Common Is PTSD in Veterans?" See also: "Traumatic Brain Injury and PTSD."

15. Kristy N. Kamarck, "Diversity, Inclusion, and Equal Opportunity in the Armed Services: Background and Issues for Congress," Congressional Research Service, June 5, 2019, accessed September 1, 2022, *fas.org*.

16. Ibid.

17. Ibid.

18. "Military Myth Busting: Check Your Knowledge of Military Culture," Returning Veterans Project, November 25, 2019, accessed September 1, 2022, *returning veterans.org*.

19. Kamarck, "Diversity."

20. "Economic News Release, Table 3: Employment Status of Persons 25 Years and Over by Veteran Status, Period of Service, and Educational Attainment, 2021

Annual Averages," US Department of Labor, Bureau of Labor Statistics, accessed August 26, 2022, *bls.gov.*

21. Melissa Boatwright and Sarah Roberts, "Veteran Opportunity Report: Understanding an Untapped Talent Pool," LinkedIn, accessed September 1, 2022, *social impact.linkedin.com.*

22. Ibid.

23. "Military Myth Busting: Check Your Knowledge of Military Culture.

24. "Fact Sheet on the Military Child," AASA: The School Superintendents Association, accessed September 1, 2022, *aasa.org.*

25. "Women Veterans Population Fact Sheet," US Department of Veterans Affairs, November 22, 2019, accessed September 1, 2022, *va.gov.*

26. Frances M. Murphy, MD, MPH, and Dr. Sherrie Hans, PhD, "Women Veterans: The Long Journey Home," Disabled American Veterans (DAV), accessed September 1, 2022, *dav.org.*

27. "Credentialing Your Military Experience," US Department of Defense Military OneSource, April 23, 2020, accessed September 1, 2022, *militaryonesource.mil.*

28. Bradbard, Armstrong, and Maury, *Work.*

29. The Conference Board Inc., the Partnership for 21st Century Skills, Corporate Voices for Working Families, and the Society for Human Resource Management, "Are They Really Ready to Work? Employers' Perspectives on the Basic Knowledge and Applied Skills of New Entrants to the 21st Century US Workforce," 2006, last accessed May 18, 2023, *eric.ed.gov/.*

30. Ibid.

31. C. Zoli, R. Maury, and D. Fay, Missing Perspectives: Servicemembers' Transition from Service to Civilian Life—Data-Driven Research to Enact the Promise of the Post-9/11 GI Bill (Syracuse, N.Y.: Institute for Veterans & Military Families, Syracuse University, November 2015).

32. A. R. Garcia, Sr., "The Science Behind Purepost" (2019), accessed May 18, 2023, *matthewjlouis.com.*

33. "The Myths and Facts of Military Leaders," PsychArmor, accessed September 1, 2022, *learn.psycharmor.org.*

34. A. R. Garcia, Sr., "The Science Behind Purepost" (2019), accessed May 18, 2023, *matthewjlouis.com.*

35. Gwendolyn Jaffe, "Reserve Forces: DOD Actions Needed to Better Manage Relations between Reservists and Their Employers," US General Accounting Office, June 13, 2002, accessed February 19, 2018, *gao.gov.*

36. Committee on the Assessment of Readjustment Needs of Military Personnel, Veterans, and Their Families; Board on the Health of Select Populations; and Institute of Medicine, *Returning Home from Iraq and Afghanistan: Assessment of Readjustment Needs of Veterans, Service Members, and Their Families* (Washington, DC: National Academies Press, March 12, 2013), Chapter 3 (Costs and Benefits), accessed September 1, 2022, *ncbi.nlm.nih.gov.*

37. Office of the Deputy Assistant Secretary of Defense for Military Community and Family Policy (ODASD (MC&FP)), "2020 Demographics Profile of the Military Community," US Department of Defense, p. 8, accessed August 28, 2022, *military onesource.mil.*

APPENDIX I

1. "Reintegration Framework," FedsHireVets, US Office of Personnel Management, accessed September 1, 2022, *fedshirevets.gov.*

2. Ibid.

ABOUT THE AUTHORS

MATTHEW J. LOUIS

Matt Louis is one of the nation's leading experts in career transition for veterans and public service professionals. He coaches individuals on their transition efforts and advises employers on hiring programs designed to successfully assimilate these valuable talent pools. He is the author of the award-winning and bestselling HarperCollins book *Mission Transition,* a practical guide for veterans in career transition, their families, and their employers.

Matt serves as the veteran transition assistance officer for his West Point class, is a national speaker for the US Chamber of Commerce Hiring Our Heroes program, serves on JPMorgan Chase's external advisory council for military and veterans affairs, advises the nonprofit Soldiers to Sidelines, and serves several other veteran collaboratives around the country.

During active commissioned service in the US Army, Matt served in the Southwest Asia combat theater and in the 194th Separate Armored Brigade. During reserve commissioned service, Matt served on the staff of the Army's Office of the Deputy Chief of Staff for Operations, and commanded multiple regions around the country for the US Military Academy's Admissions Office. He is a retired Lieutenant Colonel from the US Army and serves on the Service Academy nominating committee for his local congressman.

Matt holds an MBA in operations and finance from the Kelley School of Business at Indiana University, a BS in mechanical engineering from West Point, and is a graduate of the US Army Command and General Staff College. He is also a certified Lean Six Sigma Master Black Belt, holds the ASCM organization's Certified Supply Chain Professional designation, and is a certified Project Management Professional.

Matt is the president of Purepost (*www.purepost.co*) and heads Louis Advisors, LLC (*www.matthewjlouis.com*). He previously led global strategy and transformation projects at Deloitte, and global operational, production, and quality roles in multiple divisions of both General Electric and Procter & Gamble.

DR. ANTHONY R. GARCIA, SR.

Anthony R. Garcia, Sr., PhD (LTC USA, Ret.) is the chief science officer and board chairman of Purepost Inc. Previously, he served as the director of manufacturing operations, director of human resources, senior corporate consultant for leadership and organizational transformation, and manager of leadership and organizational development for H-E-B Grocery Company, LP. He also served as director of leadership, people, and work effectiveness for Harland Clarke Corporation, where he played a significant role in the company winning the Malcolm Baldrige National Quality Award.

Prior to his work in the private sector, Dr. Garcia served for more than twenty years in the US Army and held a variety of command and leadership positions in both the United States and Germany. He successfully commanded three times at both the company and battalion levels, and served as a certified organizational effectiveness staff officer.

Dr. Garcia has a BBA from St. Mary's University, an MHR in organizational development from the University of Oklahoma, and a PhD in leadership studies from Our Lady of the Lake University. Additionally, he is a graduate of the Army's Command and General Staff College and the Army's Organizational Effectiveness Center and School, where he gained his certification as an organizational effectiveness consultant.